Facing Forward

Residential child care in the 21st century

Edited by

David Crimmens

and

Ian Milligan

Russell House Publishing

First published in 2005 by:
Russell House Publishing Ltd.
4 St George's House
Uplyme Road
Lyme Regis
Dorset DT7 3LS

Tel: 01297-443948
Fax: 01297-442722
e-mail: help@russellhouse.co.uk
www.russellhouse.co.uk

British Library Cataloguing-in-publication Data:
A catalogue record for this book is available from the British Library.

ISBN: 1-903855-75-6, 978-1-903855-75-1

Typeset by TW Typesetting, Plymouth, Devon
Printed by Alden, Oxford

Russell House Publishing
is a group of social work, probation, education and youth and community work practitioners and academics working in collaboration with a professional publishing team.
Our aim is to work closely with the field to produce innovative and valuable materials to help managers, trainers, practitioners and students.
We are keen to receive feedback on publications and new ideas for future projects.
For details of our other publications please visit our website or ask us for a catalogue. Contact details are on this page.

Contents

About the Contributors

Dr Isabelle Brodie is a Senior Researcher in the research department of the National Children's Bureau. She has a longstanding research interest in the education of looked after children, and is currently part of the team researching the Taking Care of Education project, designed to improve educational outcomes for looked after children, in three local authorities in England.

Graham Connelly is a Senior Lecturer in the Department of Educational and Professional Studies in the University of Strathclyde and was a member of the Learning with Care – Improving Outcomes for Looked After Children project group. He teaches an elective class for trainee teachers on the education of looked after children and young people.

David Crimmens is a Principal Lecturer in the Hull School of Health and Social Care, University of Lincoln. Current research interests are in children's rights, children looked after by the state and the influence of continental European ideas on professional practice in the UK. Recent publications include Crimmens D and West A (Eds.) (2004) *Having Their Say. Young People and Participation: European Experiences*, and Crimmens et al. (2004) *Reaching Socially Excluded Youth: A National Study of Street-Based Youth Work*. David is a Trustee of the Social Education Trust and a member of the editorial board of the *European Journal of Social Work*.

Ruth Emond currently works part time in the Department of Applied Social Science, University of Stirling. The other half of her working week is spent as a social worker employed in a small project set up to provide a therapeutic service to children and parents who have experienced trauma. Her research interests are in the group and friendship experiences of children and young people, particularly those in looked after care. Since completing her PhD she has undertaken research on young people leaving care and on young people in care and their experiences of education.

Robbie Gilligan is Professor of Social Work and Social Policy, Head of the Department of Social Studies, and Associate Director (and co-founder) of the Children's Research Centre at Trinity College Dublin. He is also coordinator of the MSc in Child Protection and Welfare in TCD. He has been a youth worker, social worker, foster carer and board member of various social service organisations. He is an elected member of the Board of Childwatch International. He is a member of the editorial board of the journals, *Child and Family Social Work* and *European Journal of Social Work*.

Moyra Hawthorn worked for many years in the field of child protection and managed a child sexual abuse counselling service in Glasgow before moving to work in the field of disability. She now works part time for the NCH and at the University of Strathclyde.

Adele Jones is currently Head of the Department of Health and Social Care at Royal Holloway, University of London. She also holds a post as Lecturer and Coordinator of Postgraduate Social Work Studies at The University of The West Indies, Trinidad and was responsible for establishing both the Masters and PhD programmes in Social Work in Trinidad. Adele is a qualified social worker and has many years experience in child and family social work and as a fostering officer. She was previously a consultant at the (former) National Institute for Social Work and was also a founder member of the Bibini Centre for Young People.

Andrew Kendrick is Professor of Residential Child Care in the Glasgow School of Social Work, Universities of Strathclyde and Glasgow. He co-ordinates the research of the Scottish Institute of Resident Child Care. He has published widely on child welfare and child protection, with a particular focus on looked after children and residential child care. His current research includes studies of secure care; mentoring for care leavers; physical restraint; and design of children's homes. He is the editor of the *Scottish Journal of Residential Child Care*.

Kirstie Maclean is a social work inspector with the Social Work Inspection Agency. She was previously Director of the Scottish Institute for Residential Child Care (SIRCC) and has many years experience working in child care inspection, management, training and practice.

Jill Millar has specialised in socio-legal research on child rights and children. She was research officer for the successful joint Voice for the Child in Care/National Children's Bureau Blueprint project. Jill is currently based at Oxford Brookes University where she is a research officer for a pedagogical research project.

Ian Milligan worked in children's homes in Glasgow for a number of years before moving into further education. He has been involved with the Scottish Institute for Residential Child Care (SIRCC) from its inception in 1999 and his current post in the National Office involves training, research and policy development. Ian has written and researched in the areas of residential care policy, the education of residential workers and the mental health of looked after children.

Roger Morgan is the Children's Rights Director for England, based in the Commission for Social Care Inspection and with a statutory duty to secure the views of children living away from home or supported by local authority social services, to advise on children's rights, and to audit the work of the Commission in inspecting services from the point of view of children. Roger has previously worked in inspection, has managed local authority social services, been a government policy officer, and been a researcher into solutions to children's problems. He has a PhD in the treatment of bedwetting, and an OBE for services to children.

John Pitts is Vauxhall Professor of Socio-legal Studies at the University of Luton and Director of the Vauxhall Centre for the Study of Crime. He has worked as a youth justice development officer in a London borough, a social worker in a Remand and Assessment Centre and a group worker in a Young Offender Institution. He has researched widely in the areas of youth crime, inter-racial youth violence, the criminal victimisation of children and young people and youth justice. His publications include: *Positive Residential Practice: Learning the Lessons of the 1990s* (2000), and *The Russell House Companion to Youth Justice* (2005). He is a member of the editorial boards of *Youth Justice, The Community Safety Journal* and UNESCO's *Juvenile Justice Worldwide,* and an associate editor of *Youth and Policy.*

Satnam Singh currently works part-time with the British Association for Adoption and Fostering Association (BAAF) as a black and minority ethnic issues consultant. Satnam is also an associate lecturer with the Open University, where he has been teaching on NOLP DipSW programme for a number of years. Previously Satnam worked with Barnardo's, where he had the lead role in developing the 'Khandan Initiative' (1996–2003) which won the Community Care awards in 2001. Satnam has research interests in social policy from a race equality perspective.

Mark Smith was a practitioner and manager in residential school, close support and secure accommodation settings over a period of nearly 20 years. Since 2000 he has been a lecturer at Strathclyde University/Glasgow School of Social Work, where he developed and is course director of the MSc in Advanced Residential Child Care. His current research interests are in youth justice and in masculinity and caring. He is a regular contributor to *cyc-net,* an international on-line journal for those working in child and youth care.

Laura Steckley started working in residential treatment in the United States almost 15 years ago. After moving to Scotland in 1999, she worked in residential child care for a further four years before coming to the Glasgow School of Social Work to do related teaching and research.

Delsierene Waul currently works as a Senior Practitioner for Children and Adolescent Mental Health Services in a Clinical Psychology team with responsibility for young people looked after. She has worked in residential and fieldwork settings for many years, including seven years in the Bibini Centre for Young People (an organisation specialising in the care and support of black children and their families) where she developed and managed services to families, young people with caring responsibilities and people seeking asylum and refuge.

Jane Whiteford was formerly Assistant Director for Young People's Services at Who Cares? Scotland. She has a background in child care and training and was previously Training and Development officer with Save the Children Scotland.

Alison Williams has worked for 30 years in a variety of social care organisations specialising in work with children and families. She has a particular interest in care planning and is presently working at the National Children's Bureau developing training and consultancy for all those who work with and care for looked after children and care leavers.

Chapter One

Introduction: Meeting the Challenges of Residential Child Care in the 21st Century

Children's homes and residential schools of various kinds have undergone substantial changes in size, organisation and care practice, especially in the past two decades. Increasing use is made of residential respite or short-break services for children with disabilities, there has been an expansion of secure care of various kinds, and while the overall number of residential places ('beds') has only increased slightly in recent years, there has been a significant increase in the 'flow' of young people who experience a period of time in residential care. Staff-child ratios have improved steadily as units have become smaller. Nevertheless major questions still exist about the quality and effectiveness of different types of residential provision; questions posed just as much by those within residential services as outside it. Despite the assertion of major professional reports, from Wagner (1988) and Skinner (1992) onwards, that residential care should be a 'positive choice' for some children and young people, it has proven difficult to make the journey from 'last resort' to 'positive choice'.

Social workers make strenuous efforts to maintain children at home or to provide them with family placements and this usually means that those children and young people who are admitted to residential units have had prolonged periods of difficulty and often multiple placements. Instilling in such young people a sense of their own value, and giving them some stability is one thing, but preparing, and supporting them to leave care can be an even more demanding task. In terms of 'outcome measures' young people leaving state care irrespective of whether they were placed in a family or a residential setting, continue to do badly in areas such as further education, employment and early parenthood. The challenge is the provision of care experiences which effectively address the problems of children and young people and leaves them better placed to face the challenges of the transition to adulthood.

There has been progress in the last few years. In England the Quality Protects initiative focused on key issues such as the health and education of children in state care as well as emphasising the importance of their participation in decision making. Children's rights occupy an increasingly central place in residential practice. Since the late 1990s there have been government-funded *Young Person's Workers* in all parts of Scotland, and recent years have seen a strengthening of the role of *Who Cares? Scotland* as it has sought to deliver advocacy services to more young people in foster care. Recently they have also been funded to develop a specialist advocacy team for those in secure care. Importantly, advocacy services and participation practices have begun to extend to children and young people with disabilities. The National Care Standards and the creation of national inspection bodies to monitor their implementation creates new possibilities, to establish minimum standards and to adopt continuous improvement approaches designed to raise standards across the country. Young people themselves are beginning to play a significant role in the inspection process.

While it is not possible to critically examine every aspect of group care within a single volume the range of contributions included here address many key themes and issues. These provide both a theoretical framework for group care practice in general and highlight specific aspects of practice; from dealing with questions of ethnicity to education, and from communication to recreation. Each chapter is designed to stimulate thinking, promote debate, and provide theoretical and practical resources for residential practitioners and managers who seek to improve the quality of care provided across the UK.

The structure of the book

The book is divided into six parts:

- *The Policy Context*
- *Difference and Diversity*

- *The Voice of Children and Young People*
- *Group Care Theory and Practice*
- *Improving the Educational Attainments of Looked After Children and Young People*
- *Locking up Children and Young People Who Offend.*

Part One: The Policy Context

The first part examines the role of residential care within the wider context of childcare policy. Andrew Kendrick – the first professor of residential child care in the UK – sets the scene by exploring how some of the policy concerns around residential care for children and young people can be located within the contemporary discourses of social exclusion and inclusion. This is followed by Crimmens and Milligan, who seek to identify 'how we got here'; how residential care has changed over the last decades of the 20th century and what have been the key ideas and policies which have shaped the sector as it struggled to find its place in the 'continuum' of child care interventions.

Part Two: Difference and Diversity

This part discusses significant facets of residential provision, which are often subject to marginalisation and exclusion. Two chapters on ethnicity, one each from England and Scotland, are designed to provide a black perspective on care. They should also inform a deeper reflection on what it means to be child-centred by recognising the cultural assumptions which are often taken-for-granted by members of the majority ethnic community. Adele Jones and Delsierene Waul are black practitioners who draw on their experience in the Bibini Project to reflect on residential care of black children in England. As well as a cogent exploration of the definition of racism and the language of 'race' the authors touch on some of the tensions experienced by residential workers when trying to help young people maintain their identity and culture. Satnam Singh invites the reader to consider some common assumptions about individuality and development from an Asian perspective, with its much stronger emphasis on the 'needs of the family unit' rather than the 'needs of the individual'. In a useful link to the subsequent chapter by Gilligan, Singh offers a critique of how the resilience perspective is usually understood and applied. Children and

young people with disabilities make substantial use of residential services, albeit usually on an occasional basis rather than as a main place of residence. Moyra Hawthorn provides practical guidance in key areas, which have been little written about including sexuality and grief and loss. She aims to help readers understand some of the language issues around terms such as 'disabled children' or 'children with disabilities' and explores these and other practice issues having described some of the key policy trends which inform the recent expansion of 'short break' services.

Part Three: The Voice of Children and Young People

In 1975 the National Children's Bureau sponsored a conference which brought together one hundred young people 'in care' from all over Britain. The outcome of this event was the creation of self-advocacy organisations of young people, which have evolved as Who Cares? Scotland, in England with both the Who Cares? Trust, the Voice for the Child in Care, and more recently A National Voice. Since the implementation in October 1991 of the Children Act 1989, in England and Wales, the principle of due consideration being given to children's views is enshrined in domestic legislation. Therefore any understanding of contemporary residential childcare must be built on a foundation that articulates what young people themselves say about their experiences. This volume includes three contributions, which attempt to give expression to the voice of the child. Jane Whiteford reflects on *Let's Face it: Young People in Care Tell it as it is* (Who Cares? Scotland, 2003) which was published to mark the 25th anniversary of Who Cares? Scotland. The report enables many young people to express their views in their own words on a number of key topics, which arise from the experiences of foster and residential care. For example, the report indicates that 'restraint' is still a big problem and while young people are reporting that they know it is sometimes necessary is often not done well. The chapter also reveals the young people's sense of their own needs and what they are looking for from both their residential and social workers.

The Blueprint project, managed jointly by the Voice for the Child in Care and the National Childrens Bureau Residential Care Unit aimed to examine what a truly child-centred residential service might look like if the sector were able to start with a new beginning. Young people with experience of care were included on the staff of the project and many other children and young people were consulted throughout the project. Jill Millar, the Research Officer with the project, tells the story of the process by which the core idea of a child-centred practice was developed and highlights some of the key findings from her research. Roger Morgan is the Children's Rights Director of the Commission for Social Care Inspection, the first national organisation in England, which acts as a channel for complaints and undertakes inspections of residential services. He draws on consultations with young people, individually and collectively and distils many messages from young people, which are designed to inform the future of the inspection process – a process which will be vital to ensuring that the new National Care Standards deliver improvements in residential services.

Part Four: Group Care Theory and Practice

Five contributions are included in this section, which explores diverse ways in which group care practice can be conceptualised and what kinds of care practice might derive from these conceptions. Ruth Emond's contribution is based on her unique ethnographic research, in which she lived for a year in two children's homes, recording the young people's views and experiences. Emond reflects on her observation that staff, under pressure to be 'in control', may miss the significance of the support that young people can offer to each other. Her work encourages residential staff to recognise the reality of, and the positive possibilities of, the 'group' in group care, at a time when the *group* seems mostly an object of fear, and policy is driven by the aspiration to make units ever smaller. In recent years, Robbie Gilligan, from Dublin, and his Scottish-based colleagues, Brigid Daniel and Sally Wassell, have been responsible for introducing and developing the application of 'resilience' perspectives to work with children and families. Gilligan explores how the insights of the resilience framework can inform the practice of residential workers. He emphasises the importance of 'actively maintaining links with birth family and friends; which might be the source of ongoing support for young people in later life'.

The current volume focuses on theory and practice rooted in experience in the UK where residential child care is located within social work. However its aspirations for the development of residential childcare practice are not limited to the experiences of the UK and Ireland. Continental European traditions of 'social pedagogy' for example can provide sources of inspiration in the direct care of children and young people in various settings, residential, day care, schools and youth-work. (see for example the chapter by Jill Millar, in relation to child-centred practice). In a similar vein, 'child and youth care' embraces practice in North America, South Africa and increasingly in Ireland. It is essential that any book on contemporary child care reflects knowledge, insight and understanding drawn from these direct care professions. Mark Smith does so explicitly as he introduces readers to some of the key ideas about group care drawn from the 'child and youth care' perspective. Laura Steckley applies ideas from this perspective to the very British enthusiasm for football and explores how creative and therapeutic thinking about the experience of football training and competitive games can be utilised in residential practice. Finally in this section Alison Williams draws together her research and insight into the care-planning process. Care planning is central to British approaches to social work and care placements but it often lacks the depth and quality to adequately address the life situation of children and their carers.

Part Five: Improving the Educational Attainments of Looked After Children and Young People

In recent years the education of looked after children has risen very high up the political and policy agenda. Government in both England and Scotland have set targets and demanded regular monitoring of the educational achievements of children in residential and foster care. Isabelle Brodie summarises developments in England, particularly since the implementation of Quality Protects in 1998. She reflects on recent research carried out by the National Children's Bureau, which highlights some of the potential areas for improvements in local authority practices. Kirstie Maclean and Graham Connelly present an analysis of joined-up thinking in Scotland from both social services and education perspectives.

Part Six: Locking up Children and Young People Who Offend

John Pitts brings a critical eye to the unprecedented expansion in the use of security and custody for children and young people in England and Wales in the past decade. His chapter highlights the contradictions that inform much of government policy in this highly politicised policy area, to the detriment of the interests of vulnerable young people.

Conclusion: Informing and Improving Residential Care Practice

This book sets itself in the tradition of critical thinking about the necessary, purposeful and positive possibilities that group care of children holds out for those who can no longer live at home, whether for shorter or longer periods. (Ainsworth and Fulcher, 1985; Ward, 1993; Clough, 2000) Since the abolition in 1991 of the Certificate in Social Service (CSS) – a professional qualification aimed at residential and day care staff, when it was 'merged' with the CQSW to form the Diploma in Social Work, the study of group care as a form of social work practice has disappeared from most curricula, and few text-books make more than a passing reference to residential services. Thus it is hoped that this volume will serve those studying residential work whether within social work, social care or any other form of professional training and will inform and stimulate the thinking of those who want to engage constructively and critically with this continuously changing sector of welfare provision. The present volume aims to follow up the messages from *Positive Residential Practice: Learning the Lessons of the 90s* (Crimmens and

Pitts, 2000), which analysed the problems of the past in order to establish a baseline for improving contemporary practice. *Facing Forward* aims to provide resources for investigating key aspects of theory and practice that must be addressed if residential services are indeed to move forward and better meet the needs of vulnerable children and their families.

Facing Forward is also of relevance to those in related professional disciplines who want an overview of current issues in residential theory and practice. Thus it will be of use to social work students and practitioners, and to education and health professionals who are being encouraged to work collaboratively to meet the needs of children and young people looked after by the state (Scottish Executive, 2001; DfES, 2004).

References

Clough, R. (2000) *The Practice of Residential Work.* Basingstoke: Macmillan.

Crimmens, D. and Pitts, J. (Eds.) (2000) *Positive Residential Practice: Learning the Lessons of the 90s.* Lyme Regis: Russell House Publishing.

Department for Education and Skills (2004) *Every Child Matters.* London: TSO.

Fulcher, L. and Ainsworth, F. (Eds.) (1985) *Group Care Practice with Children.* London: Tavistock.

Scottish Executive (2001) *For Scotland's Children: Better Integrated Children's Services.* Edinburgh: Scottish Executive.

Skinner, A. (1992) *Another Kind of Home: A review of Residential Child Care.* Edinburgh: SWSI.

Wagner, G. (1988) *Residential Care: A Positive Choice.* London: NISW.

Ward, A. (1993) *Working in Group Care.* Birmingham: Venture Press.

Part One: The Policy Context

Social Exclusion and Social Inclusion: Themes and Issues in Residential Child Care

Andrew Kendrick

Introduction

In this chapter, I intend to explore the links between social exclusion, social inclusion and residential child care. I hope to show that social exclusion and social inclusion provide a useful framework for considering a number of cross-cutting themes and issues which affect children and young people in residential care, and the development of services to promote their best interests. The use of the terms social exclusion and social inclusion has become more widespread over recent years, but many of the issues are of longer standing than the concepts themselves. Like many such concepts, there is some lack of clarity, and the fact that they have been used and developed in a range of political and social arenas means that definitions and usage may be contested (Stewart, 2000; Saraceno, 2001). Levitas suggests that 'social exclusion is a powerful concept, not because of its analytical clarity which is conspicuously lacking, but because of its flexibility' (Levitas, 1998: 178), while Saraceno (2001) suggests that 'it constitutes a relatively loose set of ideas to represent the world in particular settings rather than a concept with theoretical substance and coherence which transcends national and political contexts' (Saraceno, 2001: 9). I am aware that this can lead us into complex areas, but I hope to, at least, provide an outline of the relevant ideas and practice implications for residential child care.

I will outline the concepts of social exclusion and social inclusion and underline some of the criticisms of the terms. I will look at the way in which young people who enter residential care are already frequently experiencing social exclusion. I will then consider the experience of residential child care and the ways in which this may compound social exclusion. I will discuss the process of transition from residential child care, highlighting the poor outcomes of young people leaving residential care in relation to education, accommodation and employment but highlighting the protective factors which have been identified by research. Finally, I will draw together some of the developing themes in residential care which focus on positive work with children and young people, the promotion of relationships, stability, and positive social, cultural and leisure experiences which promote social inclusion.

Social exclusion and social inclusion: definitions and issues

Social exclusion is not a new concept. Craig (2000) outlines the use of the term in French policy debates about groups at the margins of society in the 1950s and in more mainstream discussions about poverty within the context of European poverty programmes in the 1960s and 1970s. These stressed integrated approaches to tackling multiple deprivation and an emphasis on partnership and participation (Craig, 2000). Burchardt, Le Grand and Piachaud (2002) point out that the term 'social exclusion' was first used in a political climate where the Conservatives did not recognise the existence of 'poverty' and it allowed for social policy debate at the European level. Following the election of the Labour government in 1997, social exclusion came to the forefront of policy initiatives in the UK. New Labour established the Social Exclusion Unit in 1997 and its working definition of social exclusion was:

> . . . a shorthand term for what can happen when people or areas suffer from a combination of linked problems such as unemployment, poor skills, low incomes, poor housing, high crime environments, bad health, poverty and family breakdown.
>
> (Social Exclusion Unit, n.d.)

This definition has been criticised, however, for focusing on the causes of social exclusion rather than setting out what social exclusion actually is (Micklewright, 2002; Morris, 2001). In Scotland, following lobbying for a more 'inclusive' approach, the Social Inclusion Network was established (Fawcett, 2003).

Hill, Davis, Prout and Tisdall (2004) describe two overlapping meanings of social exclusion in the UK. The first is broadly equivalent to relative poverty 'signifying the way in which inadequate material resources, especially low income, make it very difficult for individuals and families to share in the social activities generally expected in the society in which they live' (Hill et al., 2004: 79). The second 'refers to the way in which certain groups are marginalised, omitted or stigmatised, usually on account of a visible feature that differs from the majority and which the majority finds hard to accept' (Hill et al., 2004: 79).

While social exclusion is closely linked with poverty, some have questioned whether the concept of exclusion adds anything to the debate, particularly over concepts of relative poverty (Micklewright, 2002; Cheetham and Fuller, 1998). However, social exclusion can be argued to be a more multi-dimensional concept (Lister, 2000; Fawcett, 2003). Barry (1998) defines social exclusion as:

> . . . *multi-dimensional disadvantage which severs individuals and groups from the major processes and opportunities in society, such as housing, citizenship, employment and adequate living standards* . . .
>
> (Barry, 1998: 1)

It has also been stressed that social exclusion focuses more on a process rather than a state; a process of being excluded by someone or something (Cheetham and Fuller, 1998; Craig, 2000).

Levitas (1998), in a critique of its use in social policy debates, identifies three social exclusion discourses: a redistributionist discourse (RED); a moral underclass discourse (MUD); and a social integrationist discourse (SID). The redistributionist discourse has a prime concern with poverty but broadens this into a critique of inequality. RED 'contrasts exclusion with a version of citizenship which calls for substantial redistribution of power and wealth' (Levitas, 1998: 7). The moral underclass discourse has many forerunners, based on fears about 'criminally-inclined, unemployable young men and socially irresponsible single mothers, for whom paid work is necessary as a means of social discipline, but whose (self)- exclusion, and thus potential inclusion, is moral and cultural' (Levitas, 1998: 7–8). The social integrationist discourse focuses more narrowly on unemployment and economic inactivity, 'pursuing social integration or social cohesion

primarily through inclusion in paid work' (Levitas, 1998: 8). Highlighting the dominance of SID and MUD discourse, she states:

> *Attention is drawn away from the inequalities and differences among the included. At the same time, the poverty and disadvantage of the so called excluded are discursively placed outside society.*
>
> (Levitas, 1998: 7)

Levitas argues that the main thrust of the reduction of social exclusion has been in getting people back into employment (see also Jack and Jordan, 1999). While few would argue that paid work is not an important aspect of social inclusion, Lister questions the assumptions underlying the social integrationist discourse of New Labour, that; paid work necessarily spells social inclusion; worklessness necessarily spells social exclusion; the only form of work of value to society is paid work; and that an inclusive society can be built on the foundations of paid work alone (Lister, 2000: 40).

Micklewright (2002) highlights that:

> *Children are very high on New Labour's agenda in its efforts to tackle poverty and exclusion. Children are frequently the chosen entry-point into the whole debate: examples of childhood disadvantage, whether labelled as exclusion or poverty, are often mentioned first in the opening paragraphs of government reports.*
>
> (Micklewright, 2002: 10)

Four of the first six reports published by the Social Exclusion Unit dealt with disadvantage among children and young people: truancy and school exclusion, teenage pregnancy, out-of-school and out-of-work young, and young runaways (Micklewright, 2002). Roche and Tucker (2003) argue that the focus of the social exclusion debate in relation to young people is on the 'highly visible disorders of youth' (Roche and Tucker, 2003: 440, see also Hill et al., 2004), and Barry (1998) points that the continuing ambiguity in New Labour about the difference between the concepts of underclass and social exclusion (Barry, 1998: 4; see also Fawcett, 2003).

> . . . *there is a danger that this discourse and the associated policy initiatives may reinforce social inequalities as characteristics located in particular social categories: teenage parents, single mothers, drug users and homeless young people. Such assumptions may further construct the 'otherness' of such groups, who are typically conceptualised as members of an 'under class'.*
>
> (Brannen, 1999: 22)

This being said, New Labour's commitment to halve child poverty by 2010 and eradicate it in a generation can be seen as reflecting the redistributionist discourse but 'the redistribution is modest in comparison with other European countries . . . and the shifts between the three discourses continue across different policy areas and over time' (Hill et al., 2004: 80).

Social exclusion prior to placement in residential care

It can be argued that all children are socially excluded. Hill, Davis, Prout and Tisdall (2004) highlight the fact that while children are one of the most governed groups in society and some of the highest users of state services (health, education and social security), they 'traditionally have had little or no input into national and local policies' (Hill et al., 2004: 78). Ridge and Millar (2000) argue that by their very status as children, they are excluded from the processes by which social inclusion is defined:

> . . . it is clear that civic, economic and social integration are all defined in adult terms, and involve social systems and institutions from which children are already effectively excluded. Where exclusion is related to the exercise of power and control, children, by virtue of being children, are already excluded from adult spheres of power and influence.
>
> (Ridge and Millar, 2000: 161)

When we focus on children and young people in residential care, then, we must ask the question, are some children more socially excluded than others? We have seen that social exclusion refers to a range of factors including unemployment, low incomes, poor housing, poor health, family breakdown and poor skills. These factors, themselves, are closely linked to the reasons why children and young people enter the care system.

While Scottish Executive statistics do not give details of the reasons why children and young people enter residential care, some indication is given by referrals to Children's Hearings. Of over sixty thousand referrals in 2000/2001, 44 per cent were on alleged offence grounds and 56 per cent were on alleged care and protection grounds. The main reasons for alleged care and protection referrals were: lack of parental care (46 per cent); victim of schedule 1 offence (27 per cent); beyond control (13 per cent). Where disposals were made by the Children's Hearings, 371 children and young people (11 per cent) were subject to a supervision requirement in a residential establishment. The proportion of children and

young people subject to a residential supervision requirement varied according to the grounds of referral. Of those referred solely for offence grounds, 212 (31 per cent) had a residential supervision requirement, compared to 101 (4 per cent) referred on care and protection grounds and 58 (17 per cent) on both offence and care and protection grounds (Scottish Children's Reporter Administration, 2002).

Kendrick (1995a), in a study of 412 residential and foster care placements, found that only 7 per cent of placements for reasons of 'family support' were in residential care, compared to 25 per cent of placements for reasons of 'child protection', and 88 per cent of placements for 'offending'. Using a different categorisation and focusing on teenagers, Triseliotis, Borland, Hill and Lambert (1995) found that the primary reasons for admission to *residential schools* were school-based difficulties, offending and family problems and each applied to approximately one-third of the residents. Almost half the young people in *residential units* were admitted because of family problems, one third because of behaviour problems and one in seven because of school problems (Triseliotis et al., 1995: 98). Similarly, Sinclair and Gibbs (1998) found that for over half (53 per cent) of children and young people admitted to children's homes, the main reason was 'breakdown of relationship between young person and family' and one in five (21 per cent) were admitted because of the 'young person's behaviour'. Other reasons for admission were 'potential/actual abuse of young person' (10 per cent); 'neglect of young person' (4 per cent) and 'family illness/housing problem' (2 per cent) (Sinclair and Gibbs, 1998: 19). Berridge and Brodie (1998), in comparing the reasons why children were admitted to children' homes in 1995 compared to 1985, concluded:

> Three main groupings of stress factors leading to accommodation were identified: behavioural problems, abuse and neglect, and, slightly less noticeably, inadequate care and relationship problems. Most children had multiple problems and had experienced severe difficulties in several aspects of their lives . . . It therefore appears that the current children's home population is much more complex and problematic than in 1985. The proportion posing behavioural problems prior to entry has more than doubled.
>
> (Berridge and Brodie, 1998: 83)

Berridge and Brodie (1998) found that although educational problems were rarely the predominant reason for a child to be in a children's home, it was considered to be a 'major' problem for 59 per cent of the children. Kendrick found that one-quarter of school age children had either been excluded or suspended before reception into care or were already in alternative educational provision. Half of the remainder were reported to have problems of non-attendance at school (Kendrick, 1995a, 1995b; see also Jackson and Sachdev, 2001).

It has long been recognised that there is a link between poverty and entry into local authority care. Bebbington and Miles (1989) investigated the family backgrounds of 2,500 children admitted to care in England in 1987. They found that only one-quarter of the children were living with both parents, almost three-quarters of their families received income support, only one in five lived in owner-occupied housing, and over half were living in poor neighbourhoods (Bebbington and Miles, 1989: 353):

Our results confirm that deprivation is a common factor among all types of children who enter care . . . poverty and adverse housing conditions are particularly common among children taken into care compulsorily.
(Bebbington and Miles, 1989: 358)

Gillham, B., Tanner, G., Cheyne, B., Freeman, I., Rooney, M. and Lambie, A. (1998) studied the relationship between poverty and child abuse in Strathclyde Region in Scotland. They looked at child abuse referral and registration rates in Glasgow social work areas and compared this to levels of unemployment in these areas. While cautioning that unemployment rates related to social areas and not to individual cases, they found that there were significant correlations to child abuse:

We were surprised by the high level of the correlations and the systematically higher correlation with levels of male unemployment. Clearly the latter is a strong index of the local ecology of child physical abuse, less so of neglect, and uncertainly in relation to sexual abuse.
(Gillham et al., 1998: 87)

They conclude that living in areas of localised high unemployment is likely to put otherwise vulnerable families at greater risk of child physical abuse and neglect (Gillham et al., 1998: 87).

Youth offending is also correlated with socio-economic deprivation, alongside factors such as parental supervision, discipline and attitude, broken homes and separation, peer

influences, school influences and community influences (Farrington, 1996). The Youth Justice Board (2001) categorise risk factors into four groups: family, schools, community, and individual. The risk factors highlighted in relation to the family include: poor parental supervision and discipline, family conflict, a family history of criminal activity, parental attitudes that condone antisocial and criminal behaviour, low income, and poor housing. School risk factors include low achievement in primary school, aggressive behaviour such as bullying, and lack of commitment to school. Living in a disadvantaged neighbourhood, community disorganisation and neglect and lack of neighbourhood attachment were linked to youth crime. Finally, individual risk factors included hyperactivity and impulsiveness, low intelligence and cognitive impairment, alienation and lack of social commitment, and attitudes that condone offending and drug misuse. Friendships with peers involved in crime and drug misuse also increase the risk of delinquency (Youth Justice Board, 2001).

The difficulties encountered in the early years may also be compounded considerably by the experience of poverty and disadvantage and the literature does identify a close relationship between crime, poverty and disadvantage. The impact of the parenting role in the context of disadvantage is highlighted as a crucial variable.
(Asquith, 1996: 10–11)

Asquith highlights the importance of changing socialisation patterns in promoting delinquent behaviour and 'the breakdown in or at least the altered patterns of informal social control exercised by parents over children and the increased importance attached to associations and friendships with peers' (Asquith, 1996: 7). Asquith also stresses what he terms 'a politics of exclusion'; the inability of many young people to actively participate in mainstream social life (Asquith, 1996: 8).

It is clear, then, that children and young people entering residential child care have experience of the multiple factors which are linked with social exclusion. While some caution against generalisation and highlight the variation in reasons for entry into care, the differences in care careers and length of stay in residential child care (Bullock, 2000), we have seen that children and young people entering residential care have experienced disruption in their families, schools and communities.

Aspects of social exclusion in residential child care

If children and young people have experienced significant social exclusion leading to their entry into residential child care, what impact does placement in residential child care itself have in relation to social exclusion. It can be argued that the very process of entry into residential child care leads to further social exclusion. Hayden, Goddard, Gorin and Van Der Spek (1999) highlight that coming into care is likely to be a stressful time for children and young people because of feelings of displacement, loss and lack of control. This can be compounded by the impact of multiple placements and schooling disruption. Literature relating to the abuse of children and young people in residential and foster care has stressed their social and geographical isolation (Berridge and Brodie, 1996; Kendrick, 1997; 1998; Kent, 1997; Nunno and Motz, 1988; Utting, 1997; Westcott, 1991). The social stigma related to residential child care has also be emphasised by children and young people themselves (Bullock, 2000; Polat and Farrell, 2002; Ridge and Millar, 2000; Who Cares? Scotland, 2004). Discussing the care system as whole, White (1999) writes (see also Micklewright, 2002):

> *They are different (socially excluded) from other children by virtue of a number of different labelling processes which make themselves felt at school, in the neighbourhood, in relation to the 'public' world of social services – and, of course, because they are palpably not included physically or psychologically in their own families.*
> (White, 1999: 73)

There are a number of aspects which highlight the way in which entry into residential child care may exacerbate the social exclusion of children and young people.

The young person's own family

We have seen that entry into residential child care often takes place because of family problems or breakdown of family relationships. The move into residential child care could mean that connections with the family will weaken. Emond (2003) highlights that over the year of her study, all of the young people in the residential units celebrated a birthday but 'a significant number received no acknowledgement of this event from their family and friends' (Emond, 2003: 329) and for some young people it seemed that their own

families had forgotten them. Family, however, is very important to looked after children and young people and feeling cut off from family has a significant impact (Dixon and Stein, 2003; Who Cares? Scotland, 2004).

Bilson and Barker (1995) in a study of parental contact found that nearly two out of five children (37 per cent) had no parental contact and less than half (47 per cent) had regular contact. They also found that contact diminished over time and only one in four of those in care for over five years had contact (Bilson and Barker, 1995: 373–4). Interestingly, however, 'the proportion having regular contact with their parents in residential care was over half as high again as for those in foster care (Bilson and Barker, 1995: 376). In addition, they found that for children aged 10 and over, the longer children were in residential care the more likely there was contact with parents, while the opposite was the case in foster care:

> *This might suggest that in residential care there is pressure leading to the re-establishment of contacts with parents which gets stronger as placements proceed whilst there is pressure in the other direction – towards diminishing contact – foster placements.*
> (Bilson and Barker, 1995: 379)

One-fifth of children and young people in Sinclair and Gibb's study (1998) had no contact with their family or had 'no family', while a further fifth had contact on a two-weekly to monthly basis. While the remainder had more frequent contact with family members, just over a third of children said that they did not see their families enough. The study found that contact was not related to length of time in care or long-term placement. Berridge and Brodie (1998) found that levels of family contact were higher in 1995 than in 1985 (Berridge and Brodie, 1998: 75).

One of the stated advantages of residential child care has been the ability to keep sibling groups together (Skinner, 1992; Wagner, 1988). Sinclair and Gibbs (1998) however, found that contacts with siblings were particularly missed; half the sample would have liked to see more of at least one brother or sister. Children and young people in the Who Cares? Scotland (2004) consultation, also highlighted separation from their siblings. Those who were in placements with brothers or sisters, however, highlighted that 'it was beneficial for sibling groups to remain together' (Who Cares? Scotland, 2004). Research has shown that (see also Kosonen, 1996):

the continuity of sibling relationships is of great benefit to children's well-being and adjustment and that children themselves valued being placed with or maintaining contact with their sisters and brothers.

(Kosonen, 2000)

Friends

Ridge and Millar (2000) suggest that interpersonal integration is a useful way into understanding social exclusion from a child-centred perspective since it allows a focus on friendship. Friendship has been described as the core relationship for young people (Cottrell, 1996). Children and young people in residential care are clear about the importance of friendship and the fact 'that the experience of coming into care and the care process itself was usually profoundly disrupting to a child's friendship networks' (Ridge and Millar, 2000: 167; see also Who Cares? Scotland 2004). Sinclair and Gibbs (1998) found that four out of ten of the residents said that they had lost touch with at least one 'important friend'. One in ten said that they were definitely lonely and loneliness was associated both with having lost touch with someone important and with not going around with particular friends. This being said, Whitaker, Archer and Hicks (1998) point out that young people's friends can be 'a mixed blessing' and we saw above the influence of the peer group in offending behaviour.

Sometimes they lead a young person into trouble – with drugs, with taking and driving away cars, burglary, or even into paedophile rings and prostitution. Sometimes they are helpful.

(Whitaker et al., 1998: 106)

In relation to what children and young people said about family and friends, Sinclair and Gibbs found that the 'associations were . . . very strong. Residents were less happy if they had left behind an "important friend" . . . happier if they were going around with a particular group of friends . . . and less happy if they wanted to see more of their family . . .' (Sinclair and Gibbs, 1998: 194).

Participation and responsibility

Hill et al. (2004) highlight the importance of participation in combating the social exclusion of children. Looked after children and young people stress the way in which 'arbitrary decision-making and lack of participation can so easily lead to negative discriminatory practices' (Who Cares? Scotland, 2004: 12). Even in the context of

formal meetings such as child care reviews, children and young people distinguish between being listened to and having influence (Kendrick and Mapstone, 1991; 1992; Thomas and Kane, 1999).

In all, participation without choice of specific placement seemed hollow to many young people and their families. Even when consulted, most young people still felt they had little influence. When such feelings persisted, the probability of success was lowered.

(Triseliotis et al., 1995: 277)

Barry (2002), in highlighting the tensions between rights of protection and rights of participation of young people in care, emphasised that young people frequently entered care from situations where they were not protected in the family but where they had 'adult' responsibilities such as caring for siblings or parents. In care they were protected, a welcome safe haven from violence, but treated as 'children', with little say in decisions or assessment of their competencies:

Once in care, their level of responsibility and autonomy was often dramatically reduced as social workers, residential workers and foster carers took over the role of ensuring their care and protection.

(Barry, 2002: 245)

This loss of autonomy and responsibility was resented by many of the young people:

As children within their families, the majority of this sample had competencies which went unrecognised by adults but growing up in care left many feeling ill-prepared for the responsibilities of adulthood. There was little continuity of support and few opportunities to exercise rights which would ensure that these young people had as smooth a transition to adulthood as possible.

(Barry, 2002: 251)

Barry concludes that the right of children and young people to be protected must be informed by 'their own assessment of their competencies, wishes and needs and they should be encouraged to participate in decisions about their welfare based on their own experiences and competencies' (Barry, 2002: 252).

Leaving care: social exclusion or social inclusion

One of the major issues facing young people in residential care is the process of transition from care to independence. Over a number of years, research has highlighted the poor outcomes for children leaving residential and foster care. Longitudinal studies which have followed up children and young people in care as part of national cohort studies present the stark contrast in life outcomes between those who have experienced care and those who have not. Cheung and Heath (1994) compare these two groups at age 33. One fifth of those who had been in care (21.5 per cent) had achieved O levels compared to one-third of those who had not (32.7 per cent); only half as many had achieved A levels (8.9 per cent compared to 16.8 per cent). Only one in a hundred of those who had been in care achieved a university degree (1.1 per cent) compared to one in ten of those who had not (10.1 per cent). Two-fifths of those who had been in care had no formal qualifications (42.7 per cent) compared to one in seven (15.6 per cent) (Cheung and Heath, 1994). This lack of qualifications converted into lack of success in the job market with three times as many being unemployed (10.8 per cent compared to 3.6 per cent) and larger proportions having manual jobs as opposed to professional or manual jobs. This is important in the context of the critiques of government social inclusion policies which have focused on entry into the job market.

Recent research in Scotland confirms the bleak picture which has previously been painted in terms of the outcomes of care leavers (Action on Aftercare Consortium, 1996; Biehal, Clayden, Stein and Wade, 1995; Stein, 1997). A survey of care leavers identified that: the majority of care leavers had poor education outcomes with only 39 per cent having one or more standard grades; over half were unemployed; many of the young people had experienced mobility and homelessness (Dixon and Stein, 2003).

In discussing young people leaving care and the concept of the 'underclass', Baldwin, Coles and Mitchell (1997) acknowledge the 'reality of deprivation, disadvantage and disenfranchisement' but argue that 'behind these gloomy statistics lie complex biographies of young people leaving care' (Baldwin et al., 1997: 91). This has perhaps been most dramatically represented in the research by Jackson and Martin on 'high achievers' from the care system (Jackson and Martin, 1998; Martin and Jackson, 2002). Of the 38 'high achievers', only one was unemployed, none were in custody, three-quarters were in rented private accommodation or their own home and only one was homeless (Jackson and Martin, 1998: 576). This contrasts markedly with the comparison group in the study and with the figures on outcomes for care leavers outlined above. The

factors identified as protective and most strongly associated with later educational success were:

(i)   *stability and continuity*
(ii) *learning to read early and fluently*
(iii) *having a parent or carer who valued education and saw it as a route to a good life*
(iv) *having friends outside care who did well at school*
(v)   *developing out-of-school interests and hobbies (which also helped to increase social skills and bring them into contact with a wider range of non-care people)*
(vi) *meeting a significant adult who offered consistent support and encouragement and acted as a mentor and possibly role model*
(vii) *attending school regularly*
(Jackson and Martin, 1998: 578)

These protective factors confirm the priorities for residential care practice with children and young people and highlight how crucial it is for residential staff to work collaboratively with schools and education staff to promote the education of looked after children (Hudson et al., 2003; Scottish Executive, 2001). Jackson and Martin stress the importance of educational success

in determining adult life-styles and ensuring social inclusion for this most disadvantaged group of children.
(Jackson and Martin, 1998: 581)

Life aspirations of young people

We have focused on some of the negative outcomes of children and young people who have experienced residential child care, but we should not forget the aspirations of these young people. Ridley and McCluskey, in a study of the health of young people in residential care, also asked about the young people's future aspirations:

Most young people thought that by the age of 22: they would have a job (81%); they would be in good health (68%); they would own a car (60%); and they would be a student at university or college (50%).

We can see that these aspirations are for conventional aspects of the socially included: job, car, education. However, as Ridley and McCluskey state,

the significant gap between young people's hopes and aspirations for the future ... represents a challenge for services concerned with improving outcomes for young people leaving care.

(Ridley and McCluskey, 2003)

Residential child care as community: the potential for social inclusion

Another important aspect of social exclusion and its relation to residential care, concerns the social context of the residential establishment itself. Within this social context are the relationships between young people, staff and the outside community.

Ward (2003) highlights that one of the distinctive features of group care is the network of relationships between the team and the group of children and young people in residential care:

> The group is the greatest resource in any group care setting, yet it is often under-used because people do not fully recognise its strengths or how to harness them.
>
> (Ward, 2003: 25)

Children and young people frequently cite the positive relationships with staff as central to their care experience (Dixon and Stein, 2003; Hill, 1999; Sinclair and Gibbs, 1998; Who Cares? Scotland, 2004).

> Even where placements had been rated by young people as being of little help, they often spoke warmly of the friendliness and helpfulness of the key worker or staff in general.
>
> (Triseliotis et al., 1995: 178)

Discussing the therapeutic community, Ward suggests that what is needed for children and young people:

> ... is both the security of a primary individual relationship and the broader base of a community of relationships with others (children and adults) who will share in the give and take of learning and developing together.
>
> (Ward, 2003: 21)

The nature of peer group relationships within residential child care have frequently been framed in the context of bullying and peer abuse. Undoubtedly this has been, and continues to be, a major issue. The negative experiences of children and young people in residential care have been starkly illustrated in recent research (Barter, 2003; Barter, Renold, Berridge, and Cawson, 2004; Sinclair and Gibbs, 1998).

There has been much less which has focused on the positive aspects of residential group living. One notable exception to this is Emond's research in children's homes in Scotland (Emond, 2002; 2003). This research has presented the nature of peer relationships in residential child care in much more positive terms. She has stressed that young people 'regarded the resident group as an important force in their day-to-day lives, their view of themselves and of their social world' (Emond, 2003: 326). Emond found that while there was no fixed group structure, 'position' or status within the group was granted as a result of subtle negotiation between individuals and the social context in which they were operating:

> ... young people had various 'competences', which were seen as valuable by the group. Status was achieved when a young person displayed the right social competence at the right time.
>
> (Emond, 2002: 33)

Emond identifies a number of competences or social currencies which were valued by the group. These included: support and advice, system knowledge, insider knowledge, humour, smoking, touch and space, verbal and physical aggression, external network and sexual/relationship knowledge (Emond, 2002). Although some of these social currencies, such as verbal and physical aggression relate to negative aspects of the peer group, Emond found that these 'were used with far less frequency than many of the other currencies identified' (Emond, 2003: 327). Emond concludes that:

> ... greater account needs to be taken of the function of 'the group' in group care for those young people who are living in it. Staff members, it is argued, need to have a clear sense of the ways in which the group is functioning and the ways in which the group impacts on individual residents. There is a sense in which the group is an untapped resource and is one that can have a positive influence on individual young people.
>
> (Emond, 2003: 335)

Resilience, social capital and residential child care

In the context of the trauma and disruption which children and young people have experienced – 'the generally under-acknowledged and largely unaddressed psychoemotional pain of the residents' (Anglin, 2002: 109) residential child care must be concerned with enhancing a young person's health, well-being and personal development. This is a social process involving growth and development predicated largely upon the social interactions with carers and others in the young person's social network.

Phelan (1999) suggests that the task for workers in child and youth care is less to address past difficulties and failings through a counselling type relationship and more to arrange and become involved in activities and experiences which allow young people to re-script their personal 'stories'. There is an increasing body of writing on resilience and its importance for the development of practice in residential care (Daniel, Wassell and Gilligan, 1999; Gilligan, 1997; 2001; 2004). Gilligan (1997) defines resilience as:

> *... qualities which cushion a vulnerable child from the worst effects of adversity in whatever form it takes and which may help a child or young person to cope, survive and even thrive in the face of great hurt and disadvantage.*
>
> (Gilligan, 1997: 12)

Three key features associated with levels of vulnerability or resilience are a secure base, self esteem and self efficacy (Daniel, 2002; Gilligan, 1997). Strategies to address this include positive relationships with residential staff themselves, as well as the work in developing relationships in the young person's formal and informal networks.

> *A key part of work with young people and of building on any potential they have for resilience is to help them 'stay connected' to key figures in their lives or their past, that is to members of their social network. A young person's social network is a key resource in their social development.*
>
> (Gilligan, 2001)

The importance of schools and of wider neighbourhoods and community has also been stressed (Cottrell, 1996; Gilligan, 2004). Similarly, the benefits of activities across a range of sporting, cultural and leisure pursuits have been highlighted (Gilligan, 2001; Sinclair and Gibbs, 1998; Whitaker et al., 1998). This links well with the concept of social capital which stresses the importance of norms, networks, know-how and culture through which people conduct informal interactions (Jack and Jordan, 1999). It is through the development of children and young people's family, community and social networks that they can become socially included in a truly meaningful sense.

Conclusion

Developments addressing the education of looked after children and young people and additional throughcare and aftercare supports are important aspects for ensuring the social inclusion of children and young people leaving residential care. It is important, however, to be clear that gaining employment, in and of itself,

does not mean social inclusion. In the context of extended transitions to adulthood (Furlong, Cartmel, Biggart, Sweeting and West, 2003), the need for vulnerable young people to draw on a variety of resources and support systems is crucial. Children and young people in residential care have experienced a variety of socially excluding influences. There is also the danger that the experience of residential child care itself can compound this social exclusion, through stigma, abusive practice and poor quality care. Residential child care, however, has the potential to provide a powerful context for the social inclusion of children and young people; leading to supportive, social networks and positive life careers.

References

Action on Aftercare Consortium (1996) *Too Much Too Young: The Failure of Social Policy in Meeting the Needs of Care Leavers*. Ilford: Barnardo's.

Anglin, J. (2002) *Pain, Normality and the Struggle of Congruence: Reinterpreting Residential Care For Children and Youth*. Binghampton: The Haworth Press.

Asquith, S. (1996) Introduction. In Asquith, S. (Ed.) *Children and Young People in Conflict with the Law*. (1–23) London: Jessica Kingsely.

Baldwin, D., Coles, B. and Mitchell, W. (1997) The Formation of an Underclass or Disparate Processes of Social Exclusion? Evidence From Two Groupings of 'Vulnerable Youth', in MacDonald, R. (Ed.) *Youth, the 'Underclass' and Social Exclusion*. (83-95), London: Routledge.

Barry, M. (1998) Social Exclusion and Social Work: An introduction, in Barry, M. and Hallett, C. (Eds.) *Social Exclusion and Social Work: Issues of Theory, Policy and Practice*. (1–25). Lyme Regis: Russell House Publishing.

Barry, M. (2002) Minor Rights and Major Concerns: The Views of Young People in Care. in Franklin, B. (Ed.) *The New Handbook of Children's Rights*. London: Routledge.

Barter, C. (2003) Young People in Residential Care Talk About Peer Violence, *Scottish Journal of Residential Child Care*, 2: 2, 39–50.

Barter, C., Renold, E., Berridge, D. and Cawson, P. (2004) *Peer Violence in Children's Residential Care*. Basingstoke: Palgrave Macmillan.

Bebbington, A. and Miles, J. (1989) The Background of Children Who Enter Local Authority Care, *British Journal of Social Work*, 19, 349–68.

Berridge, D. and Brodie, I. (1996) Residential Child Care in England and Wales: The Inquiries and After, in Hill, M. and Aldgate, J. (Eds.) *Child Welfare Services: Developments in Law, Policy, Practice and Research.* London: Jessica Kingsley.

Berridge, D. and Brodie, I. (1998) *Children's Homes Revisited.* London: Jessica Kingsely.

Biehal, N., Clayden, J., Stein, M. and Wade, J. (1995) *Moving on: Young People and Leaving Care Schemes.* London: HMSO.

Bilson, A. and Barker, R. (1995) Parental Contact With Children Fostered and in Residential Care After the Children Act 1989. *British Journal of Social Work*, 25: 3, 367–81.

Brannen, J. (1999) Children and Agency in Academic and Public Policy Discourses, in White, K. (Ed.) *Children and Social Exclusion.* (15–29). London: NCVCCO.

Bullock, R. (2000). Residential Child Care. *Research Matters: Social exclusion*, Special Issue, 34–36.

Burchardt, T., Le Grand, J. and Piachaud, D. (2002) Introduction, in Hills, J., Le Grand, J. and Piachaud, D. (Eds.) *Understanding Social Exclusion.* (1-12). Oxford: OUP.

Cheetham, J. and Fuller, R. (1998) Social Exclusion and Social Work: Policy, Practice and Research, in Barry, M. and Hallett, C. (Eds.) *Social Exclusion and Social Work: Issues of Theory, Policy and Practice* (118–32). Lyme Regis: Russell House Publishing.

Cheung, S.Y. and Heath, A. (1994) After Care: The Education and Occupation of Adults Who Have Been in Care, *Oxford Review of Education*, 20: 3, 361-72.

Cottrell, J. (1996) *Social Networks and Social Influences in Adolescence.* London: Routledge.

Craig, G. (2000) Introduction. *Research matters: Social exclusion*, Special Issue., 5–6.

Daniel, B., Wassell, S. and Gilligan, R. (1999) *Child Development For Child Care and Protection Workers*, London: Jessica Kingsley.

Dixon, J. and Stein, M. (2003) Leaving Care in Scotland: The Residential Experience, *Scottish Journal of Residential Child Care*, 2: 2, 7–17.

Emond, R. (2002) Understanding the Resident Group, *Scottish Journal of Residential Child Care*, 1: 1, 30–40.

Emond, R. (2003) Putting the Care Into Residential Care: The Role of Young People, *Journal of Social Work*, 3: 3, 321–37.

Farrington, D. (1996). *Understanding and Preventing Youth Crime.* York: Joseph Rowntree Foundation.

Fawcett, H. (2003) Social Inclusion Policy-Making in Scotland: Assessing the 'Capability-Expectations' Gap, *The Political Quarterly*, 74: 4, 439–49.

Furlong, A., Cartmel, F., Biggart, A., Sweeting, H. and West, P. (2003) *Youth Transitions: Patterns of Vulnerability and Processes of Social Inclusion.* Edinburgh: Scottish Executive.

Gillham, B., Tanner, G., Cheyne, B., Freeman, I., Rooney, M. and Lambie, A. (1998) Unemployment Rates, Single Parent Density, and Indices of Child Poverty: Their Relationship to Different Categories of Child Abuse and Neglect, *Child Abuse & Neglect*, 22: 2, 79–90.

Gilligan, R. (1997). Beyond Permanence? The Importance of Resilience in Child Placement Practice and Planning. *Adoption and Fostering*, 21: 1, 12–20.

Gilligan, R. (2001) *Promoting Resilience: A Resource Book on Working With Children in the Care System.* London: British Agencies for Adoption and Fostering.

Gilligan, R. (2004) Promoting Resilience in Child and Family Social Work: Issues For Social Work Practice, Education and Policy, *Social Work Education*, 23: 1, 93–4.

Hayden, C., Goddard, J., Gorin, S. and Van Der Spek, K. (1999) *State Child Care: Looking After Children?* London: Jessica Kingsley.

Hill, M. (1999) What's the Problem? Who Can Help': The Perspective of Children and Young People on Their Well-Being and on Helping Professionals, *Journal of Social Work Practice*, 13: 2, 135–45.

Hill, M., Davis, J., Prout, A. and Tisdall, K. (2004) Moving the Participation Agenda Forward. *Children & Society*, 18, 77–96.

Hudson, B., Furnivall, J., Paterson, S., Livingston, K. and Maclean, K. (2003) *Learning With Care: Training Materials for Carers, Social Workers and Teachers Concerning the Education of Looked After Children and Young People.* Glasgow: University of Strathclyde.

Jack, G. and Jordan, B. (1999) Social Capital and Child Welfare, *Children & Society*, 13, 242–56.

Jackson, S. and Martin, P.Y. (1998) Surviving the Care System: Education and Resilience, *Journal of Adolescence*, 21, 569–83.

Jackson, S. and Sachdev, D. (2001) *Better Education, Better Futures : Research, Practice and the Views of Young People in Public Care.* Ilford: Barnardo's.

Kendrick, A. (1995a) *Residential Care in the Integration of Child Care Services*. Edinburgh: The Scottish Office Central Research Unit.

Kendrick, A. (1995b) Supporting Families Through Inter-Agency Work: Youth Strategies in Scotland, in Hill, M., Kirk, R. and Part, D. (Eds.) *Supporting Families*. (135–47) Edinburgh: HMSO.

Kendrick, A. (1997) Safeguarding Children Living Away From Home From Abuse: A Literature Review, in Kent, R. *Children's Safeguards Review*. (143–275) Edinburgh: The Stationery Office.

Kendrick, A. (1998) In Their Best Interest? Protecting Children From Abuse in Residential and Foster Care, *International Journal of Child & Family Welfare*, 3: 2, 169–85.

Kendrick, A. and Mapstone, E. (1991) Who decides?: Child Care Reviews in Two Scottish Social Work Departments, *Children & Society*, 5: 2, 165–81.

Kendrick, A. and Mapstone, E. (1992) *Social Work Department Reviews of Children in Care*. Edinburgh: Scottish Office.

Kent, R. (1997) *Children's Safeguards Review*. Edinburgh: Scottish Office.

Kosonen, M. (2000) Role of Siblings in Relation to Children in Residential Care, in Chakrabarti, M. and Hill, M. (Eds.) *Residential Child Care: International Perspectives on Links With Families and Peers*. (125–40). London: Jessica Kingsley.

Kosonen, M. (1996) Maintaining Sibling Relationships: Neglected Dimension in Child Care Practice. *British Journal of Social Work*, 26, 809–22.

Levitas, R. (1998) *The Inclusive Society? Social Exclusion and New Labour*. Basingstoke: Macmillan.

Lister, R. (2000) Strategies for Social Inclusion: Promoting Social Cohesion or Social Justice?, in Askonas, P. and Stewart, A. (Eds.) *Social Inclusion: Possibilities and Tensions*. Basingstoke: Palgrave Macmillan.

Martin, P.Y. and Jackson, S. (2002) Educational Success For Children in Public Care: Advice From High Achievers, *Child and Family Social Work*, 7, 121–30.

Micklewright, J. (2002) *Social Exclusion and Children: A European View for a US debate*, London: Centre for Analysis of Social Exclusion. 15 July 2004, http://sticerd.lse.ac.uk/dps/case/cp/CASEpaper51.pdf

Morris, J. (2001) Social Exclusion and Young Disabled People With High Levels of Support Needs, *Critical Social Policy*, 21: 2, 161–83.

Nunno, M. and Motz, J.R. (1988) The Development of an Effective Response to the Abuse of Children in Out-of-Home Care, *Child Abuse and Neglect*, 12, 521–8.

Phelan, J. (1999) Child and Youth Care Work: Experiments With Experience, *Journal of Child and Youth Care Work*, 14, 25–8.

Polat, F. and Farrell, P. (2002). What Was it Like For You? Former Pupils' Reflections on Their Placement at a Residential School For Pupils With Emotional and Behavioural Difficulties, *Emotional and Behavioural Difficulties*, 7: 20, 97–108.

Ridge, T. and Millar, J. (2000) Excluding Children: Autonomy, Friendship and the Experience of the Care System. *Social Policy & Administration*, 34: 2, 160–75.

Ridley, J. and McCluskey, S. (2003) Exploring the Perceptions of Young People in Care and Care Leavers of their Health Needs, *Scottish Journal of Residential Child Care*, 2: 1, 55–65.

Roche, J. and Tucker, S. (2003) Extending the Social Exclusion Debate: An Exploration of the Family Lives of Young Carers and Young People With ME, *Childhood*, 10: 4, 439–56.

Saraceno, C. (2001) Social Exclusion: Cultural Roots and Diversities of a Popular Concept, Institute on Child and Family Policy Conference, Columbia University, May 3–4. Retrieved 15 July 2004, from http://www.childpolicyintl.org/publications/Saraceno.pdf

Scottish Children's Reporter Administration (2002) *Scottish Children's Reporter Administration Statistical Bulletin 2000–2001*. Stirling: Scottish Children's Reporter Administration.

Scottish Executive (2001) *Learning With Care: The Education of Children Looked After Away From Home by Local Authorities*. Edinburgh: HM Inspectors of Schools and Social Work Services Inspectorate.

Skinner, A. (1992) *Another Kind of Home: A Review of Residential Child Care*. Edinburgh: SWSI.

Sinclair, I. and Gibbs, I. (1998). *Children's Homes: A Study in Diversity*. Chichester: Wiley.

Social Exclusion Unit (n.d.) Retrieved 15 July 2004, from http://www.socialexclusionunit.gov.uk/

Stewart, A. (2000) Social Inclusion: An Introduction, in Askonas, P. and Stewart, A. (Eds.) *Social Inclusion: Possibilities and Tensions*. (1–16). Basingstoke: Macmillan Press.

Thomas, N. and Kane, C. (1999) Children's Participation in Reviews and Planning Meetings When They are 'Looked After' in

Middle Childhood, *Child and Family Social Work*, 4: 3, 221–30.

Triseliotis, J., Borland, M., Hill, M. and Lambert, L. (1995) *Teenagers and the Social Work Services*, London: HMSO.

Utting, Lord (1997) *People Like Us*. London: HMSO.

Wagner, G. (1988) *Residential Care: A Positive Choice*. London: NISW.

Ward, A. (2003) The Core Framework, in Ward, A., Kasinski, K., Pooley, J. and Worthington, A. (Eds.) *Therapeutic Communities for Children and Young People*. (21–42). London: Jessica Kingsley.

Westcott, H. (1991) *Institutional Abuse of Children: From Research to Policy: A Review*. London: NSPCC.

Who Cares? Scotland (2004) *Lets face it! Care 2003: Young People Tell us How it is*. Glasgow: Who Cares? Scotland.

Whitaker, D., Archer, L. and Hicks, L. (1998) *Working in Children's Homes: Challenges and Complexities*. London: Wiley.

White, K. (1999) Children and Foster Care: Inclusion, Exclusion and Life Chances, in White, K. (Ed.) *Children and Social Exclusion*. (71–80). London: NCVCCO.

Youth Justice Board (2001) *Risk and Protective Factors Associated With Youth Crime and Effective Interventions to Prevent it*. Research note 5. London: Youth Justice Board for England and Wales.

Chapter Three

Residential Child Care: Becoming a Positive Choice

David Crimmens and Ian Milligan

Today residential child care is a diverse sector deemed by both professionals and politicians to have an important role looking after some children and young people who are unable to live with their families for a variety of reasons. Most of the residents are teenagers, many staying for short periods while for some it is a longer term placement. Moreover the sector has become an important source of family support, working alongside foster care and community-based services. The sector is smaller than it was even a decade ago and it attracts a great deal less political and professional hostility. Children looked after by the state, come mainly from the poorest sections of the community with the poorest life chances. It was the recognition of the needs of these youngsters in the influential *People Like Us* (Utting, 1997) *For Scotland's Children* (Scottish Executive, 2001) and latterly the *Every Child Matters* green paper (2003) which ensured that the predicament of these children and young people found its way onto the present government's social inclusion agenda. This concern is evident in the higher profile and improved provision now being made for 'care leavers' (see for example, SEU, 2000). The consequent improvement in the political and professional environment in which children's homes and other residential settings function means that at long last, residential care is becoming a 'positive choice' (Wagner, 1988) for some young people.

While the overall tone of this chapter is optimistic, particularly about developments since 1997, it begins, where the previous volume ended, with the importance of learning the lessons of history (Crimmens and Pitts, 2000). Thus the first part of the chapter will give an account of what changed and why in residential child care in the period before 1991, in order to gain a better understanding of how positive contemporary developments might be sustained.

A negative choice

Little more than a decade ago there was a large question mark against the use of residential care for children and young people in need. The conventional wisdom had it that if children had to be removed from their own families, placement in an alternative family was by far the best option. Thus, residential child care was granted at best a residual function; a place to leave those who, for whatever reasons, could not be placed in foster care. As Kahan (1994) observes, the use of residential child care:

> *... has waxed and waned and waxed again depending on the fluctuations of professional and political theories and fashions and changing pressures on national resources.*
> (Kahan, 1994: 4)

However, at the beginning of the 1990s residential child care was not only waning, it appeared to be in terminal decline. The low point was reached with the publication of the *Pindown Report* (Levy and Kahan, 1991) which chronicled routine mistreatment of children and young people in residential care. Alongside 'pindown', and several other lower profile scandals, the residential child care sector in both England and Scotland had been subject to a host of other adverse influences:

- The breakdown of the post war optimism associated with the so-called welfare consensus and the efficacy of state intervention.
- A more general critique of 'institutional' care per se.
- The associated belief that the family was almost always the best place to bring up all children.
- The emergence of a social work profession.
- The rapidly rising costs of social welfare in general and residential care in particular.

An examination of these factors is important, not only because they explain the difficulties faced by residential child care between 1976 and 1991, but because they allow us to understand the continuing political and professional ambivalence towards the sector in the face of significant recent improvement.

The end of optimism and the breakdown of consensus

According to Hendrick the post-war period:

. . . was marked not only by expansion but also by a sense of optimism, a belief that it was possible to change people's lives, to enhance their experiences, in effect to patch up the consequences of economic and social deprivation.

(Hendrick, 2003: 192)

This 'period of sustained optimism'; the belief that problematic behaviour resulting from impoverished parenting could nonetheless be remedied by family-based intervention and psycho-dynamically grounded treatment, continued into the 1960s and early 1970s, despite a growing groundswell of dissent, at first in the universities and latterly in the field (Hayden et al.,1999). Nonetheless, these beliefs formed the central logic in England and Wales of the Children and Young Persons Acts 1963 and 1969, which drew no distinction between a deprived child and a child who commits criminal offences. In England and Wales and Scotland, where the Kilbrandon Report (1964) replaced juvenile courts with Children's Hearings, the focus of intervention was the *needs* rather than the *deeds* of children and young people.

However the days of these social democratic, 'welfarist', ideas in the field of child welfare were numbered. In marked contrast with the optimism of the post-war period, the 1980s were, according to Hendrick:

. . . the decade in which long smouldering tensions concerning the relationship between childcare, family responsibility and the jurisdiction of the state finally erupted.

(Hendrick, 2003: 193)

The critique of institutional care

As we have noted, the rumblings of dissent were first evident in the 1960s, and from here on a broader 'anti-institutional' movement gained momentum. In this backlash, residential child care units, no matter how well run or how well integrated into their communities, came to be viewed as 'institutions' and, as such, inimical to the interests and well-being of their 'inmates'. Perhaps the most influential of these critiques was that of Goffman (1961) whose classic work *Asylums* was based on 1,000-bed secure institutions in the USA in the mid-1950s. Yet his findings on 'institutionalisation' continue to be applied to modern children's homes, most of which accommodate no more than 5 or 6 young people.

A child's right to a family life

The 1948 Children's Act stated that the best place for a child to be brought up was in their own family, expressing a preference for family placements when it was necessary to remove a child from home. This principle has formed the basis of all subsequent childcare legislation and is a core principle underpinning the United Nations Convention on the Rights of the Child.

The emergence of a social work profession

The 1948 Act established Children's Departments in local authorities, which gave impetus to the emerging social work profession. Parker (1988) suggests that the 1948 Act marks an important turning point in the evolution of residential child care because it established *a strong orientation towards care solutions other than those in a residential setting* (6) from a profession whose identity *was partly based on the fact that it did not work in institutions* (31). Thus the social work profession supported by government policy, helped to establish the family as the central focus of child care intervention.

Rising costs

1976 was the year when the largest number of children was placed in residential care, ever, in the UK. The costs of residential provision were rising steeply as employers had to raise salaries from a traditionally low base in order to attract and keep staff (Senior, 1989). 1976 was also a year of economic crisis in the UK and the start of an era of 'cutbacks' in central government funding to local authorities. Meanwhile, the newly created social services departments were being required to assume many new responsibilities, such as the development of adoption and fostering services, by the 1975 Children Act. Government cuts, and the burgeoning salary bill, put tremendous pressure on social services departments to rationalise costs. These pressures were exacerbated by demands from residential workers for parity with field workers and access to professional social work training. The idea of reducing their reliance on the residential sector by offering support to needy children in their own homes and using foster placements where this was not possible was therefore extremely attractive to service managers.

A combination of increasing disillusionment with residential care and the rising costs of local authority services, led inevitably to the contraction of residential care and increased reliance on family casework and fostering. Not only did this shift solve some pressing logistical problems, it accorded to a considerable extent with the research evidence.

The impact of research

Contemporaneous research revealed that social workers saw reception into care as a sign of social work 'failure' (Barclay, 1982; DHSS, 1985) and this pessimism was echoed in the influential work of Rowe and Lambert (1973). Its central message was that a paucity of planning and forethought meant that large numbers of children were 'drifting in care', thereby becoming estranged from their families. There was particular concern about younger children being damaged by living in an institutional setting for long periods, and the fact that some might even 'grow up' in residential care simply because no one was bothering to return them home or look for an alternative family

Rowe and Lambert's research established a receptiveness to the concept of 'permanency' and in the 1980s this quest for permanence came to inform the strategies of social services departments and the practice of individual social workers (McKay, 1980). Permanency suggested that all children could be placed either back into their own families or in an alternative long-term family placement, which would offer them security into adult life. Permanency planning identified a hierarchy of placement options with birth family at the top followed by adoptive family, then long-term fostering and, somewhat reluctantly, temporary fostering (Maluccio, 1993: 177). Residential care did not feature at all in the hierarchy of placements and it came to be seen as a placement which should only be used on a 'temporary' rather than a 'permanent' basis.

However there appears to have been a lack of congruence between some research findings and the ideas and ideologies underpinning professional practice. As the DHSS (1985: 16) review observed, although the idea that *residential care should be a last resort*, was the implicit assumption informing much social work practice, this *extreme pessimism about care may be both unwarranted and damaging* because *the majority of parents and children felt they achieved some benefits for them*.

Parker's review of research for the Wagner Committee (1988) noted that professional interests helped to shape the fortunes of

residential care and that it was important to see residential care as part of a wider system of services. He maintained that a close relationship existed between parts of the residential child care system and foster care, citing the need for residential care as a response to fostering breakdown and for preparing children for foster placements. He maintained that this constituted a state of interdependence and that it was therefore not appropriate to regard them as exclusive options. Moreover:

> Seen from a child's viewpoint residential and foster care can be seen as sequential episodes in a string of different placements.
>
> (1988: 73)

Destruction or transition?

The prevailing environment for the residential child care sector at this time was summed up in the Short Report (1984):

> Residential care is going through an intensely difficult period, which may be optimistically typed as a process of transition but less optimistically viewed sometimes looks like a gradual process of destruction.
>
> The current prevailing public preference for family placements and the perceived expense of residential care, together with the widely held belief that residential care can often be damaging in the long term, has led to a deteriorating staff morale and a sense of purposeless in some residential homes.
>
> (para. 200)

The Short Report provides a window on some of the debates and anxieties of the times. While it contained recommendations that supported the expansion of fostering and support for families, the section on residential care declared:

> We affirm at the outset that we see a continuing and positive role for residential care, and that it should be regarded not as a second best or last resort but rather should be recognised as being the sort of care best suited for some children at some time.
>
> (para. 201)

The UK was not unique in the loss of confidence in residential care at this time. Reviewing the changing patterns of residential child care across Europe and further afield, Gottesman (1991: viii) observed that the accounts from 22 countries:

> . . . testify to two almost parallel processes: on the one hand during the last quarter of a century residential care worldwide has changed in almost all respects, mostly for the better; on the other, seemingly independent of this progress and quite paradoxically, the reservations, antag-onisms and even hostility to residential care have grown

markedly during the past few years, causing it to pass through its deepest crisis since the end of World War II.

During much of the 1980s the energy of social work managers was directed to the development of 'alternatives' to residential care, as far as resources would allow, and the hope of many was that budgets committed to residential services could be re-allocated to day care or other non-residential 'family support' services. In England Warwickshire Council gained considerable publicity and professional kudos when it closed all its children's homes (Cliffe and Berridge, 1991). In Scotland Fife Council closed all but one of its residential homes.

By the end of the 1980s some social work academics and practitioners were beginning to question the prevailing orthodoxy. As it became clear that residential care was now serving mainly as a resource for 'hard to place' teenagers, some were also beginning to identify the limitations of the wholesale application of 'permanency' thinking:

> *There is also a failure of the current permanency wisdom to address the issue of the increasing age of young people in care where permanency in the main is a non-issue and for whom residential care is often a reality.*
>
> (Frost and Stein, 1989: 112)

Indeed, placement instability and placement disruption was becoming a significant characteristic of the care system as a whole. The Short Committee had addressed this issue, drawing attention to evidence from the National Foster Care Association that:

> *Everyone working in foster care is conditioned to expect a high rate of breakdown and this becomes a self-fulfilling policy.*
>
> (1984: 191).

As Triseliotis (1988) observed:

> *Possibly our biggest failing has been in providing stable care in the lives of adolescents whether in residential homes, long-term foster home or within the adolescents own family.*
>
> (1988: 9)

Black (1988) criticised what she saw as the excessive focus upon 'drift':

> *Children who are in care at the age of 12 or over are often children newly admitted to care and not children who have drifted through care from a very early age as we knew it in the 1960s and 1970s.*
>
> (1988: 39)

O'Hara (1988), who had been a senior social work manager responsible for the development of fostering services in the Lothians, was more trenchant:

> *The approach of the mid-1970s to mid-1980s of 'No child or young person being unplaceable' was as romantic as it was unrealistic ... Older children with strong attachments to their birth families should never have been placed for adoption. Teenagers with severe acting out behaviour problems in their own families are rarely transformed in substitute families.*
>
> (1988: 31)

It was particularly significant that the Wagner Committee chose as the title of its report *Residential Care: A Positive Choice*. However, residential child care still remained relatively invisible. It was only the emergence of evidence of abuse of children living in residential institutions that thrust the issue of children looked after by the state onto the policy agenda.

1991: Pindown, meltdown and new beginnings

The publication of the Pindown Report (Levy and Kahan, 1991) led *Community Care* to launch a series on the 'Crisis in Care'. The editorial on 4th July 1991 maintained that publication of the report was a watershed for residential child care. Questions were raised about how often councillors and directors visited children's homes and who acted as an advocate for residents, in a situation where there was a lack of consultation with either young people or staff and where the provision of services was largely finance driven rather than being based on a systematic assessment of children's needs (Philpot, 1991).

In a similar vein, Payne (1991) asked how residential child care had reached its present sorry state. He suggested that the origins of the crisis lay in part in the stigma of the Victorian workhouse that was still attached to residential child care. It appears to have been generally agreed at the time that that the core problem was a failure to identify a positive role for residential child care. Kahan suggested that for some time there had been great ambivalence by senior management about residential child care. Both Levy and Kahan (cited in Cervi, 1991) stressed that children's homes were an essential part of child care, suggesting that some authorities had been too quick to run the service down. They maintained that even if fostering remains the preferred option, we should stop pretending that foster care can cope with all children in need. They insisted that despite the Warwickshire experiment there was always going to be a need for children's homes.

But this crisis in residential child care also provided a focus for examining the opportunities as well as the threats to the sector. Berridge (cited in Philpot, 1991: 14) stressed the positive possibilities emphasising that:

> ... *now is the time – there's public interest, professional concern and political interest.*

The Pindown Report turned residential child care into a public issue.

> *Publication created shockwaves brought about actions nationally and heightened awareness at local and national levels. It made a new beginning possible.*
> (Kahan, 1994: 46)

The immediate response by the government was to request the Chief Inspector's of Social Work in England and Wales and Scotland to undertake reviews of residential child care. Taken together the three reports, *Children in the Public Care* (Utting, 1991), *Another Kind of Home* (Skinner, 1992) and *Accommodating Children* (The Welsh Office, 2003) effectively established a new national agenda. In retrospect we can see that they served as the foundation upon which the recovery of residential child care in the UK was constructed. Their shared message was that:

> *The time was ripe for residential child care to enter a new phase; to be seen as an integral, essential and valuable part of services for children; for staff who work in it to be given full recognition; and for training and support to be provided for their difficult and demanding job.*
> (Kahan, 1994: 47)

Both Utting and Skinner highlighted the purposes of residential care. Skinner (1992), for example, argued that:

> *A residential home or school may offer the best placement in any of the following circumstances:*
> *a. When a young person needs care in an emergency, either because of a crisis in their own family's ability to provide care, or because they are at risk in their own home.*
> *b. When a young person needs longer-term care and a family placement is inappropriate. This may arise after a young person has had several family placements which have broken down, or when her or his need for longer-term care is not identified until she or he is well into their teenage years.*
> *c. When a young person needs care with additional specialist, therapeutic or educational services, provided on the same site.*

> *d. When a young person has complex special care and education needs, and her or his own family requires short-term support in sharing the care tasks.*
> *e. When young people and children require care which keeps them together and placement with substitute families would require them to be separated from each other.*
> (para. 1.10: 14)

Interestingly, these suggestions about groups and purposes are remarkably similar to those identified by Curtis (1946) and the Short Report (1984).

Skinner effectively put residential child care back on the agenda as an integral part of child care policy and practice. In Scotland, while there was a significant reduction in residential schools during the 1980s, they continue to play a larger part in the child care sector than in England. Skinner emphasised the positive purposes of the whole sector thus:

> *Residential care with and without education forms an important part of the range of child care resources designed to meet the individual care needs of young people and children. Residential care should be a part of each local authority's integrated strategy for child care, and should be seen as a positive means of meeting the needs of particular children, not simply as a last resort.*
> (1992: 9)

However, ongoing concerns about the potential for children to be abused when living away from their parental homes led the government to commission a review of safeguards. Government needed reassurance that the battery of regulations and guidance implemented since 1991 was effective. The protection rights in relation to the responsibilities of the state towards children living away from home were emphasised in the reports published in 1997 by Utting (England and Wales) and Kent (Scotland). Utting (1997) acknowledged that progress had been made since his first report in 1991. However, he commented that the sector remained *in urgent need of development as a national service* (para 1.12: 13) and stated his belief that the reduction in size of the sector resulted in the lack of a *critical mass to initiate improvements in standards* (para 2.7: 23). In Scotland the Children Act had been finally passed in 1995 promoting greater inter-agency cooperation but there was growing concern about the health and education of looked after children, and the quality of care-leavers support (Kendrick, 2003). The skill level of residential staff remained a major unresolved issue. Kent (1997) made a range of recommendations about the training of residential child care staff and concluded that overall *moving forward by small changes* [was] *not an option. There is a pressing need for radical change* (para 8.1: 97).

The House of Commons Health Committee Report on children looked after by local authorities (1998) identified major weaknesses in the education and health of looked after children, the lack of placement stability, and the continuing absence of an effective legislative framework for supporting children after they left state care. They concluded that:

> *The full implementation of the Children Act is a challenge awaiting the present government, and a test of the genuineness of its commitment to tackling social exclusion. If the government is prepared to invest the resources and political will that are necessary to make a real difference, it may not be necessary for our successors in another 14 years to produce another report assailing the failures of the care system.*
>
> (para 94: lxxxi)

New Labour new possibilities

However 1997 marked a major change in the social policy environment. While both Utting and Kent were commissioned by a Conservative government to carry out their reviews both reported to the New Labour government elected in May 1997. The change in government also marked a shift in the ideologies underpinning social policy and therefore in the policy objectives. The focus of policy shifted from the protection of children in state care to wider objectives of social inclusion. Children looked after by the state were identified as a key target group in the government's overall policy of tackling social exclusion and reducing child poverty. There was a noticeable change in the way in which policy was framed towards ideas of rights and entitlements and the responsibility of effective government for ensuring the citizens access to welfare. The position of children in state care becomes effectively reframed as one key target in the New Labour social inclusion agenda.

1998: drive for improvement and integration

The 'Quality Protects' initiative offered clear evidence of these commitments. Launching the initiative in September 1998 Frank Dobson, Secretary of State said:

> *Children have the right to expect the best possible care . . . children's services need reform . . . and nowhere is the transformation needed more than in the case of children in care.*
>
> (DoH press statement, 1/9/98)

Addressing an audience of local authority elected members as well as Directors of Social Services he made it clear that *we will, and must make a difference.*

Quality Protects was a radical departure from the policy frameworks for children in state care, which preceded it. Initially a three year programme, extended to five years by LAC (2000) 22, it ran until March 2004. The Local Authority (LA) circular which defined the shape of the policy, LAC(98)28, offered LAs financial incentives for compliance but it was clear that government expected local authorities to achieve the policy targets it had stipulated in relation to a wider population of children in need that included children in the care of the local state

> *Quality Protects is about improving the well-being of children in need for whom your local authority has taken on direct responsibilities.*
>
> (para 5.2)

For the first time in England and Wales, national objectives for children's services were set, outlining exactly what local authorities were expected to achieve. An explicit system of accountability was established through the requirement for each local authority to develop annual Management Action Plans (MAPs). The government acknowledged the crucial role of local authority elected members and emphasised the corporate responsibility for children who were being looked after by *your* local authority:

> *Councillors need to make sure that the interests of children come first and should do their utmost to ensure that children in public care get a good start in life.*
>
> (para 8.1)

The emphasis on Corporate Parenting was a departure from the traditions of the parish and the ideologies of the Poor Law Guardians. One of the underpinning principles of the Children Act 1989 in England and Wales and the Children (Scotland) Act 1995, was that duties under the Acts were defined as the responsibility of the local authority as a whole and not just the social services departments. However, by September 1998, 7 years after the implementation of the Act, there was little evidence of a positive impact of this change on the life chances and opportunities for children in state care in England and Wales. An SSI inspection of children's homes (SSI, 1993) for example, reiterated that it is elected members who carry ultimate responsibility for the provision of children's homes (para 20: v) and that rota visits by elected members *represented a further expression of corporate responsibility for promoting the welfare of children in public care.* While Regulation 22 ensured that senior managers were carrying out their responsibilities, however perfunctorily, to visit children's homes, rota visits by members were *a rare occurrence* (para 24: vi).

In November 1998 in his foreword to the report of the ministerial task force on Children's Safeguards, the Government's response to the second Utting Report, Frank Dobson, as Secretary of State, emphasised that *there can be no more excuses.* He indicated that the deliberations of the Task Force reflected their child-centred approach focussing on questions such as *would this be good enough for my children?*

> As a result our proposals are intended to ensure that those responsible at any level for children in care act towards them as any good natural parent tries to act towards their children.
>
> (Dobson, 1998)

Late in 1998 the Scottish Office announced their responses to the Children's Safeguards Review (Kent, 1997). Kent recommended the establishment of a National College to train residential workers (Rec. 25: 115) and the adoption of the notion of 'social pedagogue' training, through 'conversion courses', as a way of meeting the training needs of all workers in residential settings who may have had other basic qualifications in care, social work or teaching (rec. 22. 114). While the government did not follow Kent's recommendation in detail it announced that it was going to 'centralise and streamline' the training of residential workers (Scottish Office, 1998). The priority given to this was apparent in the subsequent White Paper (Scottish Office, 1999) when the training of residential child care workers was included as one of seven priorities for modernising social work.

The Scottish Institute for Residential Child Care (SIRCC) was one of the outcomes of these decisions. Established in April 2000 SIRCC is a consortium comprising the Social Work Departments of Strathclyde and Robert Gordon's Universities and Langside (Glasgow) College of Further Education, Save the Children Scotland and Who Cares? Scotland. SIRCC has a number of objectives; to develop and deliver training at all levels, from induction to Masters. One objective required the provision of full-time and distance-learning DipSW courses with a 'residential child care pathway', based on the CCETSW Pathway regulations in operation at the time (Milligan, 2003).

Registration and training

One major aspect of the modernisation agenda in social services throughout the UK has been the regulation of the profession of social work and the commitment to register all workers in social care. The responsibility for registration in England rests with General Social Care Council (GSCC) and in Scotland with the Scottish Social Services Council (SSSC). One aspect of the registration process is the requirement for minimum relevant qualifications. The government has demonstrated a continuing commitment to the sector by making residential child care workers part of the first wave of registrations along with 'field' social workers. While this indicates a move towards more parity of status between qualified social workers and workers in residential child care there are major difficulties with the registration of residential child workers. This is due to the proportion of workers in the sector who lack the basic qualification for registration, and of course the fact that the qualification itself is not at a professional level.

Recent research in England (Mainey, 2003) and in Scotland (Milligan et al., 2004) highlights the proportion of residential child care staff who remain without the relevant NVQ/SVQ child care award, the basic requirement for registration. In spite of significant investment in staff training the proportion of qualified staff in the sector continues to fall short of the targets recommended by both Utting (1991) and Skinner (1992) more than a decade after the publication of their reports. For the purposes of this chapter it is sufficient to note that the lack of an appropriately qualified workforce continues to hinder the development of the sector.

Young people's preferences

Since the passing of the Children Acts professional practitioners have been under a legal obligation to seek out the views of young people in all matters relating to their placement away from home. Research has provided inconsistent findings on children and young people's preference for placement, and one reason for this may be the changing nature of services over recent years. Several studies show strong preference for residential over foster care, for example, Sinclair and Gibbs, 1998; Berridge, 1985. Triseliotis et al. (1995: 186) found that young people were fairly equally divided in relation to the relative merits of residential and foster care and Sinclair and Gibbs (1998: 46) concluded that residents are more likely to chose residential care than any other form of care; *even those with experience of foster care chose residential care in preference to it by a ratio of three to one.* Most recently, in the context of a broader study of the views and experiences of young people about the transition to adulthood (Save the Children, 2001a), a sample of Scottish children and young people either in care or who had left care were interviewed (Save the Children, 2001b). One of the findings emerging from these interviews was a preference for being looked after in a residential setting, seeing this as providing 'a more secure, safer and longer-term environment' and therefore consistency of care' (Save the Children, 2001b).

Moving forward

This chapter has set out to demonstrate the significant gains made in residential child care since what we defined as the 'crisis' of 1991. There is, however, no cause for complacency as many challenges remain. The needs of children and families for support seem as great as ever, as evidenced for example in the mental health statistics which indicate that there are increasing levels of distress and disorder among young people (Meltzer et al., 2003, 2004). While the educational attainment of some looked after young people is improving in some places as the first fruits of better inter-departmental working, it starts from a low baseline. Many residential settings do not have the capacity to provide appropriate care for young people whose difficulties manifest themselves in challenging behaviour. The results are seen in multiple moves and further dislocation and despair. Staff to child ratios are higher than ever but the intensity of, for example, smaller units places significant demands on staff both individually and collectively.

Nevertheless it is important to recognise that significant progress has been achieved in

confronting the key issues identified above by Philpott (1991). While pay and conditions were the subject of a formal Inquiry (Howe 1992), recent research (Mainey, 2003; Milligan et al., 2004) suggests that pay in itself is not a key issue for staff working in residential child care though there are continuing concerns about aspects of the job such as 'sleepovers'. There has been a substantial investment in staff training in both England and Scotland. It is important to acknowledge that a higher proportion of both managers and care staff have a relevant qualification, while recognising that a significant proportion of staff remain unqualified. Therefore there remains a considerable distance to travel to achieve the modest targets set by Utting (1991) and Skinner (1992). National Care Standards have been developed and provide the benchmark against which residential services are inspected by the new independent, national Inspectorates. There are more checks and balances than ever before to ensure that all residential child care settings are subject to explicit and consistent accountability through independent inspection. Adults working in residential settings with young people are clearer about what is expected from them as professional practitioners, while managers and local authority members are equally clear about their responsibilities as corporate parents for children and young people looked after by the state (see for example National Minimum Standards for children's homes, CSCI (2005) and Morgan chapter below).

Developments in the implementation of Article 12 of the United Nations Convention on the Rights of the Child, and the expectations of domestic legislation that young people living in residential settings have a right to express their opinions about how they are being looked after, has raised their awareness about their rights. The growth of advocacy organisations such as Who Cares? Scotland, A National Voice and Voice for the Child in Care, the initiatives taken by the Department of Health in England in looked after children's participation as a key element of 'Quality Protects', and the commitment of national children's charities such as Barnardo's, the Children's Society and Save the Children, have all contributed towards a climate in which championing looked after children is more evident and available (see, for example, Crimmens, 2003; Willow, 2000).

The foundations are laid and the building blocks for a better service are in place. At the beginning of a new millennium, the evidence of progress made particularly since 1997 indicates that the sector is at a point in its history when residential child care can be seen to be moving forward.

References

Barclay, P. (1982) *Social Workers: Their Role and Tasks*. London: NISW. Barclay Square Press.

Berridge, D. (1985) *Children's Homes*. Oxford: Blackwell.

Black, A. (1988) Residential and Community Care: The Local Authorities View. in Wilkinson, E. and O'Hara, G. (Eds.) *Our Children: Residential and Community Care*. London: NCB Scottish group.

Cervi, B. (1991) Left to Sink or Swim? News Focus. *Community Care*. 4th July.

Cliffe, D. with Berridge, D. (1991) *Closing Children's Homes: An End to Residential Care?* London: NCB.

Commission for Social Care Inspection (2005) *National Minimum Standards for Childrens Homes*. www.csci.org.uk. accessed 4th May 2005.

Crimmens, D. and Pitts, J. (2000) *Positive Residential Practice: Learning the Lessons of the 1990s*. Lyme Regis: Russell House Publishing.

Crimmens, D. (2003) Children's Rights and Residential Care in England: Principles and Practices. *European Journal of Social Education* No.4.

Curtis Committee (1946) Care of Children Inquiry Report. House of Commons (Cmd 6922).

DHSS (1985) *Social Work Decisions in Child Care. Recent Research Findings and Their Implications*. London: HMSO.

Dobson, F. (1998) *The Government's Response to the Children's Safeguards Review*. Cm 4105. London: The Stationery Office.

DfES (2003) *Every Child Matters*. London: The Stationery Office.

Frost, N. and Stein, M. (1989) *The Politics of Child Welfare*. Hemel Hempstead: Harvester Wheatsheaf.

Goffman, E. (1961) *Asylum; Essays on the Social Situation of Mental Patients and Other Inmates*. New York: Doubleday.

Gottesman, M. (Ed.) (1991) *Residential Child Care: An International Handbook*. London: Whiting and Birch/SCA.

Hayden, C., Goddard, J., Gorin, S. and Van Der Spek, N. (1999) *State Child Care: Looking After Children?* London: Jessica Kingsley.

Hendrick, H. (2003) *Child Welfare: Historical Dimensions, Contemporary Debate*. Bristol: The Policy Press.

Howe, Lady E. (1992) *The Quality of Care: Report of the Residential Staffs Enquiry*, LGMB.

Kahan, B. (1994) *Growing up in Groups*. London: NISW, Research Unit, HMSO.

Kendrick, A. (2003) Children Looked After in Residential and Foster Care, in Baillie, D. et al. (Eds.) *Social Work and the Law in Scotland*. Basingstoke: Palgrave Macmillan/OU.

Kent, R. (1997) *Children' Safeguards Review, Report for the Scottish Office Home Department*. Edinburgh: The Stationery Office.

Kilbrandon (1964) *The Report of the Committee on Children and Young Persons in Scotland*. Edinburgh: HMSO.

Levy, A. and Kahan, B. (1991) *The Pindown Experience and the Protection of Children: The Report of the Staffordshire Child Care Inquiry 1990*. Staffordshire County Council.

Lindsay, M. (1998) Moving Mountains Armed Only With a Teaspoon: The Work of a 'Centre of Excellence' For Residential Child Care, *Social Work Education*, 17: 3, 339–49.

McKay, M. (1980) Planning for Permanent Placement, *Adoption and Fostering*, 4: 1.

Mainey, A. (2003) *Better Than You Think: Staff Morale, Qualifications and Retention in Residential Child Care*. London: NCB.

Maluccio, A. (1993) Promoting Permanency Planning, in Schaeffer, C. and Swanson, A. (Eds.) *Children in Residential Care*. London: Jason Aronson.

Meltzer, H., Corbin, T., Gatward, R., Goodman, R. and Ford, T. (2003) *The Mental Health of Young People Looked After by Local Authorities in England*. London: TSO/ONS.

Meltzer, H., Lader, D., Corbin, T., Goodman, R. and Ford, T. (2004) *The Mental Health of Young People Looked After by Local Authorities in Scotland*. London: TSO/ONS.

Milligan, I. (2003) A New Route to Professionalism? The Development of a Residential Child Care DipSW in Scotland, *Social Work Education*, 22: 3, 283–93.

Milligan, I., Kendrick, A. and Avan, G. (2004) 'Nae Too Bad': A Survey of Job Satisfaction, Staff Morale and Qualifications in Residential Child Care in Scotland. Glasgow: Scottish Institute for Residential Child Care.

O'Hara, G. (1988) Community Care for Children Who Come Into Care: Possibilities and Limitations, in Wilkinson and O'Hara (Eds.)

Our Children: Residential and Community Care. London: NCB Scottish group.

Parker, R. (1988) An Historical Background, in Sinclair, I. *Residential Care: The Research Reviewed.* London: NISW/HMSO.

Payne, (1991) What is to be done? *Community Care.* 15th Aug. 21–2.

Philpot, T. (1991) Home Thoughts. *Community Care.* 4th Jul. 12–4.

Rowe, J. and Lambert, L. (1973) *Children Who Wait.* London: Association of British Adoption Agencies.

Save the Children (2001a) *Challenging Transitions: Young People's Views and Experiences of Growing Up,* London: Save the Children.

Save the Children (2001b) *A Sense of Purpose: Care Leavers' Views and Experiences of Growing Up,* Edinburgh: Save the Children.

Scottish Executive (2001) *For Scotland's Children: Better Integrated Children's Services.* Edinburgh: Scottish Executive.

Scottish Office (1998) *The Government's Response to the Kent Report on Children's Safeguards Review.* Edinburgh: Scottish Office.

Scottish Office (1999) *Aiming for Excellence: Modernising Social Work Services in Scotland.* Edinburgh: Scottish Office.

Senior, B. (1989) Residential Care, What Hope for the Future? in Langan, M. and Lee, P. (1989) *Radical Social Work Today.* London: Unwin Hyman.

Short, (1984) *House of Commons Social Services Committee Report on Children in Care.* London: HMSO.

Sinclair, I. and Gibbs, I. (1998) *Children's Homes: A Study in Diversity,* London: Wiley.

Skinner, A. (1992) *Another Kind of Home: A Review of Residential Child Care.* Edinburgh: SWSI.

Social Exclusion Unit (2000) *Report of Policy Action Team 12: Young People. National Strategy for Neighbourhood Renewal.* London: TSO.

Social Services Inspectorate (1993) Corporate Parents. Inspection of Residential Child Care Services in 11 Local Authorities. London: SSi/DoH.

Triseliotis, J. (1988) Residential Care From a Historical and Research Perspective, in Wilkinson, and O'Hara, (Eds.) *Our Children: Residential and Community Care.* London: NCB Scottish group.

Triseliotis, J., Borland, M., Hill, M. and Lambert, L. (1995) *Teenagers and Social Work Services.* London: HMSO.

Utting, W. (1991) *Children in the Public Care: A Review of Residential Care.* London: DoH/HMSO.

Utting, W. (1997) *People Like Us: The Report of the Review of the Safeguards For Children Living Away From Home.* London: DoH/HMSO.

Wagner, G. (1988) *Residential Care: A Positive Choice.* London: NISW.

Welsh Office (2003) *Guidance on Accommodating Children in Need and Their Families.* National Assembly for Wales.

Wilkinson, E. and O'Hara, G. (Eds.) (1987) *Our Children: Residential and Community Care.* London: NCB Scottish group.

Willow, C. (2000) Safety in Numbers? Promoting Children's Rights in Public Care, in Crimmens, and Pitts, *Positive Residential Practice: Learning the Lessons of the 1990s.* Lyme Regis: Russell House Publishing.

Part Two: Difference and Diversity

Chapter Four

Residential Care for Black Children

Adele Jones and Delsierene Waul

Introduction

This chapter draws on the experiences of the Bibini Centre for Young People, a voluntary organisation established in Manchester during the period 1991–2003 to provide residential and community-based services for black children and families. The aim of this chapter is to identify important lessons for practice based on the experience of looking after black children.

In writing about black children, indeed in writing about any aspect of social life in the contemporary UK context, the subject of racism must be fore fronted. It is not that black children's experiences can be understood in the context of racism alone or that their experiences should only be defined in relation to racism. However it is the case that the black child in care is as likely to experience racism within a children's home as anywhere else and removed from the protective and resiliency factors often provided by black families and communities, children can be affected by racism in specific ways. Children's homes function as sub-systems of larger societal institutions and they are not immune to the overt and covert manifestations of racism. A failure to acknowledge or 'see' racism or the inability to address it sends a profound signal both to its perpetrators and its victims that has destructive and far-reaching consequences. Research on black children in care has often highlighted links between racism and children's reception into care or the ways in which racism can permeate decision-making processes, assessments and social work interventions thereby contributing to negative outcomes for black children. Knowledge and understanding of these issues are essential at the very least for policy and planning and at the practice level they can provide the impetus for dismantling racism whenever and however it is presented. In challenging racism, the task for the residential worker is to equip herself with knowledge and understanding and to reflect on self – for the dynamics of racism can entrap each and every one of us in a cycle of projections, responses and counter-responses that may contribute to its perpetuation. From this position,

the worker is better able to help children overcome the effects of racism and to identify and deal with its sources.

There are a number of important texts that provide a good starting point (see for example, Small, 1984; Pennie and Best, 1992; Barn, 1993; McDonald, 1991; Butt, Gorbach and Ahmad, 1991; Ince, 1998; Ince and Richards, 2000). These writers address specific issues concerning black children in care however there are also benefits to reading more widely. The work of black feminists, political activists, social commentators, poets and fiction writers for instance, are rich sources of knowledge and provide unique insights. Not only do they explore the many forms and forces of racism, they often powerfully articulate human resilience and resistance.

Much of the literature about racism refers to 'institutional' racism and 'personal' or 'individual' racism. We agree with Essed, however, who argues in her book *Understanding Everyday Racism* that this separation is artificial. We have adopted her phrase 'everyday racism' which she suggests better reflects the ways that racism permeates social institutions and is 'embedded in the routine practices of everyday life' (Essed, 1991). Essed suggests that everyday racism invades daily life for those who experience it so thoroughly that it is invisible to dominant groups who come to see it as normal. This helps to explain why many people struggle to 'see' racism and why it is easier to see black children in residential care simply as children.

A recent review of literature on the subject identifies a number of key themes drawn from the ways black people have expressed their perceptions and experiences of racism. These provide a useful basis for reflecting on how racism might impact on children and young people in residential care. Racism:

- *Is something embedded both in institutions and in everyday life to the extent that it is regarded as endemic.*
- *Is complex, multi-faceted, and cumulative involving a range of interactive processes.*

- *Is contextual in historical, geographical, institutional, social and economic ways.*
- *Can operate both covertly and overtly as well as formally and informally.*
- *Is experienced more sensitively and critically [by black people] than it is by white people.*
- *Is experienced in relation to both internal and external perceptions of self, peers and white people.*
- *Involves the interplay of stereotypes and stigmatisation with self-identity and symbols.*
- *May involve experiences of powerlessness, exclusion and invisibility.*
- *May be articulated without apparent evidence and even where evidence is presented it may be disputed or challenged.*
- *Is often experienced in conjunction with experiences resulting from class and gender.*
- *Is particularly experienced in relation to institutions and processes relating to education, employment and policing.*

(NCH – The Bridge, 2003: 14)

Other studies and literature highlight the specific circumstances of black children in care, such as the disproportionate numbers of black children of African Caribbean descent and those of mixed parentage who are in the public care system (Barn, 1993) the deprivation of community and identity for black children within the care system and the negative effects of institutional policies and practices. Additionally a number of reports published by the Department of Health have highlighted the failings of local authorities to bring about improvements for black children. Much of the literature pulls together messages from research and offers cogent suggestions for change. It is important to have an understanding of the wider context of the problems that black children in care face so that policy and practice in children's homes can be linked in meaningful ways to the broader social reality of their lives. There is nothing new about promoting anti-racist practice but it does seem that those who are genuinely committed to anti-racism often seem willing to settle for a passive non-racist stance that simply results in non-action or unwitting complicity with policies and structures that result in discrimination.

Where there is inaction against racism there is fertile ground for it to grow. Where there is ignorance about racism there is also fertile ground for the emergence of cultural and race 'experts'. Driven by orthodox, 'traditional' or narrow perspectives on culture, these experts sometimes promote prescriptions about the needs and aspirations of black children which when adopted uncritically may also be harmful. For all of these reasons, workers must acquire knowledge and understanding about racism, the skills and the will to deal with it, the capacity for critical reflection and most importantly, they must engage in action to confront it.

The issues that are discussed in this chapter are grounded in the reality of looking after black children. The issues are explored as they emerged in practice and assumptions and theory are deconstructed and put to the test. While we hope that our insights will be of value to the reader we do not provide a prescription for practice with black children. We argue for reflective practice, for transformative practice, a practice which pays attention to the needs of black children as a matter of course and within the context in which they arise. 'Good' practice or 'best' practice is not something that is fixed; it is something that is always becoming. This brings two questions to the fore. Firstly if practice is subject to constant change how do we hold on to interventions that seem to be effective and; secondly, is it possible to identify and put in place standards for all children that are indisputably universally beneficial? Both of these are possible. If practice is relevant to black children; if it enhances their potential and removes the barriers that impact on their development and if it is grounded in the reality of their lives then we can point to its effectiveness. This is also true for white children. This statement then can be said to represent a 'fixed' standard for assessing effectiveness; however 'potential', 'development' and 'reality' are not fixed concepts – they are social constructs that provide room for manoeuvre. They allow us to see that what is effective in a particular historical, social and cultural context may not be effective in another. Reflection and transformation do not mean that residential workers and managers have to operate in 'shifting sand' and asking searching questions should not prevent workers from being action oriented. These problems can be addressed by ensuring that practice is grounded in a value base (we call this a philosophy of care) that explicitly addresses the impact of racism and other forms of discrimination, a philosophy of care that is open to question and is shared by those working with black children.

We have been encouraged in our approach by the work of Foucault (1972) and other scholars.

Our association with them locates us theoretically – our discourses and interventions are produced from working with children who are on the margins of society. Foucault introduces us to the concept of genealogy as a 'history of the present' – this legitimises our critique of residential practice, for we know it has served black children badly. Our theoretical framework is based on two interlocking approaches:

1. Engaging in critical reflection and unearthing hidden knowledge – especially that which comes from marginalised voices (including black children's).
2. Discussing the ways that structures and institutions impinge upon black children collectively as well as how best to address the specificity of their needs as individuals.

The chapter makes use of these themes and explores them in relation to the residential care task. Woven throughout are questions that have been raised in our work with black children such as working with parents, the use of black role models, conflicts between children's and parent's rights, care for black disabled children, identity, education etc. and we draw on practice examples to show how they might be addressed.

Critical reflections

In discussing the care of black children it can be helpful to scrutinise and clarify concepts and perspectives. The irony of this is that as we take the reader through this process we run the risk of marginalising our own discourses. Other mainstream topics on residential care stand without the need for clarification; they are validated simply because they operate *within* hegemonic practice. Nevertheless, even this observation is useful and in any event, it is worth the risk – the knowledge we have gained over the many years of reflection on how best to serve black children and families is worth sharing.

Firstly, much of what is to be learned about caring for black children is neither unique to black children nor does it speak to the experiences and needs of *all* black children. So why write a chapter about black children at all? In his book on residential care, John Burton describes a children's home in which all the staff were white and slightly more than half the children were black (Burton, 1993). While increasingly black children may find themselves in homes in which there are some black staff,

many still experience such a huge dissonance between their emerging sense of self and identity and the care environment that loss, rage, despair and fragmentation can be compounded. Furthermore although black professionals make an invaluable contribution to social care, having black staff in homes in which power and authority is vested predominantly through white institutions does not change the nature of racism, to assume so it to misunderstand the dynamics of racism. Responsibility for meeting the needs of black children cannot rest with black staff alone, the disproportionate numbers of black children in care preclude this but in any case such a preposition rests on the premise that matching workers with children on the basis of ethnicity, race or culture will solve the problem. 'Good' quality care for black children cannot simply be equated with being black anymore than 'bad' quality care can be equated with being white.

Secondly *all* aspects of residential child care are pertinent to the care of black children including organisational and management issues; recruitment, selection, training and retention of staff; standards and quality assurance; legislation, policy and local and national procedures; registration compliance; child care, protection, rights, risk assessment and management and so on – it is simply that much that has been written renders black children invisible.

The language and practice of inclusion

Over the years we have been confronted with, and have largely resisted the requirement to define and re-define how we use the term 'black'. We adopted this approach partly because we were aware that at the same time 'white' existed as normative and uncontested. Also, what was important was *our* understanding of the term, not its defence to others. To satisfy the demand for explanation seemed to divert energy away from the business of caring for black children. Nevertheless, we are convinced that the business of caring for black children *should* begin with a reflection on language and its potential for inclusion and exclusion. This also means scrutinising the taken-for-granted status of 'white' and its position as the 'authorised' voice.

Critical reflection helps the worker to explore and articulate the meanings they give to a term that may be laden with the unstated assumptions of others. This deepens understandings about how black people are represented or choose to represent themselves, the role of whiteness and the links between racism, nation and ethnicity. Thus begins the process of developing a philosophy for the care of black children.

We use the term 'black' as a political and unifying term to refer to the 'colour' of the experience of racism rather than simply the colour of a skin. It is not a term that denotes homogeneity and on the contrary encompasses diversity and difference. The phrase 'black and Asian', common in lay speech and literature is in our view a confusing conflation of terms, with implicit assumptions about skin colour and ethnicity that reduce a complex phenomenon in simplistic and divisive ways. 'Black' has valuable currency in working with black children in that it shifts attention away from seeing the problem in terms of a specific ethnic or minority group or being attributable to a particular physiognomy. It seeks to prevent judgements about personhood based on genealogy and as with the reclamation of the term 'disabled', the concept locates responsibility for inequality and discrimination within those who perpetuate it and the broader structures and institutions of society that sustain it. However it is not a concept that has universal appeal or acceptance. It may not for example, reflect the experiences of black children from other countries who may be unfamiliar with the current landscape that characterises race relations in the UK. For some black children, and indeed for black parents and workers, the notion of an inclusive term can seem to undermine and indeed, can fuel the need to assert a specific cultural or religious identity. Furthermore, as a political concept 'black' suggests unity which in

actuality may mask the ways that ethnic, gender and class divisions fuel tensions within and between groups. While acknowledging and dealing with the source of these tensions can be important this does not mean that we should dismantle or modify a concept of value to us. Indeed we perhaps need to be mindful that the notion of whiteness is not undermined by the tensions that exist between groups of white people simply because their interests and perspectives may differ.

Generally the parents we have worked with have not required that we explain our use of the term 'black', even if they did not share our conceptualisation. What they required was evidence of their inclusion, behaviour and action on our part that made sure they did not feel excluded from any aspect of their child's care. Inclusive practice is the *approach* one takes in caring for children; it is not an abstract concept. It is tangible, is felt and has benefits for child, family and worker. There are no bounds to its possibilities. Inclusive practice is achieved for example, when a worker takes the trouble to find out how a parent wishes to be addressed; how they wish to receive information (whether it should be translated); whether an interpreter or a worker who speaks their first language would help; what the significance is to them of religious and cultural traditions (this can prevent reviews being called on particular days, for example or trips being organised at times that clash with important family events). It is also achieved when a worker takes the trouble to understand the impact that other issues may have on the parent's capacity to be involved in the care of their child. This is illustrated in the following example:

Practice Example

Joan was a young woman of 14 with learning disabilities. When she was placed at the home she had very little contact with her mother although the care plan identified increasing family contact as being in Joan's interests. It was difficult to get Joan's mother to visit and she was not sure she could manage Joan at home. Previous records suggested a lack of interest on the part of the mother however our assessment was different. This was a single mother, an African Caribbean woman with five other children and the family was living in a state of poverty. She was quiet and seemed unassertive; it appeared to us that her experiences of dealing with the social services department had left her on the outside of her daughter's care. Unable to look after her child, she did not feel she had the right to question those who did and in any event caring for her other children depleted her time and energy. She could not leave her other children to visit Joan but could not afford to pay someone to mind them. If she did come to visit she was so anxious about being away from home that it affected the quality of the visit.

Practice Example *(continued)*

We invited all of the family to come to share a Caribbean meal with us and it soon became commonplace to see her and all her children together at the home. In quiet ways she let us know that even having a break from cooking was valuable respite. Over time the family was able to see how we managed Joan's behaviour and increasingly our practice was emulated. Although we did not realize it at the time, this helped to provide a consistency of approach that eventually made it possible for Joan to spend long periods with her family. As the other children became more comfortable they would often play with the children in the home and Joan and her mother were able to spend more and more time together. When Joan's mother asked if it was OK to take Joan out on Saturdays, we offered financial assistance (to pay child minding costs, travel, meals and so on) to support the plan and did the same when she was ready, for overnight and then weekend stays.

By taking the impact of poverty into account, instead of being excluded, Joan's mother became more involved in her daughter's care. She was able to attend most reviews, she brought her family to all the leaving parties and other functions in the home and she was involved in all decisions regarding the care of her daughter. When Joan was ready to move on to a home for adults she was instrumental in finding the right placement and in developing the support plan. Additionally by involving the whole family, Joan developed a closer relationship with her siblings. As we got to know Joan's mother better we also realized she felt a considerable degree of guilt about her daughter being in care. Joan's previous placement had been with white foster parents and while they had provided very good care, Joan's mother had felt ashamed to visit her. The care and material standards provided by the white foster parents had compounded feelings of guilt and inadequacy.

So, what does the term 'black' mean in practice? The question misses the point. The concept is the summative articulation of a shared perspective; it comes out of hidden knowledge and is embedded in the practice of living. The value of the meaning of 'black' to the parent in the example above does not lie in defining it. It lies in conveying an understanding that black parents may face particular constraints that are not to do with individual inadequacy but with structural inequality. This is not to assume that *all* black parents face such adversities; that poverty and other problems *always* affect parenting or indeed to ignore the fact that some people are unable to parent their children effectively regardless of external problems; however the knowledge we have about racism and other sources of oppression must at least raise this as a possibility. The practice example shows that inclusion is not about what one *says* one's intentions are so much as what one's actual behaviour demonstrates.

Disablism and racism: a juncture for transforming practice?

The practice example above introduces the reader to the question of residential care services for black disabled children.

Disabled children's services do not adequately cater for black children and services for black and minority ethnic groups do not adequately cater for disabled children. This means that black disabled children 'fall through the net'.
(Joseph Rowntree Foundation, 2002)

This comment from research conducted into services for black disabled children holds us all to account. The writings of black disabled activists' point to a simultaneous multi-layered experience of oppression and this is the broader context for the marginalisation of the needs of black disabled children. Two measures would help in addressing this problem. Firstly services for disabled children should ensure that issues of ethnicity, culture, religion, language and racial identity are central to the care planning process and set the context in which needs arising from disability are met. Secondly where possible all services for non-disabled children should also be able to meet the needs of disabled children. For black disabled children this approach offers one possibility for lessening their isolation although it is important that specific needs relating to a disability are not neglected as a consequence. Although the concept of integrated education is well-established, we found the concept of integrated residential care difficult to establish in practice. Our building, policies, procedures, staff training and philosophy were all geared to the concept of integrated care. We could see no reason why black disabled and non-disabled children should not live together. However the practice was resisted (by professionals, not parents) on the basis that disabled children may be particularly vulnerable in care settings and may exposed to bullying and the neglect of specific needs. These problems are not however confined to settings in which disabled children are looked after and while they need to be addressed, the benefits of inclusive care can outweigh the disadvantages. It was difficult to get referring agencies to see that a children's home specialising in the care of black children might also care for disabled children. The 'black' was visible but 'disabled' was not – this seemed a reversal of the experiences of many disabled children for whom the focus is on disability and their racial, cultural or religious needs often go unseen. Black disabled children often experience isolation from friends, family and community and where they are involved with their local communities they may be subject to discrimination and disablism that need to be challenged. Supporting black disabled young people requires an approach that ensures that they are integrated within the black community – this means establishing positive relationships with black community and religious organisations and also that black disabled children have access to resources to meet specific needs.

Black role models: reflecting on a concept

The value of positive black role models for black children (and we would argue, for white children too) is largely uncontroversial and generally accepted as a good thing. The concept is usually applied in a superficial, uncritical way however, and its real value is often under-utilised as a consequence. The underlying premise is that providing black children with examples of exemplary black people in society demonstrates achievement and positive attributes to emulate, aspire to or be inspired by. The message is that black children should work today for delayed benefits tomorrow and that they can expect to be rewarded by society if they behave in exemplary ways. Unfortunately this is undermined by a more potent message. The role models they see in black communities show them that regardless of the efforts they make, black people often continue

to experience high levels of deprivation in the areas that they live and poor job prospects. Furthermore, the models we select for children to emulate are usually based on adult perspectives that fail to take into account a number of important factors:

- Children are usually targeted at a developmental stage when they are more likely to be influenced by peers than by adults with whom they have little connection.
- Young people themselves and the broader 'culture of youth' are the key determinants of role models.
- The influence of mass marketing and popular media promotes instant gratification rather than delayed rewards.
- The value to children of 'the idea of rebellion' – images that seem to usurp authority.
- Young people's perceptions of 'success'.
- The ways that feelings of inadequacy and failure can be reinforced when children are unable to live up to the ideals of others.

Moreover black children are often aware that what exemplify the positive role models they are presented with are not so much their achievements as the fact that they represent such a tiny minority within mainstream society. It is important and entirely possible within children's homes to introduce children to positive images, not just of black people but of different ethnic and religious groups, black gay men and lesbians, black disabled people and so on. While there is merit in the idea of positive role models, the concept of modelling has more benefits when viewed as synergistic with children's daily lives rather than as an influence that is external to a child's reality. For children to benefit in a meaningful way from positive role models, the concept needs to be extended, broadened and deepened in ways that reduce the emotional and psychological distance between themselves and the role models. Also it is important to see black role models as modelling not only achievement and success, but behaviour and skills that black children can learn from and connect with. Black role models in *this* conceptualisation provide a means for children to 'rehearse' the expression of their emerging identity as black young people. Indications of this can take many forms and black workers often find a child copying their hairstyles, dress, mannerisms, ways of speaking and so on. Much as a little girl might practice dressing in her mother's clothes and trying her make-up or a little boy adopts the same pose while watching television that he sees his daddy take, so black children will use black role models to explore and express who they are becoming. Celebrating black achievement is beneficial to both black and white children, however it does not equate with ensuring that black children are positively affirmed in a way that is embedded into their daily lives and becomes as familiar to them as breathing. The use of black role models should be integrated within residential homes in ways that are subtle and multi-layered. As black adults contribute to healing processes, children's sense of identity, affirmation of parents (black and white), decision making, challenging racism and other forms of discrimination, demonstrating sensitivity, creativity and compassion, experiencing and dealing with pain and stress – as black people go about their daily business and involve themselves constructively in the daily business of black children it is only then that the full benefits of the concept can be realised.

Returning to the use of the term 'black', black children are not helped by role models that promote Afrocentrism or any other form of ethnocentrism or cultural nationalism in ways that prescribe and limit how black people must behave. This is not what being positive about blackness is about. The reality for many black 'mixed parentage' children is that their parents, siblings and other family members may be white. Of itself this does not affect the use of the term 'black' however it may affect how it is modelled. If positive relationships between black and white family members are threatened by the language that is used, there may be a need to explore the source of these insecurities and fears and to provide support for the child and family to address issues that the language brings to the fore. One of the most potent affirmations of our practice centred on the ways that white parents and black workers worked together to meet the needs of children and the 'permission' (implicit and explicit) in the behaviour modelled by black workers for children to positively express and embrace the experience of being in a 'mixed parentage' family without inducing the feelings of guilt or divided loyalties that can happen when black and white adults retreat into polarised positions.

It is also the case that black mixed-parentage children sometimes experience racism at the hands of white family members. While this is very destructive and painful to the child, it is important to neither minimise the experience or to undermine the resiliency of the child and the capacity of children to love even in the face of pain. Sometimes black mixed parentage children are rejected or feel out of place because their white parent becomes involved in a new relationship with another white person. It is almost impossible to imagine the trauma to children whose racial identity presents a source of embarrassment, ridicule or rejection by people they love. The internalised self-hatred, low esteem and distorted self image that can result may lead to anti-social and destructive behaviour that can be very challenging. This in turn often leads to punitive, exclusionary measures which compound hatred towards self and anger to others. Children in this situation may also become depressed, withdrawn and inflict self-harm. It is important to understand however that most black mixed-parentage children have a healthy and positive sense of self. The difference we have found usually lies in whether the child is isolated from other black people or whether they have a positive nurturing relationship with other black adults – this is why it is important to provide children with positive black role models – not necessarily black people that have achieved success, but ordinary black people who are comfortable with themselves and can help children develop the attributes and skills for dealing with racism. When black children have been ill-treated or harmed by black parents they may associate the behaviour of their parents with them being black, particularly if their protection from harm was achieved by placement in a setting where there were no black people. Research on socialisation patterns show that from an early age children in the UK are surrounded with overt and subliminal messages and images that associate black with evil and white with good. It can be of little surprise therefore that many black children internalise negative views about black people. Positive black role models can help to dispel these views. This requires that homes:

- Employ black staff.
- Link children to black people who can befriend them outside of the home.
- Make links with black community organisations and religious organisations.
- Facilitate the greater involvement of black families in the home.

- Include black professionals in the care of children (as doctors, dentists, psychologists, teachers etc.)
- Ensure where possible that when children move on – to other residential establishments, back to families or to new families that the new placement provides positive racial, cultural and religious affirmation in a way that the child can emotionally connect with.
- Expose children to black theatre, languages, literature, music, food, celebrations, newspapers and so on as part of everyday life.

While the benefits for black children are inestimable, white children too will gain from a positive exposure to people with diverse backgrounds. As the effects of affirming white children (which happens as a matter of course) cannot be measured, neither is there any empirical evidence of the benefits to black children. For white children, even those in care, racial and cultural identity are constantly affirmed, for black children in residential care the opposite is usually true. Specific and sustained steps must be taken to meet children's needs for positive racial affirmation and identification since this is integral to positive self esteem and self image. The current policy trend towards targets and outcomes means that essential work such as this, invisible in terms of outputs, is easily neglected. Nevertheless positive black role modelling should be an integral part of residential practice and it can also be used as a specific therapeutic tool.

Practice Example

When Simon was placed at the home he was 15 years old. This was his ninth placement in 18 months and he had come from a secure unit. He had been permanently excluded from school and no other school was willing to take him. Simon was one of two children born to a white English mother and a black Caribbean father. Simon's parents were divorced and his mother had remarried a white man who was a proclaimed member of the British National Party. Simon's father was in prison. Within three days of his placement Simon was found brandishing a knife at other children and had slashed furniture. We had no way of knowing whether we would be able to change Simon's behaviour particularly given that his short term goal was to show that no home was able or willing to care for him for more than a few days and his longer term 'ambitions' were encapsulated in this statement 'I'll either be a drug dealer or dead by the time I'm 18'. He was extremely intelligent and used his intellectual ability to identify weaknesses within the staff group and to play up the fears of children – he terrorised both groups and particularly targeted female staff members; he quickly established himself as 'top dog'.

Bringing a halt to his destructive and dangerous behaviour was *our* immediate goal; if we couldn't make everyone safe then Simon would not be able to stay. Our practice always involved including any non-abusing parent or other close adult family member in the care of children. This was not just about meeting requirements to 'work in partnership' – we actually did not believe we could make it without using every resource available to children. While families were often the source of great pain for children, we were almost always able to find strengths and resources among them that we could build on. Even where families are unable to care for their own children, they usually want what is best for them and may come up with suggestions to help.

We invited Simon's mother and social worker to meet with us. Simon's mother could not attend and the social worker came expecting to be told that Simon would have to be moved. We were not prepared to quit but the situation was quickly getting out of control. Punitive measures had proved to be ineffective – as Simon's behaviour escalated, so the sanctions became more severe; the cycle simply confirmed to him that he was as bad as he set out to be. We decided to use the concept of positive black role modelling as a therapeutic and behavioural tool. We came up with a three month intensive programme involving five different black male workers with specific roles designed to (a) explore some of the underlying causes of Simon's behaviour, (b) to use cognitive behavioural approaches to help to modify his behaviour (c) to harness Simon's abilities in constructive ways, (d) to provide creative avenues for him to channel his anger and frustration and (e) to support Simon's mother in rebuilding her relationship with her son. We hoped that by placing black men in key roles

Practice Example *(continued)*

in Simon's life we would surround him with many versions of black maleness and that this might help him to envision himself in different ways from the wholly negative view he currently held of himself as a young black man:

- One male worker was assigned as Simon's key worker.
- We appointed a counsellor whose own racial identity reflected Simon's mixed parentage origins – the counsellor was contracted to meet with Simon weekly.
- We identified a youth worker as a befriender – his role was to engage Simon in positive activities outside of the home and to build up networks within the community with youth groups.
- Simon's education needs were to be met in two ways – through attendance three days a week at an education support project within the black community and by appointing a black male teacher to provide individual tuition.
- The manager of the home (a black man) was to coordinate and monitor the programme; to identify crisis points and put in place contingency measures to head them off.
- We appointed a 'floating' residential social worker as an additional staff member to give additional care and support during periods when Simon's behaviour presented particular challenges (mealtimes, evenings, weekends and holidays).
- The social worker, immensely relieved that she did not have to find yet another placement for Simon managed to get the authority to pay for the additional resources.

Although she didn't attend the meeting Simon's mother contributed to making the plan work in ways that we could not have envisaged. She offered to provide *us* with respite. Clearly unable to manage Simon's behaviour full-time, she was encouraged by the positive approach we had taken and suggested that building in regular home visits and even overnight stays might help her to build on what we were trying to achieve and would give us a break. The intensity of meeting Simon's needs was so great that as it turned out we would not have managed without this offer of help. No matter how difficult Simon was with us, he always calmed down at home; this was an interesting reversal of his former behaviour.

When we asked Simon to join the meeting he told us that he had his bags packed ready to leave. He was astonished to discover that we wanted him to stay.

The plan did not work as intended; after the first two sessions, Simon refused to meet with the counsellor; his behaviour in the school support project resulted in his exclusion and he often sabotaged arrangements to spend time with his 'befriender'. Nevertheless we persisted and even after our three-month review a number of the arrangements we had put in place continued. Simon was confronted on a daily basis with black men who were firm, gentle and cared for him. He saw them at work and at play, as workers, as husbands, as fathers, as sons; they exposed their vulnerabilities to him and their strengths. Simon's behaviour did improve although there were many times when we felt we couldn't go on.

We have no way of knowing what the deeper benefits of our approach may have been – when finally we thought we were making some headway, 12 months later, Simon was involved in a serious criminal offence which resulted in him being moved.

Reflections on caring: a philosophy of care

It is useful for children's homes caring for black children to develop a philosophy of care that explicitly addresses the effects of inequality and discrimination. Managers and staff of the home should identify what it is they hope to achieve based on values that are explicit, shared and which commit all involved in the running of the home to a pro-active stance. The point here is that it is not enough to be passively anti-racist – racism *happens*, black children's needs *are* marginalised, one cannot wait for evidence of these problems before adopting a position of care and responsibility. This is one of the powerful lessons we have learned from parents – the position of care and responsibility for dealing with these issues based on their experiential knowledge is usually something children can take for granted. Even though residential staff may not have experience of dealing with racism when they transmit care and responsibility for tackling it to black children, the dynamics the relationships in the home shift from complacency and inaction to validation of children's experiences. Adult responses to children's complaints of racism that deny or minimise its significance have nothing to do with the needs of children. They are more likely an indication that the worker lacks the skills, knowledge or commitment to work with black children or has not faced up to the impact that racism has had on the worker herself. Validating black children's experiences does not make the pain of racism go away but it builds resiliency and provides a more potent force for challenging it.

The philosophy of care should be a tool for reflection and a baseline for evaluating progress and ensuring a measure of staff accountability to black children and families. It both precedes and goes beyond the 'Statement of Purpose' (a document which sets out in a simplified form what the home sets out to do) although it should be reflected within it. The process of drawing up a philosophy of care should itself result in the personal and professional growth of staff members. It lays down the commitment staff make to black children and although not an end in itself, it brings together many of the issues we have discussed so far and applies them to the residential care task. The policies and procedures of the home must be compatible with the philosophy of care.

Residential homes need to have a good understanding of the needs of black children and should also set priorities for meeting needs. There are many texts on how to conduct a needs analysis, however while these are useful they do not often show how one can unearth hidden knowledge and we think that principles from qualitative participatory and action oriented research approaches are a better guide. Data sources might include local authority policy and planning documents; information on disability, asylum-seeking families, child protection, poverty and social exclusion, local research on service-take up; and relevant information from education and health authorities. While these sources are important, they are likely to be incomplete since they may not include the views of black service users, or equally important, the views of black families who need, but do not use mainstream services. Input from black community and faith-based organisations will help to fill some of the gaps. This exercise should enable one not only to identify the cultural and demographic make-up of the communities serviced by the home, but the extent of unmet need and ideas (and offers of support) about how best to meet needs. If for example, staff from a home meet with parents of black disabled children they may be able to unearth their views about the limitations of existing services and what they think is best for their children.

A failure to identify the needs of black children and families means that practitioners are likely to be 'shooting in the dark' – there are several examples of well-meaning organisations that have established services that do not get used by black people simply because the information on which they were based was flawed. Children in residential care do not get to 'choose' whether they will use a service or not, however the extent to which a home can effectively meet their needs depends on a having a complete understanding of what those needs are. The exercise is also important to identify needs that the home cannot meet. Unless the home is set up within the context of a larger faith-based organisation it is unlikely for instance, that it will be able to cater solely for one particularly religious group. Parents may wish to know that their child will be living in a multi-faith rather than single-faith environment. Also the needs of some children may be so specific as to exclude other children being cared for in the same home.

Practice Example

The principles that guided the Bibini Centre's philosophy of care were: inclusive, holistic services; self-determination; children's rights; supporting black disabled young people; challenging the discrimination of black young gay men and lesbians; building not breaking family and community links, and challenging racism. Innocuous in themselves each of these principles tested commitments – How could they be reflected in the policies we created? How could we make sure that each new member of staff understood and respected them?

Practice Example *(continued)*

The principles were frequently questioned both as a consequence of negotiating daily life and also by those who did not share or understand the positions that informed them. Our reflection on children's rights for example, revealed important insights. We became aware that dominant discourses on children's rights present a number of problems. Firstly rights tend to be discussed as apolitical and non-contextual – this means for example, that it is easier for workers to focus on a child's right to express their views about school rather than deal with the structural issues that might actually be preventing a child from receiving an education. Secondly children's rights are often promoted as competing with parent's rights. When the question of children's rights is raised with parents it is often done in such a way as to suggest that parental or wider family rights have less importance than individualised rights. Families seem to work best however if the rights of individual children are 'negotiated' and managed in a way that accommodates other family members. This was an approach that we found useful. Finally the concept of children's rights is socially constructed and this raised the question how do we empower young people where they have come from a culture where questioning/challenging adults can be seen as disrespectful.

Although practiced with varying degrees of success the principles did not change and indeed they were often affirmed or strengthened. This example illustrates the point.

Food for thought

The principle of 'inclusive services' requires that black children are not excluded from living in a residential home because of their religious or dietary needs. This resulted in a food policy which as well as the usual nutrition, choice, hygiene, health and safety issues also took into account concerns that had been raised by parents. The policy determined that children would regularly experience the range of foods they were accustomed to or wanted to try (cooks prepared meals as diverse as fish and chips, fufu and groundnut stew). All meat prepared was Halal and a vegetarian option was always available. The most controversial aspect of the policy was that pork was not allowed within the home. This was challenged from several quarters – one local authority social worker actually brought bacon into the home and gave it to a child who said he thought not being able to have a bacon sandwich was a breach of his rights; some staff felt the policy did not go far enough as it did not prevent people from bringing in non-Halal products (such as fast-foods) and using the home's cutlery etc. The issue of children's rights was raised – was it ethical to restrict the choice of some children in order to cater for the needs of others? We reflected on the diverse group of black children we had looked after and found that despite the policy's flaws it had meant that children from such diverse religious backgrounds as Muslim, Rastafarian, Seventh-day Adventist, Pentecostal and Sikh had been accommodated without them being set apart as needing 'special' consideration. The policy was also an important affirmation of the staff we employed, particularly those with strong religious beliefs. This was not the only way that religious needs were met, but it was important. We found that children's opposition was usually transitional – a child would often request pork one day and claim to be vegetarian the next. Children wanted options that would satisfy their expressed wishes at any given time but when asked to think through the implications of letting people eat precisely what they wanted, they were able to imagine the ways in which this could be quite damaging. It was usually professionals who persisted in challenging the policy. Workers (white and some black) found legitimacy in voicing their opposition through the guise of 'children's rights'. Parents of black children on the other hand, never took up the mantle of complaint and even when children grumbled, they signalled their appreciation in many ways and were glad when our efforts extended to identifying pizza and fast food outlets that operated a similar approach.

For the many children who were searching to re-establish links with cultural and religious practices as a means of exploring their emerging black identity eating the 'right' foods was an important step, particularly since it required little effort, no special treatment and no stigmatisation. We probed the notion of children's rights and came to understand that sometimes individual rights may need to be delayed or suspended to ensure a collective good with benefits for a larger group. We weighed up the restrictions we had imposed on black children because of the food policy with

---

Practice Example *(continued)*

the freedoms many children had enjoyed because they were able to live with us and we realised that a more liberal approach to choice often simply sustains the status quo. Meeting the needs of black children we were looking after was not about this.

Each challenge to the policy helped us to see its weaknesses and to deal with them. We never abandoned the inclusive approach we had taken but we did address the limitations and try to find better ways of communicating its benefits.

The impact of structures and institutions: meeting needs

Having identified the needs of black children a number of qunestions need to be explored:

1. What needs arise directly because of racism?
2. What needs arise out of other sources of inequality and how are these interlinked?

3. What needs arise that are specific to a particular black child – what does the *specificity* of this child's experiences mean for practice?

These questions help in identifying the different forms of action needed to create the appropriate environment for caring for black children, the resources needed and the people who can give support. Two points to consider here: firstly needs change, so the analysis will need to be subject to periodic review (over the years we identified unmet needs in relation children with learning disabilities, children of Asian descent and young asylum seekers) secondly *read* – find out what research has been done that may be of use, read the black press, ncontemporary social work theories and those emerging from anti-oppressive perspectives (feminist, anti-disablist, critical black perspectives and so on) that will help to clarify thinking and planning. Reading may seem particularly ambitious in a field of practice that can often feel like emerging from a battle field at the end of the day. Nevertheless the most effective residential workers are the ones who extended themselves in these ways.

While the impact of structures and institutions on black children is felt at an individual level some issues are common to many black children and it is possible (and necessary) to take action without waiting for children to experience problems. Black children may be particularly affected by the structures and institutions related to:

- education
- policing
- immigration
- mental health
- poverty
- drugs and crime

While these are all important, common to all black children is the need for education and most glaring of all the issues is the disproportionate numbers of black children (particularly boys) who are excluded from schools. However the problems within the education system extend further than this. Vance, in commenting on the implications for schools of the McPherson Report identified several problems that need to be addressed: inability to recognise racism, incompleteness of evidence about racism, stereotypical attitudes and lack of awareness, repeated failures to act against racism, failure to listen to black pupil's views, inability to involve the community meaningfully, mistrust by local black communities, inadequate complaints systems and flawed curriculum. Additionally there are particular problems for many children in care, not least the effects on learning of instability and emotional distress. While it is not the responsibility of residential workers alone to address these problems, they have a vital role to play. Action is needed to make sure that black children are at least able to access schools. Even this can be difficult. The negative stereotyping of black children is compounded by the stigmatisation of care – schools want children who will enhance their league tables and black children in care do not usually fit such criteria. Using the formal education authority procedures to obtain school places may be appropriate but it can be time consuming, over-bureaucratic and may take a very long time. Meanwhile the child becomes increasingly alienated from the school environment, further behind with their work, socially isolated from other school children and will often internalise or externalise the anger generated by powerlessness and such overt rejection in harmful ways. By the time a school is identified, the child is often expected to fit in some way during the term when friendships and groups have been formed. The feelings of isolation, difference (particularly where there are few other black children) and stigma (everyone knows this is a child with a problem) are heightened and the sense of anxiety can be overwhelming. The child is forced to adopt a masquerade to survive. This may include pretence – pretending to understand work that they struggle with. It may mean accepting the role of victim – this can be particularly the case for young asylum seekers who have to deal with popular discourses that position them as war victims and needy recipients of help. It may mean playing the stereotypes conveyed overtly and covertly to the child - the trouble-maker, the 'gangsta'. It may mean adopting the wallflower approach – to blend in. These behaviours speak to the resilience of the child; however they can also thwart a child's development and undermine achievement. The school is a reluctant recipient of the child and the child is made a reluctant pupil – the stage has been set for further problems.

Practice Example

When we started out caring for black children, it was impossible to find schools willing to take our children. The ramifications of attempting to provide education support within the home environment for the majority of our residents can be imagined. Each time a child was placed we had to start the process of finding a place all over again – the social worker would approach the education authority and the long process of allocating a school place would begin. The children and staff were frustrated and so we decided to take an alternative approach.

While education as part of each child's care plan was the primary responsibility of the key worker, we allocated a senior staff member to take lead responsibility for making links with schools that had a more positive approach to black children. We identified the schools that had a good reputation among parents. We asked to see the policies schools had for dealing with racism and bullying. We found out which schools were actively involved in local community initiatives and routinely involved parents in the life of the school. The senior worker identified a number of key people from schools in the area and began to build relationships. He went to schools and talked about the needs of our children in a general sense; he made sure that the home supported school events and got our children involved in fund-raising events. Together with other professionals, educational psychologists, school social workers, teachers etc. he identified the ways that we might work together to resolve problems that might come up.

Our strategy was a major success; we found school places for all of our children and thereafter we were always able to identify a school place for a child coming to live with us even before they arrived. We drew up a support plan for children based on their individual needs. This approach had come out of the meeting with professionals. It ensured that we had measures in place *before* problems got to crisis point and that schools felt supported. It also ensured that residential workers were more closely in touch with what was happening at school and additional supports, for homework etc. could be put in at home when needed.

Conclusion

A great deal of what we have shared in this chapter on residential care for black children is also applicable to white children. It has often been said that anti-racist practice is simply good practice. This is so. What we have described is a practice that not only attempts to meet individual needs but which also acknowledges and deals with the ways that oppression impacts the lives of black children and families – there are universal benefits in such an approach. Parents of black children looked after have often talked of the ways in which they felt they were pathologised and shut out from their children's lives. This has an added dimension because of racism; however the experience of exclusion is debilitating and disempowering for *all* parents and practice based on principles of inclusion has benefits for all. The practice we have shared is also child-centred practice.

Effective residential care for black children, as for white children, is about the particularities of the residential care task, undoing the effects of previous harms and helping children achieve the aspirations we might have for our own children. Beyond this effective care for black children must be rooted in a willingness to understand and deal with racism in all its manifestations; to meet needs that arise for black children, including those that are linked to racism, those that emerge out of different sources of inequality, those that are 'simply' to do with them being children and those that are to do with being a specific child with specific needs, history, background and life experiences in a specific context.

While this is a chapter about many things, we are aware that many important areas have been omitted. For instance we have not been able to examine the impact of globalisation, particularly in regard to the needs of the children of asylum-seeking families and children affected by immigration trends. Neither have we been able to explore the specific challenges that black young people leaving care face or the attachment and loss implications of black children separated from their families (such as young asylum seekers). We have not discussed ethnic record keeping and monitoring for residential care homes; recruitment and retention of black staff; developing links with black communities, training or assessment. It is not possible within one chapter to provide an in-depth examination of all the issues involved in the residential care of black children and the reader is encouraged to explore other literature on the subject. Despite the limitations, we have attempted to demonstrate that there need be no gaps between theory and practice. We have argued throughout the chapter for the worker to engage in critical reflection and by linking knowledge, experience and practice together we hope we have shown that reflection is not an academic exercise distant from the trials of residential care but is essential to its transformation.

The Bibini Centre evolved out of the 'Black and in Care movement' – the collective impact of a number of black-led initiatives aimed at highlighting racism in policy and practice as it affected children within the public care system. Key organisations (some no longer in existence) included the Children's Legal Centre, the Lambeth Black Families Finding Unit, the REU (Race Equality Unit) the National Black Caucus, ABSWAP – the Association of Black Social Workers and Allied Professions, BAAF (British Agency for Adoption and Fostering) Black Perspectives Committee and a string of voluntary groups made up of black young people in and ex-care that sprang up in places such as London, Manchester, Liverpool and Nottingham.

References

Association of Black Social Workers and Allied Professionals (1983) *Black Children in Care.* Evidence to the House of Commons Social Services Committee.

Barn, R. (1993) *Black Children in the Public Care System.* London: Batsford.

Bebbington, A. and Miles, J. (1989) The Background of Children who Enter Local Authority Care. *British Journal of Social Work.* 19: 5.

Burton, J. (1993) *The Handbook of Residential Care.* London: Routledge.

Butt, J., Gorbach, P. and Ahmad B. (1991) *Equally Fair?* London: REU.

Department of Health. https://www.the-stationery-office.co.uk/doh/pgacn.htm

Essed, P. (1991) *Understanding Everyday Racism.* London: Sage.

Foucault, M. (1972) *The Archaeology of Knowledge.* London: Tavistock.

Ince, L. (1998). *Making it Alone: A Research Study on the Experiences of Black Young People.* London: BAAF.

Ince, L. and Richards, A. (2000) *Overcoming the Obstacles, Looked After Children: Quality Services for Black and Minority Ethnic Children and their Families.* London: FRG.

Joseph Rowntree Foundation (2002) *Providing Better Access to Short Breaks For Black Disabled Children and Their Parents.* York: Joseph Rowntree Foundation.

McDonald, S. (1991) *All Equal Under the Act?* London: REU.

NCH – The Bridge Childcare Development Service (2003) *Racism and the Lawrence Inquiry: A Literature Review.* Unpublished paper, NCH.

Pennie, P. and Best, F. (1992) *How the Black Family is Pathologised by the Social Services System.* London: ABSWAP.

Small, J. (1984) Transracial Placements: Conflicts and Contradictions, in Ahmed, J., Cheetham, J. and Small, J. *Social Work with Black Children and Their Families.* London: BAAF.

Chapter Five

Thinking Beyond 'Diversity': Black Minority Ethnic Children in Scotland

Satnam Singh

This chapter is focused on the conceptual and practice dilemmas regarding 'looked after' black minority ethnic (BME) children in Scotland. Although many of the issues raised will be of relevance to practitioners working within the residential care setting, the intention here is to take a broader approach and look critically at our understanding of child care policy and practice. An anti-racist perspective is adopted throughout the discussion and all the changes advocated to practice and policy are predicated by such an approach.

The first section of the chapter, presents the wider context issues concerning the representation of BME children in the care system, the terminology that is frequently used in discussions of 'race', and the legal framework for child care policy. The second section is ideological in nature, concerning the conceptualisation of 'identity' of BME children and in particular of black children of 'mixed' parentage. The final section addresses the pragmatic questions of how practitioners can re-orientate their traditional practice wisdom and knowledge, towards something that approximates anti-racist practice.

The social and legal context

BME children: demographic trends

According to official Scottish Executive data, Scotland is home to approximately one million children under the age of 16 and a further 326,000 who are aged between 16 and 21. Scotland has some of the highest rates of relative child poverty in the developed world. Although the research data provides a very clear statement of the social exclusion experienced by a significant proportion of Scottish children, it does not in any way establish the situation of specific marginalised groups, such as those from BME communities.

The 2001 Census identified that:

• Around two per cent of the Scottish population identified themselves as being from a minority

ethnic community. The census also shows that BME people reside in every single area of Scotland, albeit in very small numbers.

• BME communities reside principally in and around the urban centres of Glasgow and Edinburgh. In these areas the figure is thought to be closer to four or five per cent.

• BME communities are significantly younger than Scotland's white communities: 56 per cent of the BME population is aged under 30, compared with only 35 per cent of the white population. 22 per cent of Chinese, 23 per cent of Indians, and 33 per cent of all Bangladeshi, Pakistani and other South Asian communities, compared with 19 per cent of the white population.

Such marked demographic shifts in the BME composition of Scotland's population have not until recently been widely acknowledged, partly because of a legacy of 'we don't have many of them' thinking that has been a dominant feature in Scotland. At present, some service providers continue to think that there is a relatively small BME population but this is unlikely to be the case if national trends continue. Recent arrivals of 'new' BME communities, whether refugees or asylum-seekers from various war-affected parts of the globe or 'economic migrants' who are being encouraged to settle here, are already in evidence in all parts of Scotland.

BME children: social exclusion

There has been a history of well documented research evidence (mainly in England) that indicates the over-representation of black and mixed parentage children in the public care system. For example, Batta and Foren (1970) found that mixed parentage children are almost eight times more likely to enter the care system than white children. Other studies undertaken in the mid and late 1970s demonstrated that these mixed parentage children not only entered the care system in higher numbers but also at a much younger age (see for example Batta et al., 1979).

Other evidence from research has equally demonstrated the disadvantage experienced by black children of mixed parentage. For example, Bebbington and Miles (1989) found that black mixed parentage children were two and a half times more likely than other children (either black or white) to enter local authority care. This over-representation is replicated across the spectrum of social welfare: black children in the public care system, black people subject to compulsory admissions to psychiatric units, the juvenile justice system and in school exclusions (Skellington and Morris, 1992; Barn, 1999; Barn, Sinclair and Ferdinand, 1997; Social Exclusion Unit, 1998).

In Scotland, there is less certainty about the actual numbers of BME children who are 'looked after' or 'accommodated' by local authorities. Recent data published by the Scottish Executive showed that as of March 2003 there were:

- 225 black and minority ethnic children 'looked after' by Scottish Local authorities.
- 100 (45 per cent) of these children were described as being of a black mixed parentage.

Although the overall number appears to be small, it is important to recognise that owing to the current lack of robust research data we only have a glimpse of the real picture. Anecdotal information within local professional networks suggests that for around fifty per cent of 'looked after' children in Scotland ethnicity is simply not recorded.

Singh and Patel (1998) highlighted the importance of recording and monitoring ethnicity in Scotland as a way of planning and delivering equitable services for children. They also found that the BME voluntary sector was (and probably remains) the main provider of social work/social care services to black children, with statutory agencies only becoming involved when the situation deteriorates to warrant compulsory measures of care. As the BME voluntary sector is staffed largely by unqualified or poorly qualified staff, very few of whom have professional social work training, the question emerges not about 'over-representation', as is the case in England, but about the 'colour blind' provision of services which fail to reach vulnerable sectors of the community in an appropriate and timely manner. Research evidence in Scotland has consistently demonstrated the low level of priority given to the needs of BME communities (for example Cadman and Chakrabarti, 1991). More recently

the audit of research on 'race' undertaken by Netto et al. (2001) has shown that across Scotland and across all areas of social care, health, education, leisure, justice and housing, BME families and children are disadvantaged, excluded and marginalised through a failure of institutions to address or understand the complexity of need. This results in what McCluskey (1991) described so clearly as 'a non-White population, which is expected to "fit in" with existing (White) services'. It is important then that planners, managers and others in leadership responsibility for Children's Services take account of the changing ethnic diversity in the planning and delivery of services for children and their families.

Terminology: the 'mixed' and 'BME' categories

UK Census 2001 data indicates that inter-racial unions are becoming increasingly more common. Coleman and Salt (1996) found that, forty per cent of black men and twenty per cent of black women, who had a partner, were with a white partner. Estimates suggested that in 1996, there were about 350,000 individuals in the UK who are of 'mixed-race' parentage; it would not be surprising to find that a small but significant proportion of this group will be living in Scotland. Recent figures from the 2001 Census indicate that just over 12.5 per cent of the BME community in Scotland is of a 'mixed' heritage, and indications suggest that this figure is likely to grow.

The category of 'mixed' as it has been used in the National Census is by no means a straightforward matter. Ballard (1996) suggests that 'race' and 'ethnicity' refer to far less easily objectifiable personal attributes than such routine categories as age, sex or marital status. The categories used in the Census and subsequently in other forms of ethnic monitoring often confuse such factors as skin colour, religion and country of birth; it also uses the very broad and generic categories of 'mixed' and 'other'. This further compounds the difficulty of accuracy on statistical returns. It is therefore important to be clear at the outset about the use of terminology, including that used throughout this discussion. The term 'black' as a political category encompasses all 'non-white' (or what in the USA is termed 'people of colour') groups who have a current or historical experience of racism, through 'white' colonialism, slavery and imperialism is well known in anti-racist discourses in Britain. However, this approach has been challenged by black communities and professionals in recent years and is being replaced by such terms as 'black and Asian', 'black and ethnic minority', 'black/minority ethnic'. The term 'black' continues to be used in its broad ideological, inclusive sense, but in England, at least, it appears to increasingly refer to people of African and Caribbean origin whose history of location and whose experience has been so fundamentally influenced by the Atlantic slave trade. This latter tendency is less pronounced in Scotland where the term 'black' continues to be favoured by many black professionals and academics working within an anti-racist perspective, to provide a sense of solidarity and community that is particular to the Scottish demographic context. However, there is pressure from policy makers, at least, to adopt the less political terminology and discourse of 'ethnicity and diversity', but that is a debate for another time.

The question of 'mixed parentage' is however important to address here. When referring to the category of 'mixed' parentage, I do not use it in its literal sense, i.e. to include those who have parents from different white ethnicities, say German and English parents, or indeed Scottish and English. By 'mixed parentage', I very specifically refer to BME children who have one white parent and one BME parent or grandparent. It is these 'visible minorities' that experience the most disadvantages in every sphere of their lives. It cannot be accepted that there is anything inherent in being black or of mixed parentage that predisposes an admission into the 'looked after' system. If children of mixed parentage are over-represented in the care system, or if the child care services are ignoring the needs of BME families, it seems more likely that the reasons lie in the way that institutional systems, structures and process impact on the lives of BME communities.

Legal framework

Child care practice in Scotland is principally governed by the Children (Scotland) Act of 1995, which places the welfare of the child as the paramount principle. The requirements of the 1995 Act are underpinned by a number of important over-arching principles; listening to

children, minimum intervention, the presumption of contact and the right to family life. In addition to these overarching principles, the 1995 Act was also a piece of landmark legislation, in that for the first time Scottish child care legislation introduced the requirement that authorities had to give due regard as far as is practicable to the child's racial origin, religious persuasion, linguistic background and cultural heritage:

- Section 17(4), when making any decision concerning a child they are or may be looking after.
- Section 22(2), when providing services for children in need.
- Section 95, when an adoption agency or court is reaching a decision.

(Children (Scotland) Act 1995)

What the legislation makes clear is that there is a clear *duty* on local authorities and relevant agencies to pay attention to children's race, religion, language and culture *whenever* a decision is made or a service is provided:

In addressing their needs (Black children) it is important to take account of their individual characteristics. Race, culture, language and religion are amongst the most important of these.

(Scottish Office, 1998)

These duties are entirely consistent with the United Nations Convention of the Rights of the Child that states:

Every child, regardless of race, colour, sex, language, religion or disability should be protected from every kind of discrimination.

(Article 2)

In addition the Children Scotland Act (1995) complements the Race Relations Act 1976 and the Race Relations Amendment Act (2001) both of which place a general and specific duty on public authorities, including local authorities, schools and colleges to promote race equality and to eliminate discrimination.

It is these very principles, outlined in the range of legislation indicated above, which raise real and fundamental concerns about how the needs of black children and black children of mixed parentage are conceptualised, and how well the care system is complying with the legislation. On the one hand the central tenet of the legislation and therefore the policies and practices of work with all children is the principle of 'the child's welfare as paramount'. However, the legislation suggests that for some children, i.e. black children, a child's welfare can be separated from considerations of the child's race, religion, language and culture, if doing so would prove to be impracticable.

This then raises important questions for social workers and for agencies about how we understand and define 'welfare' and second, in what circumstance and instances is it possible and ethically permissible to give paramount consideration to a child's welfare while at the same time disregarding the child's race, religion, language and culture because it is considered to be much too impractical.

This issue of *practicable vs. impracticable* is one which comes into the realms of 'institutional racism' and to the 'racialisation' of child care practice. If systems, structures and processes are set up in ways that disadvantage BME children in this respect, then it is clearly 'institutional racism'. Institutional racism can be defined as; those forces, social arrangements, institutions, structures, policies, precedents and systems of social relations that operate to deprive certain racially identified categories equality. The Macpherson Report (1999) that looked into the circumstances surrounding the murder of Stephen Lawrence, placed clear responsibilities on local authorities to consider their systems:

> It is incumbent upon every institution to examine their policies and the outcome of their policies and practices to guard against disadvantaging any section of our communities.
>
> (Macpherson, 1999)

Re-conceptualising the issue of 'identity' of BME children of 'mixed' parentage

One of the concerns that has been expressed repeatedly by practitioners is the complex matter of the identity that is bestowed on BME children of 'mixed' parentage (e.g. Tizard and Phoenix, 2001; Katz, 1996; Prevatt-Goldstein, 1999; Alibhai-Brown, 2001). The issue is two fold: on the one hand there is the question about the system of classification, categorisation and resulting terminology that is employed. The various debates argue that the term black in its political sense is of little value, as it does not allow any recognition of the complex ethnicities of mixed parentage children. This may be true at the level of service provision when it may be

important to know a child's particular racial and cultural origins together with an understanding of their current social milieu. However, it is important to remember that services for children need also to be planned strategically and it is this regional or national planning that requires an understanding of the socio-demographics of the population of children served. Hence the importance of black as a unifying political entity that helps to focus on the strategic, systemic issues that impact negatively on the lives of black and minority ethnic children regardless of their ethnicities, origins and linguistic attributes. Put simply, black children are disadvantaged, regardless of which religion, language, culture or race they belong.

The second, and more problematic issue, is about 'identity' itself, including how a child's sense of identity can be promoted and protected, amidst these complexities. One young black person speaking about his identity said:

> I am like Nescafe, I am a special blend from several ethnic backgrounds, incorporating the best from each or so I would like to think. Ethnicity is always tricky for me as I feel that it pigeonholes an individual into a specific category.
>
> (22 year old male)

Social workers, foster carers and residential workers have sometimes been faced with situations where black children may display negativity about their skin colour, about their cultural traditions, about their associations with their history and general distancing. In this situation discussions about identity have traditionally tended to pathologise the black child in terms of identity confusion and self-hatred. Prevatt-Goldstein (1999) suggests that such pathologising locates the problem with the individual child and diverts attention from the real focus of systemic and structural issues that contrive to disadvantage children. In simplistic terms what this means is that the fact that black children may display negativity about their skin colour, about their cultural traditions and about their associations with their history and general distancing. What this means is that when a child is distancing themselves from their black heritage it tends to be viewed by professionals as an indication of either the child's inability to assimilate into the dominant culture, hence a personal weakness or failing, or the child's inability to develop pride or self-esteem in their difference, again a personal weakness or failing.

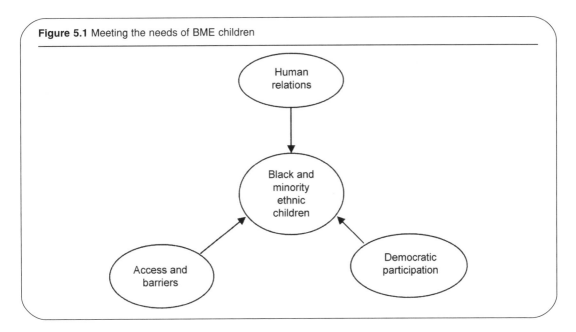

Figure 5.1 Meeting the needs of BME children

What such interpretations fail to recognise is that it is the 'nature' or the 'essence' of the society in which we live that conspires against black or mixed parentage children. For example, research from Child-line Scotland found that black children 'endure unrelenting racism on an almost daily basis' (Child-line, Scotland, 1996). Despite this black and black mixed parentage children continue to develop, in most cases meaningful and positive identities that are not deterministic in nature, but rather are fluid and adapting in relation to the external forces that help shape them.

Developing an anti-racist approach in professional practice

A framework for action

In my discussion this far, I have raised two main issues concerning professional practice. Firstly how do child care professionals conceptualise questions of identity of BME children of 'mixed' parentage, and secondly how does the care system as a whole address the social exclusion and disadvantage experienced by these children when they enter the public care system. The two issues although related to some extent are mutually exclusive of each other and I am proposing that it is important to address some of the barriers that disadvantage BME children of 'mixed' parentage, regardless of how we or they

conceptualise their identity. I do not mean that we disregard their identity, but that service delivery does not have to be contingent upon it.

To help understand this it may be helpful to consider a three-dimensional model (Figure 5.1, adapted from Almeida Diniz, 2004).

This model proposes that in addressing the needs of BME children it is important to consider at least three dimensions, each being as important as the other.

Most often we see discussion and energy focused on the area of 'Human Relations'. This is the area that is the focus of 'cultural diversity' or 'multi-culturalism' and addresses notions of how we understand, value and celebrate differences between us and how we learn to enjoy each others' food, music and traditions. In terms of black children of mixed parentage it is this level that requires a discussion and understanding of the children's 'mix' so that practitioners can ensure that 'all parts' of their ethnic background are valued and promoted. However 'multiculturalism', 'human relations', 'valuing diversity' is limited to a superficial engagement with the real issues that disadvantage black children. Domenilli (1998) identified that it was the efforts to overcome the weaknesses of the assimilationist approach that led to the 'multi-cultural approach' much favoured during the 1980s. These approaches that focused on 'human relations' were seen as the embodiment of equality between different 'races' and cultures drawing on equal opportunities, cultural diversity and tolerance (Cheetham, 1982). However these approaches have been severely criticised from black perspectives for failing to acknowledge the structural and systemic inequalities that exist in society. Gilroy (1987) described multi-culturalism as being a 'diversionary tactic' that has ultimately reinforced the victim mentality by blaming those at the receiving end of racism, instead of tackling, confronting and challenging the social forces that enforce. In simple terms, although it is important to ensure for example that a Muslim child is provided with Halal food, whilst in a residential unit, this does not in any way address the multiplicity of factors that probably contributed to the child being perhaps inappropriately placed there in the first place, perhaps through a lack of Muslim foster carers?

If we shift our focus to consider the other two areas of the proposed model, that of 'access and barriers' and 'democratic participation' we then have to attend to the structural issues that are inherent within the systems that we operate. Focus on these areas is not dependent on an understanding or celebration of any individuals' background, religion or ethnic makeup.

The focus on 'access and barriers' requires us to look critically at the features of our systems, methodologies and interventions which disadvantage black and minority ethnic children, the disadvantage being well documented in the research literature in terms of health, education, leisure and employment (e.g. Netto et al., 2001). This links very closely to the early comments on 'institutional racism'. If we are serious about social justice, and creating a Scotland where 'everyone matters'; 'A Scotland in which "every child matters", where every child, regardless of their family background, has the best possible start in life.'

Focusing on this area means that practitioners and policy makers will need to look at the structural barriers that prevent BME people accessing services in an equitable manner. For example, it means looking at the way that the agency delivers its services, prepares and disseminates information, and reviews its procedures and protocols. For example, the Khandan Initiative (Barnardo's, 1999; Singh et al., 2002) in Edinburgh was an attempt by one national children's charity to focus on this very issue and develop a range of services for BME children in need of substitute family placements. In developing the Khandan Initiative, the agency

looked at a range of its standard practices. Information leaflets were not only translated, but widely circulated through minority ethnic community groups, training and preparation for BME foster carers and adopters was undertaken in separate groups, and assessment procedures were carefully reviewed to ensure that BME applicants were sensitively and appropriately assessed. BME people were recruited to sit on the fostering panels. Almost every area of policy and practice was reviewed to ensure that there were no unnecessary barriers to BME people accessing the service

Democratic participation requires us to address the relationship that agencies and institutions have with black and minority ethnic people, and requires a critical examination from a perspective of power and disadvantage. Who is it that is providing the service, to whom and on what terms? In what way do the black and minority people have the opportunity to 'give voice' to their issues, concerns and views and furthermore, in what way are they enabled to play an active and meaningful part in the decision making process of the 'systems' in which they have become a part? An example in relation to BME young people would be looking at the degree to which young people are consulted and included or engaged in the way that services are run or structured. This means that agencies would need to invest in ways of building the capacity of local communities, engage in meaningful dialogue and identify appropriate mechanisms for supporting the involvement and engagement of these disadvantaged groups.

Reconsidering child care theories, from an anti-racist perspective

The notion of 'family'

One of the challenges to practitioners in addressing issues of access and barriers and democratic participation whilst working with black children is that all the tools, theories and perspectives at their disposal have been developed from Euro-centric perspectives. This means that the 'lens' through which black children are viewed is 'myopic' and can only interpret the world from one particular perspective. Nobles (1978) describes this as a process of 'conceptual incarceration' meaning that Euro-centric perspectives can only illuminate Euro-centric realities. Euro-centric theoretical approaches can also be considered 'hegemonic' in so far as they can 'control without force'. Before looking critically at two such dominant theories, and offer alternative perspectives for each I want to briefly highlight how pervasive Euro-centric thinking is within our culture and how completely it shapes our 'common sense' understandings and interpretations of our social world.

From a white Euro-centric framework, for example, families are generally conceptualised as being one generation, nuclear and focused on the promotion of individual strength, achievement and identity. This conceptualisation does not sit well in a cross-cultural context, where in South Asian families at least; the emphasis is on multi-generation families, including not only grandparents, but also uncles, aunts and cousins. In addition, the values systems within South Asian families are orientated towards communal achievement and shared identities.

The table below highlights a number of key differences across a range of different domains. What we see is how it challenges our understandings of what is 'normal' in terms of parenting and child care practices. I do not propose to address separately each section in Table 5.1 as the majority of the points can be subsumed in the dichotomy posed by the relationship between 'self and other' or the 'individual and the collective'. I want to explore this tension very briefly.

The notion of individuality is deeply rooted into western consciousness in that it forms part of the development tasks of adolescents whom, according to Erikson, struggle between 'ego-identity' and 'role confusion'. It is such that western psychology has posed a dichotomy between the individual and the group. From a Euro-centric perspective it is this individuation of a young person that indicates a healthy development into adulthood. Cross-culturally however, individuation of young people that leads to a separation of the self into a new ego-identity separated from the identity of the family, tribe, community or history is one, which may in some contexts be considered to be faulty. For South Asian young people, an individuation into a new ego identity needs to occur successfully in the context of the family and social milieu; it needs to incorporate both 'self' and 'other'. South Asian young people need to develop an ego, which to some extent is more regulated by the norms values and traditions of duty responsibility and *izzat* (social honour), than would white young people.

Adolescence is a stage where all young people have to negotiate the very same 'crisis' identified by Erikson in moving from childhood to adulthood, but the resolution is one, which is very different for different ethnic groups. It is these 'resolutions' of identity that challenge practitioners working cross-culturally with black children and young people.

Attachment

Attachment theory, developed by John Bowlby in the early 1950s has influenced and informed social work practice with children and young people for many decades. However, attachment theory focuses on the psychological relationship between the child and primary care givers only, and takes little account of the social, cultural and political context within which that care giving takes place. So for example, although a secure attachment experience allows a child to successfully separate from their primary care givers, attachment theory does not tell us how this happens where the 'outside' world is 'essentially' racist. Not necessarily always overtly, but in the ways that the systems and structures function.

In a critical sense attachment theory does not account for the role of 'belonging', as opposed to attachment. This sense of belonging, described by Owusu-Bemph (2000) as 'socio-genealogical inter-connectedness', refers to the sense of belonging that we all have to some degree to family and community, and in a much broader way to the sense of belonging to a history and culture and a traditions. It refers to being able to answer the questions 'where do you come from' in the broader sense. It explains the popularity in Scotland of films such as 'Braveheart' that speak directly to this communality of experience rooted in a shared history. Nick Banks (1992) a black psychologist described this sense of belonging in a political sense as to 'who is on your side'. Banks writes that an indication of what he calls a 'consolidated identity' or an 'integrated identity' is one where the individual is able to view themselves positively, both as an individual and as part of a group with ease. An integrated identity being one, which enables a black person to have balanced views about their own black community and about the white majority community.

Table 5.1 Individual vs Family

Euro-centric view of family	Asian view of family
Emphasis on meeting the needs of the individual.	Emphasis on meeting the needs of the family unit.
Concept of family is nuclear.	Concept of family is wider, e.g. grandparents, uncles and aunts.
Families not necessarily living close together.	Families living within a close community network.
Ethos in the home is to help individual reach full potential.	Ethos in the home is to strengthen the bonds with brothers and sisters.
Emphasis is placed on toys for children, e.g. Christmas presents.	Emphasis placed on playing with each other and developing family relationships (e.g. Eid, Diwali, new clothes and going out).
Roles of parents may not be traditional.	Roles are traditional in the main.
Children can negotiate some rules.	Rules are largely made by parents.
Older people have to earn the respect of young. Can call by first name.	Older person gets the respect because they are older. Don't call older person by first name.
Holidays are an important part of the culture.	Visiting family and friends is an important part of culture.
English is most likely to be the dominant language of the home.	Urdu, Punjabi, Gujerati or Bengali may be the dominant language in the home.
May have links with relations in other countries.	Most likely to have strong links with relatives in other countries.
Food and clothing more Western.	Food and clothing more likely to be Eastern.
Autonomy/independence is seen in a positive light.	Caring for and helping the family is seen in a positive light.
Religious label is not seen as a necessity. Marriage is largely by choice. Couple sort out their marriage plans.	Religious label is seen as a necessity. Marriage is largely arranged and relatives help to sort wedding plans.
Boyfriends/girlfriends are an acceptable part of the culture (hence the emphasis on sex education).	Boyfriends/girlfriends are not seen as an acceptable part of the culture (hence the lack of sex education).
Individual choice is respected. (Drawback is that there is a danger in ignoring experience).	Individual choice needs the approval of the others. (Danger is that experience takes over and quashes individual choice).
Education is not necessarily seen to include religious education.	Religious education is seen as part of mainstream education.
Second and third marriage and living together outside marriage is becoming more common.	Second marriage is uncommon for a woman, as is living together outside marriage.
Individual who strays from the norm can find their way back into the fold easier.	Individuals who stray from the norm have to work harder to get back into the fold and sometimes can't get back in.
Families not necessarily living close together.	Families living within a close community network.

Resilience

Daniel, Wassel and Gilligan (1999) have recently helped to popularise the idea of resilience, as a way of conceptualising the care needs of looked after children. The shifting away from the systems and procedures that help to provide a sense of permanence or security for children, to thinking about what are the 'conditions' that children need within which they can grow into healthy adulthood, is an orientation which is particularly applicable to black and minority ethnic children. Daniel and her colleagues argue that children develop resilience through the development of at least three facets: these are 'self esteem', 'self efficacy' and 'secure base'.

In order to demonstrate the efficacy of this approach I am going to deconstruct some of the key concepts from this theory from a black perspective and suggest alternative ways of re-conceptualising the central questions which the above writers pose in order to guide application of a resilience perspective.

- **Is there purposeful contact with family members and other key adults in the child's life?**

For children who are looked after or accommodated away from home, purposeful and consistent contact with birth family members, parents, siblings grand parents and uncles and aunts is well recognised as being of importance, to the extent that it is legislated for in the Children (Scotland) Act 1995. Although the same principles apply for black children and children of mixed parentage, there are additional factors that need to be considered. Many black children of mixed parentage are often, but not always, living with a white mother. If care is not taken then this 'contact with family' may only be with the white mother and family. A practice that is underpinned by expediency and the attachment theories discussed above. If we consider both the identity needs of black children and the 'belonging' needs, then it is clear that contact with 'black' family members is important. Where this is difficult, then contact with other black 'key adults' needs to be established. These key adults could be 'mentors' or 'befrienders'. It is only then that a black child of mixed parentage can develop a sense of belonging through the availability of culturally appropriate role models.

- **How are positive experiences at school being encouraged? E.g. sports, homework, links with staff? (High but reasonable expectations are vital here)**

School experience is significant for all children. For black children however, school can take on an even greater significance. For example, recent research (CERES, 2004) found that an average of just less than two racist incidents were being recorded everyday by schools within the City of Edinburgh alone. In thinking about children's school experiences, it would be helpful to ask if the school is providing a positive multi-cultural experience. Are there other black or mixed parentage pupils in the school? How does the school value other faiths?

- **How are the child's' friendships with peers developed and sustained?**

Friendships and peer relations are central to a child's development, however for black children, there will be additional questions and pressures that will need to be considered. How will the child be helped to develop friendships with peer relationships with people from their own cultural background? How will cross cultural and inter-racial friendships be viewed. In addition there will be questions about how the child will learn about cultural norms, for example children will need to be supported to access culturally appropriate music, clothes and fashion, and language, in order to fit in.

- **Does the child have a talent, skill, and aptitude and how is this being encouraged?**

There is a danger that for 'looked after and accommodated' black children it is only the 'dominant culture' talents and skills that get promoted. As an example an Asian young person in foster care had a musical talent that was rightly promoted by giving him the opportunity to learn to play the bagpipes. He went on to win awards for his piping. However, it may have been more appropriate and helpful to have encouraged him to think about South Asian musical traditions as well, such as 'Dhol' a form of drumming which is very popular with young people or 'Bhangra', traditional dancing, also becoming increasingly very popular with young people.

- **What help is available in observing, practicing and rehearsing problem solving and coping skills and strategies?**

Problem solving and coping skills and strategies are essential for all children to enable a development into healthy adulthood. For black children it is important to consider how the child's cultural context and role of older relatives is taken into account in developing these important skills and strategies. What this means is that whereas it might be appropriate to encourage self reliance and initiative, for black children these skills would need to be complemented by the skills that are required to seek advice and guidance from elders in the community, in some cases this may include learning how to consult with a church leader, or Imam.

- **How are pro-social skills being developed and encouraged? For example, a capacity for self-awareness and empathy?**

These pro-social skills are derived from the concept of 'independence' discussed earlier. For black children pro-social skills of interdependency, kinship relations and appropriate deference and courtesy need to be promoted and explored. How does, for example, a young Asian male learn about 'empathy' for the family and community? How do black children learn an awareness of their own efficacy in relationship to other older adults in the community of origin?

Conclusion

We have seen throughout this chapter that being black or being BME of a 'mixed' parentage in Scotland is far from straightforward. If we add to this the additional exclusionary barriers placed on children when they are 'looked after' or accommodated, then it is not hard to see the responsibility on residential workers and on social work agencies to ensure that these children are not further disadvantaged. Even a brief examination of the various theories and perspectives highlights the pervasiveness of Euro-centric perspectives in modern child care practice. This practice undermines the distinct experience of black children and children of mixed parentage and serves to further obscure their needs to the point of invisibility. Theoretical perspectives rarely develop in isolation from other systems. In the case of children's services, child care practice is underpinned by a whole raft of procedures and policies which do little to deal with 'difference' and instead take a utilitarian view in that 'need' is defined by 'numbers'.

In this context it appears that black and mixed parentage children do not yet provide the 'critical mass' deemed appropriate by policy makers.

I have indicated that any child care agency which intends to meet its legal obligations and provide an appropriate service to black and mixed parentage children, needs to move beyond a focus on 'diversity' or 'human relations' or 'multi-culturalism'. This was popular throughout the 1970s, and prevails almost unchallenged in modern discourse. Agencies need to embrace a post-modern, multi-dimensional approach that focuses clearly on the issues of democratic participation, and takes seriously questions of access to services.

Agencies will only truly develop 'inclusive practices' when they tackle the systems, structures, policies and practices that are currently blind to the needs of an emerging cohort of black and minority ethnic children, many of whom are of a mixed parentage.

References

Alibhai-Brown, Y. (2001) *Mixed Feelings: The Complex Lives of Mixed Race Britons.* The Women's Press.

Ballard, R (1998) Asking Ethnic Questions: Some Hows, Whys and Wherefores. *Patterns of Prejudice.* 32: 2, 15–37.

Banks, N. (1992) Techniques for Direct Identity Work with Black Children. *Adoption and Fostering.* 16: 3, 19–25.

Barn, R. (1999) Racial and Ethnic Identity, in Barn, R. (Ed.) *Working with Black Children and Adolescents in Need.* London: BAAF.

Barn, R., Sinclair, R. and Ferdinand, D. (1997) *Acting on Principle: An Examination of Race and Ethnicity in Social Services Provision for Children and Families.* London: BAAF.

Barnardo's (1999) *In on the Act.* Edinburgh: Barnardo's.

Batta, I., McCulloch, J. and Smith, N. (1979) Colour as a Variable in Childrens' Sections of Local Authority Social Services Departments. *New Community.* 7: 78–84.

Batta, I.D. and Foren, (1970) Colour as a Variable in the Use Made of a Local Authority Child Care Department. *Social Worker,* 27: 3.

Bebbington, A. and Miles, J. (1989) The Background of Children who Enter Local Authority Care. *British Journal of Social Work.* 19, 349–68.

Bowes, A. and Sim, D. (Eds.) (1991) *Demands and Constraints: Ethnic Minorities and Social Services in Scotland.* Edinburgh: SCVO.

Bowlby, J. (1970) *Attachment.* Basic Books.

Cadman, M. and Chakrabarti, M. (1991) Social Work in a Multi-Racial Society: A Survey of Practice in Two Scottish Local Authorities, in *One Small Step towards Racial Justice.* London: CCETSW.

CERES (2004) *Minority Ethnic Pupils Experiences of Scottish Schools.* Edinburgh: Scottish Executive Education Department.

Cheetham, J. (Ed.) (1982) *Social Work and Ethnicity.* London: George Allen and Unwin.

Childline Scotland (1996) *Children and Racism.* Childline.

Coleman, D. and Salt, J. (1996) *Ethnicity in the 1991 Census. Volume 1: Demographic Characteristics of Ethnic Minority Populations.* London: HMSO.

Commission of Human Rights (1989) *Convention on the Rights of the Child.*

Daniel, B., Wassell, S. and Gilligan, R. (1999) *Child Development for Child Care and Protection Workers.* London: Jessica Kingsley.

Dominelli, L. (1998) *Anti-Racist Social Work.* 2nd edn. Basingstoke: Macmillan.

Gilroy, P. (1987) *Problems in Anti-racist strategy.* Runnymede Trust.

HMSO (2000) *The Race Relations* (Amendments) Act. HMSO.

Katz, I. (1996) *The Construction of Racial Identity in Children of Mixed Parentage: Mixed Metaphors.* London: Jessica Kingsley.

Macpherson, W. (1999) *The Stephen Lawrence Inquiry.* London: The Stationery Office.

McClusky, J. (1991) Ethnic Minorities and the Social Work Service in Glasgow; in Bowes, A. and Sim, D. (Eds.) *Demands and Constraints: Ethnic Minorities and Social Services in Scotland.* Edinburgh: SCVO.

Netto, G., Arshad, R., De Lima, P., Almeida Diniz, F., Macewen, M., Patel, V. and Syed, R. (2001) *Audit of Research on Minority Ethnic Issues in Scotland from a Race Perspective.* Edinburgh: Scottish Executive.

Nobles, W. (1978) Toward an Empirical and Theoretical Framework for Defining Black Families. *Journal of Marriage and the Family.* 679–87.

Owusu-Bemph, J (2000) Socio-genealogical Connectedness. *Child and Family Social work.* 5: 2 107–16.

Prevatt-Goldstein, B. (1999) Black with a White Parent: A Positive and Achievable Identity. *British Journal of Social Work.* 29: 2, 285–301.

Scottish Executive (2001) *For Scotland's Children.* www.scotland.gov.uk/library3/education/fcsr-00.asp

Scottish Executive (2004) *Analysis of Ethnicity in the 2001 Census: Summary Report.* Office of the Chief Statistician.

Scottish Executive (1999) *Social Justice: A Scotland Where Everyone Matters.* Edinburgh: Scottish Executive.

Scottish Office (1995) *The Children (Scotland) Act.* Edinburgh: HMSO.

Singh, S. and Patel, V.K.P. (1998) *Regarding Scotland's Black Children.* Barkingside: SBWF/Barnardo's.

Singh, S. (1997) Assessing Asian Families in Scotland: A Discussion. *Adoption and Fostering.* 21: 3, 35–9.

Singh, S., MacFadyen, S. and Gillies, A. (2002) To Attach and Belong; Scotland's Black Children in Family Placement, in Sachdev, D. and Van Meeuwen, A. *Are we Listening Yet?* Barkingside: Barnardo's.

Skellington, R. and Morris, P. (1992) *Race in Modern Britain Today.* Newbury Park: Sage.

Social Exclusion Unit (1998) *Truancy and School Exclusion Report.* London: HMSO.

Tizard, B. and Phoenix, A. (2001) *Black, White or Mixed Race? Race and Racism in the Lives of Young People of Mixed Parentage.* London: Routledge.

End notes

1. Forthcoming reseasrch by Singh and Almeida Diniz. Assuring equality in childrens services.
2. Personal communication. The model has been used in researching services for BME communities in education, social care and housing.

Chapter Six

Dismantling the Barriers: Giving a Voice to Disabled Young People in Residential Care

Moyra Hawthorn

I think the attitude of professionals was that I would never amount to any thing and that's the message I got.

(Morris, 1995: 17)

Introduction

The history of residential care for disabled children and young people shows a mixed bag of provision over the years; long stay hospitals, 'colonies', residential homes and schools, often many miles from the children's family home. Research indicates the quality of such provision was often very poor (Morris, 1995, 1998a, 1998b; Oswin, 1998). Anecdotal accounts from some parents suggest that until recently, they were 'offered the opportunity' to place their child in residential care and that by refusing, they felt that this was seen by agencies as absolving them from the responsibility to support the child in the community.

In her book, *Gone Missing* Jenny Morris (1995) includes a wealth of personal accounts by disabled adults who spent a significant part of their childhoods in residential care, most of which was negative. It would be comforting to believe that the experiences of disabled children in residential care were now radically different, and in some respects they are in that Community Care legislation has brought about the closure of long stay hospitals. In her subsequent work however Morris found that despite the UN Convention on the Rights of the Child, and the Children Act 1989:

> While many service providers and social workers do attempt to adopt a child-centred approach to their work, assessments rarely include the child's point of view and there was a predominantly service-led response to parents' requests for support.

(Morris, 1998b: 115)

Furthermore the research revealed that social service departments were failing in their statutory duty to consult children about decisions about their care and there was evidence of reviews of placements being overdue in a significant number of cases. There was often little social work input with children who use 'respite' care services and there was also a lack of information about children spending time away from home either in long-term placement or short break services (Morris, 1998b: 115).

This situation need not persist however. There is an increasing amount of literature and practical material on how to involve disabled young people in consultation about service provision and about their own packages of care (Morris, 1998c; Ward, 1997; Marchant and Jones, 2003; Kilbride, 1999). There are also examples of services which are 'breaking new ground' in trying to move away from traditional models and to develop provision which is socially inclusive and child-centred. This chapter will therefore serve as in introduction to the task of the residential practitioner and manager in supporting disabled children and young people to lead full and stimulating lives, promoting their participation and citizenship in the community, be they included in 'mainstream' services or services specifically designed for disabled children and young people

Models, meaning and the experiences of disabled children

Discussion of disability as a social construct can initially sound abstract and only marginally related to the practical task of supporting disabled children and young people in residential care. However without understanding the nature and impact of the marginalisation of disabled young people, support can be at best well intentioned but misguided, and at worst highly abusive. Black, disabled children are often further disadvantaged in that disability considerations have often overridden racial and cultural needs in placing children in schools or residential homes some distance from their home community (where the commonality is disability rather than other factors in respect of their personal identity) (Middleton, 1999: 125). These factors need to be borne in mind when providing services for disabled children from ethnic minority groups. It is beyond the scope of this chapter to offer a comprehensive critique of the social exclusion of disabled people when combined with factors such as age, disability, race or ethnicity, and there are several quality texts which offer this (Middleton, 1996, 1999; Swain, Finkelstein et al., 1993; Oliver and Barnes, 1998; Thomas, 1999 amongst others). It is however important that staff teams have a shared value base in respect of disability and a sound grasp of both the nature and implications of the medical and social model of disability in order to help young people and their families make sense of their experiences, and tackle the barriers to their full inclusion.

Traditional explanations of disability place responsibility for disabled children's failure to achieve a quality of life comparable to their typically developing peers as 'the inevitable outcome of individually based impairments and/or medical conditions' (Barnes, 1997: 6). This is the basis of the use of 'the medical model' of care which has been severely criticised by disabled people and their supporters. As a consequence of such explanations it is common to hear disabled children and young people referred to in terms which suggest they are eternal, asexual children with 'special needs' who need 'treatment' or who are 'tragic' (Hevey, 1993: 116). This kind of thinking also underpins the fragmentation of services between agencies, in particular health, education, social services, and voluntary agencies which makes it difficult for young people to receive a seamless package of support to ensure a full and stimulating life experience and 'to facilitate active participation in the community' (UN Convention on the Rights of the Child Article 23). This is particularly problematic if their physical and emotional health needs fluctuate or if they have a degenerative condition. The medical model has also been criticised as encouraging the use of various treatments which may be intensive in terms of time and commitment of young people and family members and at the cost of wider experiences while young people may think they have to be physically 'normal' to be fully accepted. For example some people view Conductive Education with its emphasis on intensive physical training, in this light. Middleton gives various other examples of such treatments – e.g. *Suspended Inverted Rotation* whereby as part of the 'treatment' the child

apparently has their feet tied together, hung upside down and spun around, as a prevention of scoliosis or curvature of the spine (Middleton, 1999).

A social model of disability is now widely promoted in nearly all agencies and has been accepted by professionals in most sectors. Using this model young people are perceived as being disabled as a consequence of social barriers which prevent their full participation in the wider community. Mason and Rieser's account (1992) of the social model describes how:

> *Disabled people's own view of the situation is that – while we may have medical conditions which hamper us and which may or may not need medical treatment – human knowledge, technology and collective resources are already such that our physical or mental impairments need not prevent us from leading perfectly good lives. It is society's unwillingness to employ these means to altering itself rather than us which causes our disabilities . . . (The Social Model) puts the problem outside of ourselves, back onto the collective responsibility of society as a whole.*
>
> (Morris, 1995: 32)

Using this model, the young person's functional limitation such as cerebral palsy, or epilepsy for example is often referred to as an *impairment* rather than a *disability* in order to separate the condition from the disabling effects of social barriers. Children are then referred to as 'disabled children' i.e. disabled by social barriers rather than 'children with disabilities' which identifies them by their functional limitations. The social model values diversity and promotes the inclusion of disabled young people in the community, seeing them as having the same rights, needs and vision of their future as other more typically developing children and young people. Many would now challenge the notion of disabled children having 'special needs' arguing that they have the same needs as any other child, but may need additional help to meet these needs. The difficulty for parents and carers lies in meeting their needs in a society which places barriers in the way of achieving their aspirations. These barriers may initially appear to be physical, e.g. poor access to buildings, lack of appropriate equipment in 'disabled' toilets, but they are rooted in individual, organisational and institutional discrimination and appear in many guises. Examples given by young people, parents and experienced practitioners include the following:

- Information not being available in accessible formats.
- Young disabled people's opinions not being sought on important matters such as individual and family support packages, placement outwith the family home despite legislation to the contrary (Children Act 1989, Children (Scotland) Act 1995).
- Education and leisure services being segregated with the quality of support to promote inclusion being variable.
- Appointments not being organised so that young people and parents need only make one visit (Beresford 1995: 28).
- Facilities appearing at times to be resource driven rather than needs driven and varying geographically depending on the priorities of the purchasing agency.
- Sexuality and relationships only being addressed with the young person on a reactive basis rather than a proactive basis in preparation for the changes of adolescence.

New thinking leads to new practices

While there are now some excellent examples of families and services working together to challenge these barriers, these are isolated, hence disabled young people cannot be assured a smooth transition into adulthood or inclusion in the community in which they live. There is however a role for the residential care workers and managers to challenge these barriers, either directly in the day to day support of young people and in the organisation of service, or indirectly by supporting young people and parents to do so and participating in local forums where such issues are addressed. To bridge the gap into local youth groups for example, it may be necessary to help the group leaders develop an understanding of the disabled child's world and 'what works' so that they in turn can facilitate the young person's inclusion, rather than simply accompany the young person to the club. Connors and Stalker give some interesting feedback from young people about personal support, specifically in respect of Special Needs Assistants at school. In some instances their involvement was reported as an 'ongoing source of difficulty' (2003: 72–3). While this is in the educational context, there are some important messages for anyone involved in supporting the inclusion of young people be it in the educational or recreational setting. There is also a task for

residential care workers to consider the inclusion of disabled children in 'mainstream' residential care provision. Anecdotal accounts show a marked reluctance, usually on account of a very real concern about the risk of bullying by emotionally troubled residents or about inexperienced staff with insufficient skills and knowledge to manage this process effectively. There are however isolated examples, where other factors have taken precedence over impairment in order to keep children in their local community. In at least one local authority in Scotland staff teams have opened themselves up to the challenge of developing new knowledge and skills in order to integrate a disabled young person to a 'mainstream' unit, and young people have been helped to understand and value the contribution of their disabled peer to the residential community.

The residential task in the 21st century

The task of the residential care worker in relation to all young people is to promote their growth and to provide opportunities to bring about change. Empowering and supporting through the maturational tasks is part of this process. The residential worker's task with disabled children and young people is no different. When viewing the life path and expectations of disabled children and young people and their families, it is important to recognise how frequently their experience is significantly different in an important way to that of children who are more 'typical developing'. Those differences persist despite skilled professional intervention at critical periods. For example there are often no celebrations at the birth rather anxiety and uncertainty as to how to respond to parents. Milestones which are normally the cause of celebration such as baby's first steps and first words are often not present or very much delayed. As years go by, children's friends do not live nearby due to segregated schooling, and 'sleepovers', such a significant feature of modern child and youth culture, are replaced by professional services such as residential short breaks. Personal decisions such as future career or packages of support are discussed in reviews and planning meetings when the young person is sometimes not present and often not invited to make a contribution. Young people and their families are therefore often unaware until mid adolescence of options in respect of future lifestyle, such as living outwith the family home, getting a job etc. and the people who are able to advise, such as Community Learning Disability Nurses, Community Care Social Workers are introduced on a resource led basis, at the age directed by services rather than being triggered by the needs of the young person. The total impact on young people is that they are not encouraged to have an active vision of their future, rather they are socialised to be passive recipients of services and find it difficult to challenge or disagree with adults. Attempts to protest are often seen as 'challenging behaviour' rather than a young person's communication of dissatisfaction, frustration or confusion, which are actually quite common in adolescence (Sinason, 1992; Hawkins, 2002).

It is important therefore for everyone working with disabled children and young people to make it a priority to develop an understanding of the young person's communication and to use this to gain insight to their world. Communication is central to empowerment. Within some residential care environments, examples exist where young people have been involved in consultation and review of their own care, in aspects of the running the unit and sometimes to take on more complex tasks such as being involved in staff interviews, or challenging access in the community. All of which are good examples of children's rights being respected as well as good preparation for the challenges facing them in adulthood.

For many years, services for disabled children were managed separately from those for non-disabled children and located with services for disabled adults where the commonality was disability rather than childhood. The UN Convention on the Rights of the Child, The Children Act 1989 and The Children (Scotland) Act 1995 made it clear however that provisions contained in them apply equally to all children including those who are disabled. As Middleton (1996: iv) reminds us however:

The attempt to refocus attention on the disabled child as a child first is sometimes misunderstood as meaning that the disability ought to be ignored or something to be ashamed of . . . Quite the contrary this kind of thinking is unhelpful as the disabling condition is very much a part of the child's reality.

The rest of this chapter will consist of exploring key aspects of practice; communication, care

planning, health, death and grieving, and sexuality.

Communication

She can't communicate at all, but I understand everything she says.
(Rachel's foster carer, of Rachel who had no verbal communication in Morris, 1998a: 43)

She does not communicate at all – everyone says there is no point in even trying.
(from a professional's report – Marchant et al., 2001)

The latter example serves to demonstrate the lack of awareness on the part of some professionals about their role in communicating with disabled children. Equally the foster carer appears to be a very effective communicator, attuned to Rachel's sounds and body language. Referring back to a social barriers model of disability, Jenny Morris describes a child's *communication impairment* as the fact that they cannot speak, their *disability* is the fact that 'you won't take the time and trouble to learn how to communicate with me' (Morris, 1995: 33).

Communication is a very basic human need, evident from birth until death. At the most simple, communication is about the passing of messages between people – not only about having our basic needs for survival met, but also about what happened yesterday and about what may happen tomorrow. It is about how we see ourselves in relation to others, about spirituality and emotional well being, as well as expression of fears, fantasies, hopes and dreams. There are of course many non-verbal ways we communicate such as body language, facial expression, body piercing, smell, hand gesture, dress. Because the majority of people use spoken language to communicate those who don't find that their way of communicating is unrecognised and undervalued. The disabled young people in the video *Two Way Street* give both positive and negative experiences about communication with adults, citing positive examples of being consulted about programs of medication, and how they wanted to be introduced at a new school, but also of being ignored and professionals asking questions of a parent rather than of the young person herself. The UN Convention on the Rights of the Child makes it clear that children have the right to give their views on matters affecting their lives and for these to be taken seriously (Article 12). The spirit of the UN Convention has been integrated to the Children Act 1989 and Children (Scotland) Act 1995, therefore the views of disabled children and young people should be sought about matters such as using residential and short break services, support packages etc. but it is clear that this is still not happening. Reasons given are similar to those quoted at the start of this section, when responsibility for communication was left with the young person rather than the adult having responsibility to learn how to communicate with the young person.

Residential workers are often very experienced communicators however and in this respect they can be a very powerful advocate for disabled children and young people.

Sometimes describing the communication as 'intuitive' they are in fact very quickly receiving a non-verbal message sent by a young person, e.g. tapping on the table, 'interpreting' the meaning i.e. on the basis of experience and knowledge it indicates that the young person is becoming irritated, then sending a verbal or non-verbal message back 'I wonder if you're getting a bit annoyed by this, maybe we could go and' in a tone of voice which is supportive and non confrontational. A key task of the residential care worker is helping young people become more aware of their emotions by helping them recognise what they are experiencing, naming this, and helping them find a way of dealing with them more effectively.

Stuart Aitken (Aitken, Pease et al., 2000: 26–9) describes how communication requires:

- Someone to communicate with.
- Something about which to communicate.
- A reason and intention to communicate.
- Some means to communicate.

In respect of children and young people with a communication impairment, it can be helpful to have a full assessment by a speech and language therapist depending on their value base, and they can be very powerful allies. The assessment should however be informed by those involved in the young person's care as well as in their formal education. This may well involve the residential care workers. Like the foster carer above, they are often in a strong position to advise on the child's preferred method of communication, and what certain non-verbal gestures and behaviour means. The lack of such services however should not prevent residential care workers working effectively in supporting a young person's chosen communication method. Communication needs to be built around the child's lifespace, using everyday tasks to develop close relationships, predictable boundaries and routine, and building in opportunities where these are lacking.

Reflecting further on Aitken's four requirements of effective communication, however there are many ways in which the residential worker can support communication.

Aitken's four requirements in a residential context are:

Having someone to communicate with, begins in infancy by adults using opportunities of children's personal care, leisure activities etc to learn their preferred method of communication, and to ensure that this is respected. Failure to do so can result in children withdrawing into a world of self stimulation and possibly self harm. Depending on the child's experiences of communication partners prior to residential care, the residential worker may have to carry out some 'remedial' work using all opportunities offered by personal care and support of the young person, firstly to develop a relationship, secondly, to help the child realise that their communication will be responded to. Aitken also reminds us that it is important to treat disabled children and young people as children first, with feelings, likes, dislikes and individual interests, showing that you are happy to be with them, and talking about what you are going to do. It is important to ensure that the child recognises you before you begin or resume an activity. Aitken suggests using tone of voice or objects such as particular jewellery or colour. He also suggests joining in a preferred activity, e.g. copying their body movements, sharing their space in a non threatening way. These can be very powerful opportunities for developing relationships and communication.

Having something to communicate about, Aitken suggests, requires carers to help build the child's physical and social world by offering information about and experiences with the people, events and places in the physical and social world. This is best done by structuring experiences for the child to discover themselves, encouraging the child to take a lead in exploration rather than directing their interest, giving time and patience to explore objects in their environment. If children and young people's efforts to communicate are ignored, they may withdraw, seeing no point in communicating. Equally they may become frustrated and aggressive, trying to assert some control over their world.

Having a reason to communicate, Aitken proposes, means that children and young people need to be offered real choices that are valued. It is important that the choice is in a form which the child can manage, hence the need for observation and assessment to ascertain the most effective method, be it eye pointing or finger pointing to the object, picture or symbol.

Having a means of communication is equally important. Observation when interacting with children and young people will highlight their preferred method of communication e.g. reflexive responses, like crying, skin pallor, pulling back etc, or signals, throwing an object away, or using objects such as fetching their jacket as an indicator that they want to go out. They may use methods involving some symbolic representation such as an object, photograph, picture, symbol or word to denote the thought or idea. Like all of us, children use a mixture of methods to communicate. It is therefore important to respect their chosen method and to organise the residential environment so that it is a total communicating environment, with 'objects of reference', pictures etc readily available in a predictable place for use by children as well as staff. Laura Pease makes many helpful suggestions in her work *Creating a Communicating Environment* (Aitken et al., 2000).

In a communicating environment, the residential unit will use all of the above, but also capitalise on different senses, using e.g. a different essential oil in a burner for each day of the week, to give a sense of rhythm and routine for the young people, different table mats for each meal, a different floor surface, smell, or texture in each room or next to each door to give a sense of the structure of the building. There may be calendar charts, of activities for each day of the child's week or short break, talking walls of staff and young people who are new to the unit, who have left, or simply who will be working over the next 24 hours. Individual children and young people may have their own box or bag of 'objects', some of which will accompany them on outings. There may be pictures or symbols on cupboard doors to denote the contents such as snacks, drinks etc. For young people using short break services, it may be helpful to have a picture of the unit and a picture of a bed for each nights stay. The young person can then take one down each morning, helping them determine how

many 'sleeps' they will have before returning home. Young people may also have safe access to the kitchen and encouraged to be present during preparation of meals. This can help develop a sensory understanding of the process of food preparation and mealtimes, smells, tastes and textures as well as having fun. Being involved in cooking can in fact help some young people who are reluctant to eat take more of an active interest in their food.

Communication between staff is clearly also critically important when supporting young people's communication. There are many different ways of recording young people's preferred means of communication, but often a simple easily accessible method is most effective, such as that used by Sanderson, Kennedy et al. (1997: 99) in the following case examples.

What we need to do to respond to Derek's communication

When/Time of day	When Derek does this	We think it means	And we should
Any time of the day	Derek goes into the kitchen	Derek is hungry or thirsty	Support Derek to eat or drink. Derek usually sits on the floor or stands and watches while it is being prepared

What we need to do to communicate with Derek

We want to let Derek know	To do this we encourage Derek	And to help we
It's time to go out	Show Derek his boots	Put his boots on and walk to the door

Communication is not only at the heart of human relationships, it gives children an opportunity to say 'yes, no, don't know' and so to give an opinion which is important when consulting with them about their lives, be it social life, school, residential placement, or plans for the future. It is also the essence of helping disabled children and young people stay safe and healthy. It is beyond the scope of this chapter to address the complex issues around child protection and safe care of disabled children and young people. This is however comprehensively addressed by others such as Briggs (1995) Westcott and Cross (1996) Middleton (1996) as well as practical materials such as ABCD pack (Cross et al., 1993) *My Book My Body* (Peake, 1989).

On the subject of communication it may be opportune to leave the last word to the young people from the Triangle:

- Listen very carefully.
- Stay calm and give yourself time.
- Say if you don't understand and don't pretend you did.
- Ask the child to repeat words if necessary.
- Check back with the child to see if you have understood.
- Let the child choose someone to help you understand them.

(Marchant, 2001)

Care planning

To ensure effective care planning, the residential worker needs to 'get along side' the young person and ensure that the care plan is empowering, child-centred and reflects their lifestyle choices both now and for the future. Terminology is important both within and out of hearing of the young people e.g. staff being asked to 'support or help James to have his meal' rather than 'feeding James' to 'help Mhairi have a bath rather than 'bath Mhairi' the latter of which have passive connotations of dependency. It is important for the staff to spend time discussing their value base as well as language and terminology. They need to understand the way in which the use of language can influence our practice and the perception of others as well as show respect for the young people. Other young people in the unit involved in peer support can be included in such discussions, regardless of whether or not they too are disabled and inappropriate language be gently challenged.

Disabled children and young people lack disabled role models. They often know what they are unable to do, but not what they will be able to 'have a go at'. It is important that they too are encouraged to have visions, dreams and ways of realising them (Connors and Stalker, 2003). Children and young people test out plans for their future from infancy onward through play and chat. If a young person wants to live initially in their own flat with a friend and work in a hotel, what support will be available to make this reality. However it is unfair to patronise a young person and encourage unrealistic aspirations such as being a truck driver when they take epileptic seizures. Sally French, herself a disabled person, supports this view, proposing that:

> *While I agree with the basic tenets of (the social model) and believe it to be the most important way forward for disabled people, I believe that some of the most profound problems experienced by people with certain impairments are difficult, if not impossible to solve by social manipulation.*
>
> (French, 1993: 17)

The residential task is to research and create opportunities and to help young people differentiate social barriers from the very real limitations of their impairment. Staff groups who have tackled this seriously are then in the position to support the young person; identifying their hopes and plans for the future while sharing disappointments and exploring other ways of achieving their vision. Understanding our personal limitations and learning to deal with disappointments is an important stage in the maturational process and defusing the myth of disabled adults being like 'eternal children'.

Health

Recent research (Grant, Ennis and Stuart, 2002) indicates that the health needs of young people who are looked after and accommodated are often not fully realised by residential care workers. It is particularly important that staff are not only aware of the young person's health care needs, have these recorded in care plans and review them regularly, but that they also understand the assessments and are prepared to research services available from the range of agencies – occupational therapists, speech and language therapists, physiotherapists, teachers, educational and clinical psychologists and dieticians, as well as the range of specialist community nurses, paediatric, learning disability, continence, epilepsy, neurofibromatosis to mention but a few. There is also a wealth of information available from voluntary and self help agencies. For the disabled young person in residential care when early medical and developmental records are often incomplete, opportunity for comprehensive assessment and coordination of an appropriate support package can be missed.

It is also important to see the health needs of disabled children extending beyond their impairment. Changes in a young person's well being such as self harm or mood swings are sometimes seen as part of their primary impairment when in fact they are due to a new and different condition e.g. pre-menstrual tension, reaction to prolonged use of medication, or stress. They may also be signs of abuse or related to other factors such as attachment disorder. Medical advice should be sought and behaviours monitored and recorded in a way to assist in identifying the cause. Knowledge of health conditions is also important in relation to properly carrying out daily care tasks such as supporting someone have a meal or move from their wheelchair.

Staff not trained in health care can initially feel quite deskilled when faced with the complex personal care needs of some disabled young people. This can lead to them adopting 'over protective' or highly limited views of the possibility of more independent living. These staff tendencies to elevate health care needs becomes one of the blocks to disabled young people living in 'mainstream' residential units, hence facing segregation in 'specialist resources' often a long way from their home area. Without minimising the importance of quality personal care or indeed the value of specialist resources, most staff can be trained to carry out the clinical care tasks expected of parents. The agency should however have comprehensive clinical procedures and a competency framework for training, testing and refreshing staff skills and knowledge base. These would include any procedures required by the young people resident, epilepsy awareness, safe storage and administration of medication (including emergency medication) enteral feeding, suction, risk assessment and safer people handling. While trained nurses do not need to be present, realistic staffing levels, organisation of the rota or involving support people from the child's home care package in a short break service can ensure that competent and experienced staff, familiar with the needs of the young people are always available.

Turning to emotional well being and mental health, although this is equally relevant to able bodied and disabled young people, priorities may differ for some disabled young people. Resources such as psychiatrists, psychologists and learning disability nurses with experience working with disabled children and young people however are not universally available. The risk is then that young people with emotional difficulties or whose communication is misconstrued and who

are perceived to be 'challenging', do not receive the appropriate assessment and support and may be prescribed anti psychotic drugs. While not diminishing the relief which appropriate use of such medication can offer, it should not be seen as a substitute for therapeutic services that would be offered to emotionally troubled children and young people who are not labelled 'disabled'. There is however an important role for the residential worker in promoting the mental health of disabled children and young people. Some of this is referred to above (appropriately) challenging social barriers, promoting social inclusion, ensuring that the unit is a total communicating environment and making best use of the young people's lifespace.

As with all young people however, disabled young people will often raise a personal thought or mixed up feelings obliquely, consciously or unconsciously through their behaviour. This may be specifically about their impairment, or about a more general worry e.g. health, relationships, changes associated with puberty etc. Television 'soaps' offer invaluable opportunities for checking with young people their hopes, aspirations and feelings, following them up with 'what do you think about . . .', particularly if a young person appears to be dwelling on a particular scenario. More personal issues arising from such chats or from other such observations can be raised in privacy using the young person's preferred words. 'I noticed when Sarah was talking about her boyfriend/baby/flat etc. you were very quiet/annoyed. I wondered if you ever thought about yourself having a boyfriend/baby/flat'. Alternatively, 'A lot of people think that because they use a wheelchair and have 'fits' they can't get a job . . .' Music also provides a helpful medium as it offers a wide spectrum of emotional expression easily available on CD, from angry and aggressive through to soothing and reflective be it rap, rock, pop, classic or country and western. Not only are you providing an opportunity for exploring worries and feelings, you are showing that you are able to talk about very sensitive, sometimes socially taboo subjects. Thus residential workers can help disabled young person understand the physical and emotional implications of the impairment on their lives, e.g. managing epilepsy, spasms or incontinence while helping them value themselves as sensual and sexual young people.

On reflection then it is hardly surprising that some disabled young people are emotionally troubled. As outlined above, their life experience is often significantly different to their peers who are not disabled, although their hopes and dreams may be very similar. In addition, experienced practitioners report that some aspects of their lives have almost taken on the status of being 'taboo', often not addressed effectively by professionals, in particular those areas of death and sexuality. Sheila Hollins, professor of psychiatry of disability at St. Georges Hospital, London, has identified what she sees as the 'three secrets' of 'mental handicap', – the 'handicap' itself, sexuality and death (Sinason, 1992).

Death and grieving

One possible difference in respect of care planning with disabled young people is that of their awareness of death and its meaning for them. Practitioners report that disabled children and young people are likely to be confronted with loss and bereavement on a more regular basis than their able bodied peers, but people in their lives are more reluctant to include them in the grieving rituals, often requesting admission for a short break because of the death of a loved one. A more appropriate role for the residential team however may be supporting the young person before, during and after the funeral in the security of their family home. In addition, the not infrequent reports of the loss of school friends from conditions such as cystic fibrosis, muscular dystrophy, chest infections etc can be harrowing for young people and staff alike – even more so if it is a fellow resident who staff have helped support and who the young people knew. Not only is the young person grieving the loss of a friend, they are often also seeking to understand death itself and to be reassured in respect of their own mortality, particularly if they too have a life limiting condition. Before being able to support young people effectively, staff need to feel supported themselves however. Only then, when secure in their own position, can they be confident in allowing young people to open up with their questions, fears and mixed up feelings. Sometimes such worries can be masked e.g. as school refusal when in fact the discussion is about 'why should I go to school when I might have died by the time I am 20?' Sinason recognises the complexity of the care task, observing that 'it is not surprising that some workers defend themselves against the pain of their clients'

meaning' (Sinason, 1992: 223) Again it is helpful to discuss death and dying as a matter of course in the unit, through events such as the death of pets or animals found when out for a walk, the coming and going of the seasons, and using TV programmes. Some of the euphemisms used around death are also not helpful such as pets being 'put to sleep' or people 'passing away in their sleep'. From experience this results in a marked resistance to going to bed!

The death of a young person, particularly while in the residential unit is always highly distressing, but it helps if staff members are clear as to what to do and understand what will happen next before having to deal with it in practice. Staff fears of death can block effective work with the young people, particularly those with a life limiting condition. It is therefore particularly important that external line management are aware of the possibility, that a written procedure is readily available and that staff feelings and anxieties are spoken about openly in team meetings and supervision. It is also important to work closely with others involved in the young person's care outwith the unit and with the young person themselves in order to gauge their level of understanding and to clarify cues as to their wish to talk and with whom. Often young people are in fact trying to protect the adults around from too much worry and welcome the knowledge that they can be involved in decisions about their own care. Practical activities such as involving the children and young people in the ritual around death, talking about memories, keeping a memory box, planting a memory tree, visiting the graveyard and other such ways of keeping the person's memory alive are helpful for both staff and young people coming to terms with the loss of a friend or loved one. Children's Hospices and Children's Hospitals provide an invaluable resource in this aspect of the work. Literature is also available which gives practical ideas on supporting disabled young people with such painful fears about death, either their own or others (Sinason, 1992; Hawkins, 2002; Brearley, 1997) as well as several quality children's books about death and dying.

Sexuality

Ann Craft writes that:

> To be a human being is to be a sexual being. Although there may be a range of intensity, varying over time, we

all have sexual needs, feelings and drives, from the most profoundly handicapped to the most able among us. Although we can shape (and misshape) sexual expression, sexuality is not an optional extra which we in our wisdom can choose to bestow or withhold according to whether or not some kind of intelligence test is passed.

(Downes and Craft, 1997)

Sexuality still remains an unspoken 'secret' in some residential units however, with staff remaining uncomfortable talking about it. The very structure of the regime in hospitals for disabled children and adults until recently was rooted in the Eugenics movement in the early 20th century when there was an attempt to make laws allowing only 'intelligent', physically fit people to 'breed' (Oswin, 1998). Despite the closure of such institutions and the powerful drive of the disability movement, many disabled young people still receive little support to explore and express their sexuality. For many years there was criticism of a number of the sign and symbol systems used by young disabled people as there were gaps about intimate body parts such as bottom, or breasts, or personal activities such as masturbation. Recently, the agency Triangle in consultation with young people developed an image vocabulary, funded and supported by NSPCC to fill the gap (Marchant and Cross, 2002). Other systems are also now expanding their vocabulary in response to demand. It is not uncommon however for professionals to describe young disabled people as 'presenting challenging sexualised behaviour'. While undoubtedly some disabled young people's behaviour can be sexually aggressive and they need help to address this, for many they are simply trying to make sense of the normal physical changes of adolescence, having received no preparation for the physical and emotional impact. If kept in the dark, young people can find puberty frightening, believing the physical changes to be further deterioration of their physical condition. Again there are examples of good practice, where young people's sexualised behaviour has been seen as communication, that they are unsure about what is happening to their body rather than being perceived as a challenge. Such behaviour can be sensitively put back to them using simple language, and the terminology the young person uses 'I wonder if you are thinking that you are growing hair on your legs and around your privates etc. and are wondering why'. This is often sufficient to open up dialogue using words, or pictures about body changes, feelings, fears

and relationships. As with all young people, however, disabled young people will only trust staff with a 'big worry' if they have been helped in a non-judgmental way with lesser worries and if they feel that people involved in their support are comfortable with their own sexuality.

It is therefore important to have addressed sexuality as a staff team to ensure that all staff are comfortable with addressing this and are coming from a shared value base. This gives an opportunity for staff to address their own fears and lack of knowledge in a relatively safe environment and to agree what words they will encourage the use of when the young people's own vocabulary is lacking. It also gives an opportunity to plan how to involve parents to ensure that all are working in partnership while ensuring the confidentiality, safety and well being of young people and staff. With a few exceptions, parents often welcome the opportunity to discuss either in privacy or in a group, their fears, feelings and practical ideas as to how to address their young person's developing sexuality. Caroline Craft and Anne Downes have designed a comprehensive staff development pack which helps staff teams on this journey (Downes and Craft, 1997). Good practical resource material is also often available from health promotion units or family planning units run by area health boards and such services will support staff development and training if resources are available. Agencies such as learning disability nurses and speech and language therapists can also play a valuable role in how best to communicate with young people using objects of reference, symbols or simple text about forthcoming body changes, or acceptable sexual behaviour. They can be particularly helpful if the young person has an impairment which means that their sexual development will be atypical. Sexuality is more than just the mechanics of sexual relationships however. It is about our whole way of being, gender, sensuality, self expression and it is important that young people's care plans reflect this, how they wish to explore sensuality and sexuality through touch with others, private time to explore their body, as well as dress, fashion, hairstyle, music and relationships, in fact, like typical adolescents.

The way forward

For the twenty-first century, it remains to be seen how society will support and respect children with severe impairments who are surviving babyhood due to advances in medicine; how the new forms of hospice care will develop for these children, and whether children who cannot communicate and move will be given real choices.

(Oswin, 1998: 40)

Some experienced practitioners predict a reduction in residential care for disabled children as there is an increase in social inclusion in practice and as alternatives such as inclusive recreational activities develop. Residential short break services and residential schools may become a historical relic, like the large hospitals and 'colonies'. Another possibility as we move towards smaller residential units and a more skilled and qualified workforce, is that disabled young people are integrated to 'mainstream' services. Whatever the future of residential resources for disabled children and young people, for those involved in their care the task remains the same, listening to young people and working along with them to rid society of the 'disabling barriers' (Swain, Finkelstein, French, Oliver et al., 1993).

This chapter can only serve as a brief overview of the task facing residential workers who support disabled children and young people in any setting. We have only touched on the abuse of disabled children and have not even begun to explore the complex task of working in partnership with parents, both of which are areas of practice meriting a chapter in themselves. But leaving the last word to disabled young people:

We are different and we should be proud that we are different. But it doesn't mean that we are completely different.

(young woman – Barnardo's, 1999)

Really listen and understand.
Learn from young people.
Show an interest in us – make it more than just a job.
(young people – Marchant et al., 2001)

References

Aitken, S. (2000) Understanding Deafblindness, in Aitken, S. et al. *Teaching Children Who Are Deafblind: Contact, Communication and Learning.* London: David Fulton.

Barnado's (1999) *Playback Video Resource Pack.* Edinburgh: Barnado's.

Barnes, C. (1997) A Legacy of Oppression: A History of Disability in Western Culture, in Barton, L. and Oliver, M. *Disability Studies: Past Present and Future.* Leeds: The Disability Press.

Beresford, B. (1995) *Expert Opinions.* Bristol: The Policy Press.

Brearley, G. (1997) *Counselling Children with Special Needs.* Oxford: Blackwell.

Briggs, F. (1995) *Developing Personal Safety Skills in Children with Disabilities.* London: Jessica Kingsley.

HMSO (1995) *The Children (Scotland) Act (1995).* London: HMSO.

HMSO (1989) *The Children Act (1989).* London: HMSO.

Connors, C. and Stalker, K. (2003) *The Views and Experiences of Disabled Children and their Siblings: A Positive Outlook.* London: Jessica Kingsley.

Cross, M., Gordon, R., Kennedy, M. and Marchant, R. (1993) *ABCD Pack.* Leicester: ABCD Consortium.

Downes, C. and Craft, A. (1997) *Sex in Context (Safeguards in Systems Handbook).* Brighton: Pavilion.

French, S. (1993) Disability, Impairment or Something Inbetween, in Swain, J. Finkelstein, V. French, S. and Oliver, M. *Disabling Barriers: Enabling Environments.* London: Sage Publications

Grant, A., Ennis, J. and Stuart, F. (2002) Looking After Health: A Joint Working Approach to Improving the Health Outcomes of Looked After and Accommodated Children and Young People. *Scottish Journal of Residential Child Care.* 1: 1, 23–9.

Hawkins, J. (2002) *Voices of the Voiceless: Person Centred Approaches to People With Learning Difficulties.* Ross-on-Wye: PCCS Books.

Hevey, D. (1993) The Tragedy Principle: Strategies For Change in the Representation of Disabled People, in Swain, J. et al. *Disabling Barriers: Enabling Environments.* London: Sage Publications.

Kilbride, L. (1999) *I'll Go First.* London: The Children's Society.

Marchant, R. et al. (2001) *Two Way Street.* Training Video and Handbook. Hove: Triangle and NSPCC.

Marchant, R. and Jones, M. (2003) *Getting it Right.* Hove: Triangle Services for Children.

Marchant, R. and Cross, M. (2002) *How it is: An Image Vocabulary for Children About Feelings, Rights and Safety, Personal Care and Sexuality.* Hove: Triangle with NSPCC www.howitis.org.uk

Mason, M. and Rieser, R. (1992) The Medical Model and the Social Model of Disability, in Rieser, R. and Micheline, M. *Disability Equality in the Classroom: A Human Rights Issue.* London: Disability Equality in Education.

Middleton, L. (1996) *Making a Difference.* Birmingham: Venture Press.

Middleton, L. (1999) *Disabled Children: Challenging Social Exclusion.* Malden: Blackwell Science.

Morris, J. (1995) *Gone Missing.* London: Who Cares Trust.

Morris, J. (1998a) *Still Missing? Volume 1.* London: Who Cares Trust.

Morris, J. (1998b) *Still Missing? Volume 2.* London: Who Cares Trust.

Morris, J. (1998c) *Don't Leave Us Out.* York: Joseph Rowntree Foundation.

Morris, J. (2002) *A Lot to Say.* London: Scope.

Oliver, M. and Barnes, C. (1998) *Disabled People and Social Policy: From Exclusion to Inclusion.* London: Longman.

Oswin, M. (1998) An Historical Perspective, in Robinson, C. and Stalker, K. (Eds.) *Growing Up with Disability.* London: Jessica Kingsley.

Peake, A. (1989) *My Book My Body.* London: The Children's Society London.

Pease, L. (2000) Creating a Communicating Environment, in Aitken, S. et al. *Teaching Children Who Are Deafblind: Contact, Communication and Learning.* London: David Fulton.

Sanderson, H., Kennedy, J., Ritchie, P. with Goodwin, G. (1997) *People Plans and Possibilities: Exploring Person Centred Planning.* Edinburgh: SHS.

Sinason, V. (1992) *Mental Handicap and the Human Condition.* London: Free Association Books.

Swain, J., Finkelstein, V., French, S. and Oliver, M. (1993) *Disabling Barriers: Enabling Environments.* London: Sage Publications.

Thomas, C. (1999) *Female Forms: Experiencing and Understanding Disability.* Buckingham: Open University Press.

UNICEF (1989) *United Nations Convention on the Rights of the Child.* London: Children's Rights Development Unit.

Ward, L. (1997) *Seen and Heard: Involving Disabled Children and Young People.* York: The Joseph Rowntree Foundation.

Westcott, H. and Cross, M. (1996) *This Far and No Further: Towards Ending the Abuse of Disabled Children.* Birmingham: Venture Press.

Part Three:
The Voice of Children and Young People

Chapter Seven

Let's Face It! Young People Tell us How it is

Jane Whiteford

Introduction

This chapter tells the story of contemporary residential life in the words of children and young people. The experiences and views of the children and young people presented here are extracted from the report *Let's Face It! Young People Tell us How it is* produced by Who Cares? Scotland in 2003.

Consisting largely of the words of young people themselves it was developed following an extensive process of consultation. As the majority of national consultations about residential child care tend to be policy-driven, it was decided that in this case the initial participation process involved young people identifying *their* priority issues. The production and the publication of the report was the highlight of the year for Who Cares? Scotland and it was launched at a conference to mark the 25th anniversary of the organisation. This chapter explains how the report was developed and includes substantial extracts from the report itself giving the young people's views and also adding some commentary to put these comments into context. Following a brief explanation of the purpose and work of Who Cares? Scotland and the methodology, the rest of the chapter will contain the views of the young people with the responses grouped under a number of headings: the first section is *My care experience*, the next is *My safety in care* and the final section is entitled *Mental health and well-being*. The author believes that the material contained within this chapter illustrates the sensitivity and wisdom of young people and demonstrates that they have a great deal to contribute to any discussion about improving residential care policy and practice. More than that many of the points made by the young people show that improvements are indeed required.

Who Cares? Scotland

Who Cares? Scotland was set up in 1978 and over the years it has grown from small beginnings, relying mainly on a few volunteers, to having over 30 staff providing a service to 'looked after and accommodated' young people all over Scotland. The organisation operates independently and works in partnership with local authorities, The Scottish Executive, The Scottish Institute for Residential Child Care, and other organisations and agencies. It provides a range of services for children and young people with experience of care up to the age of 25, and this includes children and young people in all settings; foster care, residential care, secure accommodation, residential schools, in supported accommodation, and 'care leavers'.

Organisational aims

- To provide an advocacy service throughout Scotland, accessible by all children and young people with experience of being looked after and being accommodated.
- To provide information to children and young people about their rights.
- To enable these children and young people to come together to identify issues of importance to them and to campaign for improved policy and practice.
- To ensure that their opinions are included in all decisions and discussions which affect their lives.

The work of Who Cares? Scotland

The foundation of the organisation's work is its relationships with children and young people. These relationships are based on mutual trust and aim to provide the child or young person with advocacy, advice and support outwith the formal 'care system'. To many children and young people the value of their relationship with Who Cares? Scotland lies in the independence of its staff from the bureaucratic structures of local government. For many children and young people the freedom to speak about their concerns to *their* Who Cares? worker is of great importance to them.

As for Who Cares? Scotland itself, all its work – dealings with policy-makers, educators, carers, public authorities, and its publications and research – is based upon direct knowledge of the current experience of young people and an understanding of their rights and needs. Over the years many of the employees of the organisation have had experience of the care system themselves and young people hold half of the places on the Board of Directors. The desire of the Board is to ensure that the views of young people in care are at the core of the organisation and its work.

Methodology

In the original report the purpose of the consultation process was twofold: the first aim was to identify the most important issues for young people who are looked after and accommodated in Scotland and, secondly, to further develop themes within the identified issues. The purpose of the first aim was to avoid producing a policy-led document and encourage young people to identify the issues that were most important to them and therefore produce a report shaped by the young people themselves. In order to ensure the reliability and validity of the information contained within the report, a number of methods were utilised at a number of consultation events during a fourteen-month period. At each event Who Cares? staff acted as facilitators; there was a social programme and a number of activities to allow people to get to know each other and to become comfortable about expressing their opinions, and a specific period was allotted for the purpose of the consultation.

Consultation process

The consultation process consisted of a one-day event, then a two-day residential nine months later. This was followed by twenty in-depth interviews with individual young people. The two group events are referred to by the names of the centres hosting the events: Kilgraston and Inverclyde.

Kilgraston
A one-day event for young people. A total of thirty-four young people, 12–19 years old, worked in groups facilitated by Who Cares? Scotland staff.

During the consultation young people were given over ten different issues and blank cards (for their choices) to prioritise in terms of

importance to them. The areas to prioritise were Friends and support (which the young people then chose to separate); my quality of care; health; money; safety and protection; family; relationships with staff (which young people related to quality of care); where I live; education; food; hobbies. (Young people raised the issue of discrimination independently although viewed it as something that permeated the other issues rather than a stand-alone issue. The young people also raised being happy and contact with partners.)

The key areas identified by young people were:

- safety and protection
- relationships with care staff/trust and quality of care
- family
- friendship and support

Inverclyde
A two-day residential event for young people. A total of sixty-two young people were involved (25 male, 37 female) at this event. The intention of this stage of the consultation process was to allow them the opportunity to further develop themes around these issues and also to identify ways of making things better. Young people were placed randomly into eight focus groups working together over the two days. Each group was facilitated and scribed by Who Cares? Scotland staff, and facilitators were asked to identify young people who would be willing to participate in interviews at a later date. Young people who consented had their details recorded.

Individual interviews

The next stage involved undertaking semi-structured interviews with the 20 young people identified at the Inverclyde residential event. Prior to the interviews, young people who had previously consented were provided with further information regarding the interview process and issues about which they were to be consulted. This allowed them to provide informed consent or to decide to withdraw from the process.

Two senior staff conducted the interviews, which were tape-recorded and then transcribed. Each young person was interviewed about two of the four main issues identified. Normally the interviews took place in the presence of their local Young Person's Worker, although in some cases this was not possible and in these instances the young person could choose another suitable adult to provide support.

Young people involved in the consultation process:

In total there were 90 young people involved in the consultation process. Local Who Cares? Scotland Young Person's Workers selected delegates randomly. Whenever possible there was an attempt to maintain a gender balance while representing a variety of experiences, views and care settings. The young people who participated represented 29 Scottish Local Authorities and the age range was from 13 years to 19 years old. .

Summary of young people involved in the Consultation Process

	Male	Female	Total
Residential unit	23	32	55
Foster care	6	10	16
Residential school	8	3	11
Secure accommodation	1	0	1
Supported accommodation	4	3	7

Total young people involved in the consultation process: 90 (42 Male, 48 Female)

A. My care experience: Young people tell us how it is

> *I didn't really lead a life before I went into care so my life is care basically.*
> (male, 15: received in to care age 1)

Just under half of the young people at the conference placed 'relationships with staff and quality of care' as one of the top three most important issues to them. Additionally, 'where I live' was placed in the top three by a quarter of the young people. Therefore the following account is a representation of the views expressed at Inverclyde and during the interview process. Many of the young people's recorded views can be related to more than one heading however for the purposes of the report their views were separated into discrete themes: values, attitudes and discrimination; trust, listening and decisions and familiar faces and more strangers.

Values, attitudes and discrimination

In residential care, young people are aware of the tensions involved in living in a group setting and they articulate issues around individuality and

group living very well. They make important points about equality, individual identity and individual preference. These issues are complex due to the very nature of bringing any group of people to live together in order to share common living space, with all that this implies for relationships, rules and practice. Nonetheless, many young people refer to the difference between general rules for all and the unnecessary assumptions, labelling and stereotyping that can become a part of the practice and culture within a unit. Their examples highlight how arbitrary decision-making and lack of participation can so easily lead to negative and discriminatory practices.

Some young people spend only short periods of time in residential care; either before they return home or pending a transfer to a foster placement. Over two-thirds of the young people who took part in the interviews have been in care more than ten years. Therefore while this group may not be typical of all young people who spend time in residential care in any one year, they have substantial experience of residential and foster care. The young people talk candidly about their lives and the links between family members unable to look after them and the reasons they remain in care. A common plea from young people is for residential care staff (and the public) to understand that there are significant reasons for being looked after and accommodated and therefore not to blame them for the separation from their families. As one young woman put it:

> *Spread the word that it's not children's fault for being in children's homes because they think it's you and you've done something wrong, but for us it was our parents that had the problem and not us. The minute people look at you, they look with disgust, and they say that you're in a bad boy's or bad girl's home, as if to say you have done something really violent, and we haven't done anything wrong.*
> (female, 15)

As this seems to be a persistent stereotype, it is important to ask whether the adults working with young people may be influenced by such prejudice and even perhaps contribute to it. Young people want to be valued and respected and this is illustrated in a component of the Inverclyde consultation which focused on staff attitudes, and what young people viewed as being helpful and unhelpful treatment. The focus group summary indicated that on the one hand, all of the groups referred to respect, fair treatment and understanding as helpful attitudes. However on the other hand, at least four out of the six groups referred to aggression, mockery and disrespect as unhelpful attitudes that they had come across.

One sixth of this group of young people were from foster care and two thirds of interviewees had experience of foster care. The most important area of discrimination was the foster carers' different treatment of them compared to their own children:

We used to think that they were treating us unfairly [and] my social worker noticed that as well. I know it's hard trying not to favour your own kids over your foster kids, but I find it really not fair because I used to get treated very differently – I used to get sent to my bed earlier, used to get told to sit at the table and eat, used to get told to do this and do that – but their real kids were out having fun, getting taken everywhere. Me and my brother had to stay in and do chores which I didn't think was fair, and I just thought they weren't nice to us, didn't think they were nice at all, I really didn't -I wouldn't want ever to go back again. They're trying to get foster parents for me leaving school but hopefully they'll be nice ones this time.

(male, 14)

Given the preference for fostering which most local authorities operate it is important that more is done to look into children's foster care experiences, which have been relatively undocumented to date. The young man quoted above makes an important point as he recognises the application of different [negative] rules, behaviour and treatment by foster carers *because* he is looked after and accommodated. This prejudice and discrimination should be identified, explored and challenged with foster carers. The striking use of the term 'real kids' for foster carers' children touches a nerve in respect of what foster children are if they are not 'real children'.

Trust, listening and decisions
The importance of young people being listened to and participating in decision-making is central to establishing relationships and respecting their rights. Components of the United Nations Convention on the Rights of the Child are included in the Children (Scotland) Act 1995, which governs the work of social work departments, and indeed provides a framework for the rights and responsibilities related to children and young people. The importance of listening to children and young people has

gained recognition over recent years both in government reports such as *For Scotland's Children* (2001) and in research such as that carried out by Save the Children (2000).

[It] is important for all young people to have people to listen to them. The one and only main thing to having a good experience and good relationships with staff, is trustworthy relationships, trust is the key part to any relationship.

(male, 16)

Moreover, the right to participate and be involved in decision-making is made clear throughout child care policy and literature (The Scottish Executive 2001 and 2002; Skinner, 1992; Kent, 1997; Murray and Hasslett, 2000; Sinclair, 1999) to name but a few examples. The issue is not whether the decision reflects the young person's desired outcome, it is that professionals have to demonstrate that children and young people's views have been heard and taken into account within the decision-making process. One young woman states:

I have a key worker, she's really good. She used to work in a unit I was in before and I really trust her. She'll sit down and let me talk. She helps me understand the decisions that have been made about me.

(female, 14)

Another young man states:

The staff sat you down and told you what the decisions were and explained why and how. You get some staff that you don't even need to go to for support because that staff is there for you. There were two staff in the home that I was in and they were amazing. Every time I was in they would talk to you and you didn't need to be sat down and told what decisions were made and why because they made it clear when they were talking to you.

(male, 17)

Absence or negation of young people's views can only further alienate them. Such responses can cause at best despondency and at worst fear, distress and anger. When facing decisions in relation to rules, it is not the inconsistencies in themselves that cause young people to be perplexed, if not frustrated, it is the lack of explanation to help understand particular changes or preferences within staff decision-making:

I also wish people would explain rules more. It's always better to explain rules rather than just tell you that's the way it is, that's what you have to do. So sometimes when there are rules and I think 'I don't know why that rule's there', they just tell me 'that's just the rules', and you just have to get on with it.

(female, 14)

Confidentiality is another complex area of practice. Confidentiality is not absolute and therefore staff need to get into discussion and negotiation with young people about what can be kept confidential – *and what cannot* – and why. Such discussions would build more constructive relationships between staff and residents. In a group care setting, with numerous staff, questions will often arise in relation to what kind of conversations can remain private and confidential, the reasons for sharing information, who it is being shared with, and the framework of this process. Not only does this help the young person understand issues of care, concern and risk, it helps staff to monitor and question the need or requirement to share information about young people.

Trying to find a member of staff to trust appears to be linked to staff responses and what kind of approach they take with young people. One young man thinks that bossiness does not help the relationship and that a different approach is required. He thinks some people are 'gifted' in this respect and associates this ability to relate with people who have had a similar experience, he states:

I think they should really come across to you a bit less bossy. When the staff talk to you there was a bit of them authority wise, it was always that they were the big ones, they were there to tell you what is what and that's it. I think there is an easier way instead of them not talking to you or saying things to you. There was always a couple of staff you'd get that was naturally gifted that way. There was actually one staff that had been through our situation, so he was better to talk to than most staff because he could come across easier and less bossy.

(male, 17)

A positive and sensitive approach can have many benefits for young people particularly when they are struggling and experiencing difficulty. One young man illustrates the importance of affection, tenderness and care during emotionally turbulent times:

They were just there for me, and gave me a hug when I needed one, gave me support when I needed it, gave me love and attention when I needed it and that's what I wanted and needed at that moment in time. I really owe a big deal to them, to the staff in my unit I owe a lot to them for doing that for me. They were just there for me to understand me, listen and be there for me and I appreciate it very much.

(male, 14)

Familiar faces and more strangers

Two common issues arose from approximately one half of the interviewees: a sense of history i.e. relationships with staff they have known in previous residential placements, and also the negative impact of a high turnover of new staff. There appears to be a security in knowing members of staff from previous placements particularly if young people re-established relationships with staff who have worked with them as small children. Fortunately, the relationships tended to be positive ones and the young people felt a sense of their own history and the meaningfulness of long-term relationships:

One of the staff who was in a home a few years ago with us is in the same home now with us. It's like old times again. Yes, she was our keyworker for us back then and now she's my keyworker. She knows what [my sister and I] have been doing, she knows our history. Probably because she was there when we were growing up and she still is really. She's a part of my history because I was close to her back then and I'm still close to her now.

(female, 15)

Young people highlight the importance of some form of continuity in their lives and that, somewhat unusually, compared to other living situations; they have an adult in their lives who remembers them as a child.

There's some people that I know who say they don't feel they can talk to anybody but I get on with quite a lot of the staff because when I went into the home [some of them have] known me since I was four. A lot of the staff that worked with me then are in the home now.

(male, 16)

These young people illustrate the (lack of) shared history for young people who have been in care since early childhood. There appears to be an invisible childhood for many young people in that the adults caring for them cannot share retrospective stories, observations and memories about the young person as a child. The cultural norm of looking back at childhood with other people who were a part of that experience is not open to many young people who have been in long-term care. The same young man describes one of the good things about his re-established relationships as getting access to photographs of him as a child:

It's good [that I have previously known them] because I never saw any pictures or anything and now they'll bring me pictures.

(male, 16)

It is deeply concerning that some young people in care have few or no photographs of early childhood, care staff and their home. It is curious in this case that the photographs were held by the unit staff rather than with the child. It may be an overstated point but surely children and young people in care have the right to photographs of themselves and their history and that they too, as with so many people, can enjoy or cringe at the visible reminders and memories of their relationships and experiences.

B. My safety in care: young people tell us how it is

In this section the vitally important issue of safety is addressed in terms of protection from aggression and violence, and highlights that, despite units becoming smaller over the years, bullying is still a significant feature of some young people's experience. Although young people experience bullying in general, young people in care have an issue that is usually out with the home (e.g. school, leisure areas, the street etc) brought in to their home. Even more serious is the fact that some young people report concerns about staff 'bullying' and in particular that approved procedures for 'physical restraint' are either not or inappropriately used – young people know when these are being wrongly and abusively applied. Young people's views reflect many of the messages highlighted and discussed in *Children's Safeguard Review* (Kent, 1997) *Edinburgh's Children* (Marshall, Jamieson and Finlayson, 1999) and the *Feeling Safe? Report* (Who Cares? Scotland, 1997).

I think some people would be shocked if they knew what some people have gone through.

(male, 16)

Since I was born my life hasn't been very good. It's been a hard knock life!

(male, 15)

From the beginning of the consultation process the issue of safety and protection has been uppermost in young people's minds. At the Kilgraston conference over one third of young people placed safety and protection as one of the top three most important issues for them. During the focus groups at Inverclyde four out of six groups highlighted bullying and restraint as key safety issues in care:

I think it's important to feel safe because if you go somewhere and you don't feel safe then you shouldn't be there – that's an automatic reaction. You shouldn't be at that place if you don't feel safe. You need to be somewhere that you feel safe and comfortable, and you feel comfortable around the people you're with. Automatically, when you walk into their hands you've got to be comfortable and think you're going to be comfortable there and going to be safe. If you walk in there and you think that it's not going to be the right place for you then you shouldn't be there.

(male, 14)

Irrespective of the many complications in finding the appropriate placement to meet a young person's needs, this young person's statement summarises one of the most important factors in providing care for young people and that is when they 'walk into your hands' the young people are safe. There is little doubt that the need for safety in care is often emphasised because of children and young people's experiences before being looked after and accommodated. Connections with previous experiences and what is happening in care are apparent throughout their comments.

Bullying by peers

Bullying is a key safety concern for looked after and accommodated young people. Their views convey the complexities of living in fear, how they cope and what they hope residential care staff can do to protect them:

Bullying in residential care is really frightening for young people. I've tried to tell staff and they sort it out for you but sometimes they can't be there all the time and bullies find a way of getting you on your own.

(female, 14)

The fear associated with bullying by peers is intense and young people are aware that due to the very nature of group living and the staff to young person ratio, it is almost impossible for residential child care staff to 'be there' on an ongoing basis. However one young person demonstrates the level of fear and distress for him and the subsequent staff response:

They knew something was wrong with me and eventually I told them what was happening and they sorted it out. It was all the staff working together, [they] had a team meeting and spoke about it and said 'this is what we're going to do' and then went and done it and sorted it out, and now I don't get bullied at all basically. Well, I do get bullied a wee bit but not as much as what it used to be, now it's just now and again verbal bullying from this one person that I don't like.

(male, 15)

One young woman talks about the difficulties of living in a unit where the age range of children and young people is too wide. Some of the children are as young as five and she is one of the oldest at fifteen. She describes how the needs of young children are different from teenagers and also recognises that the children's need for attention from staff tends to be greater and more time consuming. Moreover, she points out that vulnerable, young children struggle to protect themselves from bullying:

I don't think he bullies us, but I think he tries to bully us. We just don't have it because we're older and stand up to him. The little ones run away and tell one of the staff or they'll tell one of us and we'll go down and stick up for them.

(female, 15)

Furthermore, when asked, she describes the response to her complaint about the situation i.e. where it had got to and why she feels her views are taken seriously:

Yes, [I think it is taken seriously] because an independent chairman went up to [the children's services manager] and [the service manager] was agreeing with every single word that we were saying.

(female, 15)

Most of the statements indicate that bullying situations improve through residential child care staff's careful identification, consideration, support and action in response to bullying. Each young person needs an individualised response and, importantly, consultation on any prospective action as some young people fear repercussions.

Bullying by the community

From outside, I get hassle from the people on the streets too. I get shouted at outside. Some of those that shout at me know the bully in the unit and so they now know I'm in care. They say things about me, the way I look, and I hate it; it stops me from going outside.

(female, 14)

This young woman recognises connections between the residential unit and the community and that bullying can cross over into the local environment and result in young people being afraid inside and outside their home. Another young person describes an escalation of bullying at school and starts with the dilemma of how people got to know he was in care, a resistance against shame associated with being in care and also an argument that it is his right to choose to tell people:

Yes, [I was bullied] because I was in care. Everybody knew I was in care and I don't know how they found out because I didn't tell anybody. I don't usually tell people, but if someone asked me and I was out with my pals, I would say I'm in care as I'm not ashamed to say I'm in care, but sometimes I don't want to tell anybody and sometimes I don't care if I'm in care. If they want to say anything about me being in care on they go, I don't give a stuff what [they] say.

There is little doubt that the young person is holding on to his own sense of self worth however the bullying is directly related to being in care and verbal bullying has painful consequences. Unsurprisingly, the bullying escalates into physical assaults which not only results in fear and violence, but also has cost to his education by staying away from school:

Then it ended up they started to hit me because I was in care and they thought they could get away with it until one day I turned around and smacked one of them and that's when they all started verbal bullying me, then it went into more physical, then I got battered, and that's when it started getting even more physical and I started running away so I didn't need to go to school. I started dogging school and running away.

(male, 15)

Restraint: safety or staff bullying?

Most times in care I do feel safe, there's only a few times that I don't feel safe and the only times I don't feel safe is when I'm getting bullied or if I'm getting a restraint done which is being done wrong. If a restraint that's getting done on me is done correctly then I feel safe because they're stopping me from hurting myself, hurting somebody else or doing something stupid.

(male, 15)

Yes, [restraint is the] last resort but in some cases that just doesn't happen.

(male, 16)

Throughout the interviews it was largely the young men who referred to restraint. Overall their criticisms are around too many restraints when risk is not an issue, badly handled restraints and the use of too much force/aggression, including too many people holding them down. It seems that some young people understand the concept of restraint as a last resort when they pose a serious risk to themselves or others however it is their opinion that this is not often the case:

A couple of times when there were restraints, some of them are a bit heavy. I was 9 and 10. There was this one staff who restrained and always got too heavy handed it happened to me once but I didn't struggle – I did prefer that than getting my face scrubbed on the carpet. Then the next day they try to talk to you and you're like 'Who are you trying to talk to? Get away from me.' They would just say it was for your own good.

(male, 16)

This young man struggles at the normality of staff resuming the relationship after a restraint; there is for him a contradiction in being physically and aggressively handled and residential child care staff apparently unaware of the impact on the relationship. He felt that, in his case, restraint was not acceptable and that it is an issue of equal treatment and respect.

One young man is adamant that many restraints are not done properly and that some residential care staff do not adhere to the guidelines set out by social work departments and associated agencies. He is clear that young people are getting hurt and makes a link to young people being hurt and not being liked in the process.

I've been restrained about 6 or 7 times from in here and only one of the restraints out of the 6 or 7 have been done correctly. That's bad because the staff are trained to do TCI [Therapeutic Crisis Intervention] which is a restraint and they're trained to do it correctly, well when they're doing it to boys, some boys that they don't like, they're doing it wrong and they're hurting the boys.

(male, 15)

To promote safety within care, young people have a right to make a complaint, both to the agency that is looking after them and to the independent inspectors – the Care Commission – and therefore it is important that they understand the process of that procedure and that they know their complaint will be taken seriously and responded to promptly. The majority of local authorities' Children Services Plans refer to a complaints procedure and Children's Rights Officers and Who Cares? staff can offer support to understand the complaints procedure and advocacy, representation and support throughout the process. Additionally, there is evidence to suggest that protection and participation are linked: if young people are expressing their views to adults and experience their views as taken seriously then there is a forum for discussing their safety (Sinclair, 1999).

Overall, the picture is gloomy in relation to restraint. During the work of Who Cares? Scotland it has been both young women and young men who have raised the issue of restraint, however, in the interview sample all of the young

men referred to restraint and none of the young women raised the issue. There are questions to be asked about how [male] residential care staff exert physical control, how young men's needs and challenging behaviour are responded to and why physical intervention with some young people [men] becomes part of common practice rather than a last resort.

C. Mental health and well being: young people tell us how it is

This theme in the chapter arose from young people's comments about safety and the emotional and psychological issues implicit within it. Three quarters of the interviewees made some form of reference to their self esteem, feelings of fear, stress and anxiety, the impact of trauma and loss, and experiences of low mood, depression and suicidal thoughts. Whilst these issues are disturbing, it is important to convey the seriousness and extent of feeling in order to understand young people and the meaningful support required.

One young woman gives an insightful account of how she feels she has no control over her encroaching low mood and feelings of depression. She describes how those negative feelings contribute towards different problems in different aspects of her life:

You know some people in their lives go through a bad time and [now is] maybe my time. You don't really know what's wrong with you. I feel like I'm in this dark dimension and I can't find the light, I can't get out and I'm trying my hardest to find the light. It's like I've got problems with school, problems with my friends, problems with this and that, and I'm trying to be good at school, and it's working, but then just at the wrong time, the wrong place, I do something and I get into trouble for it. It feels like this dimension is holding me back, every time I'm trying to get out of it, it's pulling me back in again.

Many of the comments convey low self-esteem, worthlessness and, worryingly, how they often believe one answer is not to live. For example, a young man describes this desperation and yet how he then allowed staff to support and care for him, and then, in turn, wanted to return the care and protection. One reason for having mental health as a separate theme is to illustrate the lack of safety and protection in young people's lives from a young age and how they connect their [lack of] safety and protection in care with earlier experiences and the intensity of negative feelings, particularly about themselves:

You feel like when you're safe you're on top of the universe, like nothing can get you down. You feel like in Titanic when she says she feels like she's flying, and makes you feel so great. I felt that but a limited amount of time. Anything can put you down. The worse scenario is that you feel suicidal and maybe depressed. Both of them together brings back the feeling of being unwanted. If you're unsafe and no one protects you it makes you feel unwanted and you feel that you can just end it all there and then.

(male, 16)

Different people, situations and experiences can 'bring back' childhood memories and make links with painful memories where [lack of] safety and security has been an issue:

Even now I still get flashbacks of my mum and dad. I also get flashbacks of some old carers I've been with and I just keep getting flashbacks all the time. Sometimes I like the flashbacks and sometimes I don't but it's not depending on the mood that I'm in, it depends on what flashback it is that's coming back to me. If it's anything to do with my mum and dad, I hate those flashbacks because that's what makes me go to my room.

(Male, 15)

Having lived in institutions, off and on, for most of his young life it is not surprising that this young man identifies the experience of living in a residential setting as a major cause of overwhelming, negative feelings:

Keep me out of care; well keep me out of residentials because residentials make me even more insane than what I am. They make me feel bad with myself, like I've been a bad boy, then it leads on and my head's been all bad then I end up saying something to somebody and I start getting bullied and it all builds up in my head.

Self-harming

Self harming is an issue for a number of young people in care and as one young person wanted to put in a reminder that it is not only the behaviour of self harming that needs attended to by staff:

Remember, people are harming themselves because they have a reason.

(male, 16)

Young people often describe a sense of feelings building up, overwhelming them and needing some form of release. Some describe intense feelings of self-loathing and hatred believing they are responsible for what has happened to them. Such self-blame and hatred can be related to parental rejection, coming into care, bullying, restraints, and to experiences of abuse and feeling

responsible for its occurrence. These possibilities are not mutually exclusive and illustrate that safety and protection are at the core of young people's well being and mental health.

[Self harm] was discussed on a limited number of occasions. The only time I know for sure it was discussed was when I became depressed. They didn't know it was because of the feeling I was unprotected, but I knew, but you don't want to tell anyone because you don't want people thinking you're a plonker. They say you're safe but you don't feel it at times. No one knows that the two things are related.

(male, 16)

Whilst one young man makes links with depression, lack of protection (historically and currently) and self harming, another young man makes connections to getting bullied, 'wrong' restraints, fear and lack of safety, and therefore self harming:

I have tried things in the past since I've been in care that I don't really like doing but I've tried it. You can probably guess what that is which is self-harm basically. I've tried it a few times and I've spoken to a psychologist guy on self-harm that I've read [about it] as well. Since I've come here I've felt safe mostly all the time except for the time when I was getting bullied when I first came in and when the few restraints that got done wrong, they're the only times that I don't feel safe and then it gets too much and you just want to hurt yourself.

(male, 15)

He speaks candidly about the need for staff to cope with levels of fear and apprehension in relation to self-harm. There is a vivid account of what residential care staff need to witness and work with as a young person is self-harming. In amongst all of this he is able to identify what he perceives is safe and unsafe practice in relation to him:

I've sat on the bed and tried to self-harm and some staff have talked me through it and helped me handle it. Others have watched and don't know what to do. Sometimes they've pushed the knife away and this has felt more dangerous.

He goes on to advise staff about how they can further support young people who self harm:

Ask them why they do it. They'll tell you willingly. They'll tell you their secrets if you want to listen. I've sat and told my teddy. Tell people, we need to be listened to and they would do it [self-harm] far less.

(male, 16)

Another young man expresses his fear about self-harming is able to identify that residential staff are disconcerted and afraid of self-harming and its relationship to anger and release:

[I] tried [self harming] but got scared of it. If they asked why [I harmed myself], I'd say 'anger, release', that would put them off. They'd leave it to settle down a bit but they don't come back to speak to you and that's when you feel unwanted and low again.

(male, 14)

Loss

Another issue arising from the interviews on safety is separation, loss and bereavement. Out of the random sample of young people interviewed over a half of the young people had experienced the death of one parent and approximately one third had experienced the death of both parents. The rest of the group had been separated from one or both parents for a significant number of years as they had been looked after and accommodated at an early age (from one year to five years old).

Although young people were not asked about issues of loss and bereavement they make connections themselves as to the impact of these experiences on their mental health and indeed one young man could not envisage dealing with the loss of his parents at this current time because of the other stresses and pressures in his life:

[I was] 6 when my mum died and 7 when my dad died. I've got over it a little bit at least, I'm actually quite glad that it happened when I was young because if it had happened now then I would be in jail probably. I wouldn't be here just now, I'd be in jail, I would have ended up doing something stupid. I've got loads to cope with just now, and if I added that on it would make me go mad.

(male, 15)

The young person is asked if he had help to support him with his bereavements. He feels that specific bereavement work with other young people who have been bereaved was immensely supportive. He not only highlights the need for therapeutic services for young people who are bereaved, he further demonstrates the degree of trauma young people are coping with as part of their lives:

I [got help from] the social work and I done Seasons for Growth with a group of three boys and a girl. There was four of us altogether and we knew each other very well, we were all pals and we all used to sit at lunchtime in this wee room that we were allowed to go into, and just sit and talk about things that happened either the night before or if anybody wanted to talk about anything the 4 of us would sit and talk about it. We used to always sit and talk about the family that we've lost, and I used to talk about my mum and dad, and my uncle who was stabbed to death.

That was another thing that nearly killed me, I nearly killed myself when I found out that he died because he was my favourite uncle, but I've got a new favourite one now.

(male, 15)

This young person is clear that specific support to help him talk about his feelings with other young people and adults allowed him to share the traumatic experience and, importantly, allow him to know that other young people could understand what he is going through. He found that being listened to and listening to others with experiences of bereavement helpful.

Another young man highlights the vulnerability of young people at night and their need for assurance and security. Going to bed and being alone in a bedroom is a particularly lonely and frightening time for him and the connection between why he was brought in to care and his fear is apparent:

At times I don't feel safe, to be honest with you, when I'm lying in my bed at night I always need to know that my roommate, the person next door to me, is in another room, I've always got to know that he's there. I've always got to know that there are people sitting with me or that there are people thinking about me and are out there and are just there – I don't like thinking that there's nobody there, that there is nobody in the bit where I am. I feel scared at times, I feel that somebody is going to come and get me at times, just things I've gone through.

Moreover, there is also faith in the residential care staff that they understand his fear and would respond with understanding and care:

If they're there for me, they sit with me until I fall asleep or they sit with me until I feel less scared, I'm happy. At night when I'm in my bed, that's when I usually feel scared at times, so I just get up and tell them that I'm not feeling very happy and a bit scared and can I sit with them and talk to them, lie here and go to sleep because I know there's going to be somebody in here with me, so that's what I usually do.

(male, 14)

A young woman is able to describe living in residential care with her siblings and how this prevented isolation as well as an element of safety and security:

[You can feel unsafe] because you don't know what the people are like, you don't know what they'll do to you. We've been in that place for 5 years so it's been a long time that it's been like that so I don't know. We've always had our sisters so we've never had the experience of being [alone], like felt unsafe because we've always had each other.

(female, 15)

Conclusion

There are numerous constituent elements that make for a high quality residential care service for young people. Young people are telling us what they need and we have had tomes of learned recommendations from reports and inquiries. Until now, what has not been achieved is valuing the service sufficiently at local and national level. Moreover, by valuing the service users, by strictly observing their rights and tackling the stigma and discrimination that surrounds them, and by giving residential care the status it should merit, both young people and staff may begin to receive the respect they deserve.

And finally, let's face it, there are many lessons to learn from young people in care. As well as giving voice to the young people the *Let's Face It!* report makes a number of recommendations. Many of the recommendations laid out in the full report emphasise improving the life and life chances of the young people and how we can look after them better. The quality of care experienced by children and young people across Scotland varies considerably, and some of it is clearly failing to properly meet the needs of a very vulnerable group. Yet even the best units need to be open to the voice of young people to make sure that they are really meeting needs in a way that respects the dignity and promotes the development of the young people. Looked after and accommodated young people are vulnerable but they are also often very resilient. It is the commitment, drive, determination, wit and wisdom of children and young people that energises Who Cares? Scotland. For everyone involved in the care of these young people there are many messages here. Young people have told us how it is, are we ready to listen?

References

Kent, R. (1997) *Children's Safeguard Review*. SWSI, Scottish Office.

Marshall, K., Jamieson, C. and Finlayson, A. (1999) *Edinburgh's Children: The Edinburgh Enquiry into Abuse and Protection of Children in Care*. Edinburgh City.

Murray, C. and Hasslett, C. (2000) Young People's Participation in Decisions Affecting Their Welfare, in Jenks, C. (Ed.) *Childhood: A Global Journal of Child Research, Volume 7*. London: Sage.

Save the Children (2000) *Challenging Transitions: Young People's Views and Experiences of Growing Up (Young People's Summary)*. London: Save the Children.

Scottish Executive (2001) *For Scotland's Children: Better Integrated Children's Services*. Edinburgh: Scottish Executive.

Scottish Executive (2002) *National Care Standards: Care Homes for Children and Young People*. Edinburgh: Scottish Executive.

Scottish Office *Children (Scotland) Act 1995, Regulations and Guidance Volume 2: Children and Young People Looked After by Local Authorities*. Edinburgh: HMSO.

Sinclair, R. (1999) Children's and Young People's Participation in Decision-Making: The Legal Framework in Social Services and Education, in Hill, M. and Aldgate, J. *Child Welfare Service: Developments in Law, Policy, Practice and Research*. London: Jessica Kingsley.

Skinner, A. (1992) *Another Kind of Home: A Review of Residential Child Care*. SWSI, Scottish Office.

Who Cares? Scotland (1997) *Feeling Safe? Report*. Who Cares? Scotland.

Chapter Eight

Child-Centred Residential Care: The Blueprint Project

Jill Millar

Introduction

The purpose of this chapter is to highlight some of the issues raised by the Blueprint project (a joint Voice for the Child in Care and National Children's Bureau programme) which have particular relevance to current approaches to residential child care. The basic aim of the 18 month project was to take an independent view of what the current care system, including residential care, looks like and to come up with a vision of what it could look like.

In order to achieve this aim the Blueprint project has drawn on evidence from three main sources – what children and young people say, what research says, and what practitioners and policy makers say. Information from these different sources was obtained in several different ways including:

- A series of creative thinking groups involving mixed groups of researchers and practitioners from the United Kingdom and Europe. The groups were described as *creative thinking groups* rather than focus groups or similar, because the aim was to provide fora for innovation and new ideas.
- Pilot projects with eight English local authorities.
- A review of current research and literature.

Building on the evidence obtained from this wide ranging exercise a detailed Blueprint document entitled *Starting with the Child: a Blueprint for a Child Centred Approach to Children and Young People in Public Care* was launched in February 2004.

A central theme of the Blueprint vision is that care should be child centred. Starting from the child, being child centred, means developing positive ideas of children and young people, and challenging negative ones. Several key elements to a child-centred approach have been identified. These include: respecting and valuing young people as individuals with something to contribute; understanding children's and young people's perspectives; and respecting the competence of children and young people. These values have helped to shape both the Blueprint programme and the final recommendations contained in *Starting with the Child*.

One such recommendation is that residential child care should be seen as a positive option in placement choice. This proposal takes into account the views of children and adults involved in the Blueprint programme, many of whom had direct experience of residential care as residents and staff. Their views will be discussed in more detail below. First the current policy and research context in relation to residential care will be briefly considered.

Policy perspectives, research messages

Policy

Residential child care continues to have a place on the policy agenda, that much is clear from statements made in the recent government Green Paper *Every Child Matters* (2003) and work being done under the auspices of Choice Protects. The Green Paper recognises that there is a population of young people in residential care, often teenagers, often vulnerable, and also that this form of care 'can be suitable' for looked after children who reject foster care (2003, para. 3.27). Equally, the residential sector has been involved in the Choice Protects review, including being invited to be represented on the *Partnership in Planning Forum*, which is charged with developing a 'strategic agreement on the way that services for looked after children.are commissioned and planned' (DfES, 2004a), as well as being a focus of research commissioned by the Department of Health on the costs and effectiveness of services for children (DfES, 2004b).

The Green Paper discusses residential care along with fostering and adoption in connection with the key objective of achieving permanence for those looked after children who cannot go home. Residential care is identified as a potential step towards that permanence, but in itself it is *unlikely* to deliver it. Similarly considerable emphasis is given in the Choice Protects programme on improving fostering services, rather than residential care, as a way of securing placement choice and stability for children who are looked after long term.

Whilst this focus on foster care reflects the current reality that the majority of looked after children are in foster care, it also reflects the continuing strength of the family model of child care, as endorsed by the Green Paper when it states that 'All children deserve to grow up in a loving and secure family' (2003: 39). Within this model only rehabilitation home, fostering or adoption can provide a long term solution, because only these forms of care provide a family environment. Residential care therefore becomes a stepping stone towards a long term family placement or a placement for those young people who choose a residential placement or those who cannot cope with family care.

Research

In addition to having a place on the policy agenda, residential child care continues to be a focus of a wide ranging body of research which addresses both its problems and potentials.

Problems identified in current research include concerns about the impact of staff and peer relationships and culture in residential care. For instance, Sinclair and Gibbs (1998) found that 21 per cent of 223 young people that they surveyed were not in school. Allen (2003) in a study into the engagement of young care leavers in education and employment, found that young people felt that residential homes, in contrast to fostering, were unsupportive of education, staff were lax and peers dismissive. The participants in the study by Jackson et al. (2003) into care leavers and higher education, were equally negative about residential care, finding themselves unusual among peers in wanting to do well, *one young woman was so badly bullied by the other children that she took an overdose* (2003: 34). Gibbs and Sinclair suggest that well-being, which they describe as *happiness*, was adversely affected by bullying and sexual harassment (2000). At the same time, Farmer and Pollock suggest that many homes have particular difficulties in dealing with abnormally sexualised behaviour, with negative consequences for well-being and health (2003).

In marked contrast, research by Harker et al. (2003) suggests that children in residential care have some positive advantages in relation to educational attainment (see Chapter 15). Emond's recent ethnographic research in two residential units in Scotland (2002) provides positive examples from residential experiences. Emond's focus was the dynamics of the peer group among unit residents, and most especially the way young people experienced group living. She found that young people's status within the group was variable. 'Put simply, young people had various 'competencies' [such as humour], which were seen as valuable by the group. Status was achieved when a young person displayed the right social competence at the right time. The group members used their various competencies to moderate group behaviour, and to respond to new residents, staff and to their environment more generally. Group members valued being in a group, with other young people who had had similar experiences. They did not want to be in foster care, and 'while they could not control who they lived with, the group served as a mechanism by which they could control how they lived with them' (2002: 35). This research therefore highlights some of the positive benefits for young people in group living. Emonds chapter in this volume provides further details of these experiences.

Mainey's (2003) research indicates that, contrary to popular assumption, residential child care workers in England are also largely positive about their work in residential care. She found that staff morale is good in the majority of children's homes in her sample, and that there are high levels of individual job satisfaction. Care workers tended to be positive about management style and stressed the importance of teamwork in maintaining good morale.

In identifying the importance of teamwork Mainey's findings feed into a current body of research on the culture of children's homes. In this research there appears to be a consensus about the significance of a sense of *cohesion* within and beyond the residential unit. Whitaker et al. (1998), suggest that cohesion is important in helping staff teams deal with difficult situations within the home. Sinclair and Gibbs (1998), relate difficult social environments within homes to a lack of cohesion between staff and managers, objectives and roles. In such difficult environments young people were more likely to behave delinquently, staff morale tended to be low, and relationships between residents and staff and residents could be poor. They argue that a positive social environment is produced by a head of home who is clear about the objectives of the home; who feels that the roles of the unit are mutually compatible and a staff team who are agreed about how a home is run.

Linking residential units with external structures, Brown et al. (1998), suggest that where there is cohesion between broader social goals (as exemplified by legislation and guidance), local residential policy and procedures and the values of managers and staff, this produces a healthy staff culture. They go on to link such a culture with staff who can support the aims of the unit and deliver positive outcomes for young people. Following this analysis it is significant that Mainey suggests that while many residential staff worked well as a team, they also felt unsupported by external contacts, such as field social workers, and expressed the view that residential care continues to be seen as a Cinderella service. This suggests a lack of a sense of cohesion between residential work and broader social structures and goals, with potentially adverse implications for a healthy staff culture.

Developing ideas of changes in culture and approach, some researchers have recently been considering what the European social pedagogic tradition may have to offer to English social policies, including residential care (Higham, 2001; Petrie, 2001). Social pedagogy is both a theoretical and practical discipline, which covers the whole range of services offered to children and adults. Petrie suggests that it is explained as 'as bringing up children, looking after their education in its widest sense (not just schooling) nurturing and socialisation' (2002: 34). Such a holistic approach is a hallmark of pedagogy, it not only covers the whole range of activities involved in bringing up children, it also looks at the child as a whole person. In terms of residential care this broad but in depth approach translates into sharing:

> children's everyday lives, eating with them, taking them to school and to the dentist, helping with homework, watching television, mediating quarrels, comforting them, liaising with parents, and building children's self-esteem through enjoyable pursuits.

More generally residential care is seen as something that is potentially beneficial to young people.

Current research reflects the problems and potentials of residential care. *Caring For Children Away From Home Messages from Research* DoH (1998) the Department of Health overview of all the research into residential child care it

commissioned after the first Utting report (1991: 2) suggested that residential child care is 'a set of services at the cross roads'. Debate continues about the role and direction of residential care. The experience of the young people and adults involved in the Blueprint project has direct relevance to this debate.

Young people's perspectives

The Blueprint participation programme involved young people's events held country wide and a peer consultation exercise. There were also groups and meetings held for black and ethnic minority young people, young people in special settings, disabled young people, gay and lesbian young people and asylum seekers.

As part of the programme young people were asked to talk about what life was like in their current placement and what could and should be changed about it.

What follows below reflects directly the views expressed by the young people.

Many of the young people involved in the exercise, most of whom were over 10, had experience of residential care, and made both positive and negative comments about it, including:

> *Staff team is good.*

> *Staff are good listeners.*

> *I don't prefer either foster care or residential units, but if I had to choose I'd choose foster care as you have more of a chance to be good as you haven't got loads of other disruptive kids there.*

> *I don't know what advice I'd give to a RSW [residential social worker] – I never engaged with or got to know any RSW 'cos I knew I'd only be moving on again. No point in making friends. I'd just keep to myself and go out or stay in my room.*

They also talked about their environment, what residential homes should look like and how they should be run. One group suggested that they would change:

> **Rules!** *Bedtimes, pocket money [and] put an extra 3 grand in the budget, decorate the house better.*

The young people came up with a broad range of comments and ideas and these are set out in the Blueprint document. This discussion will concentrate on two particular issues that young people regularly referred to and which are crucial to child-centred care:

- participation in decisions ranging from house rules to family contact
- relationships with family and friends as well as professionals.

Participation

Many of the comments that young people made about participation suggest that they want to participate in the sense of being involved in decisions. Being involved, specifically being involved on their own terms, was particularly raised in connection with reviews:

> Reviews could be more entertaining – social workers could dress up and give us a laugh. Reviews are a bit like assemblies at school – boring.

Combining comments made by young people, a 'good review' would include: the young person choosing who comes (and who does not); the young person choosing the venue; people turning up on time; and the review not lasting too long.

Effective involvement demands information:

> Often with the big things that are going on you are left in the dark. e.g. Me – 'When can I go home?' Social Worker – 'When a risk assessment is completed.' I don't even know what a risk assessment is.

Young people suggested that they should be involved in discussions before deciding what decisions get made and that the why and how of decisions should be made clear. The ideas reflected in these comments suggest that young people want more than simply to be involved, they also want a sense of control. The feeling of being completely out of control within the care system is graphically illustrated by the comment that:

> I was in a residential unit for a year, but I don't know where it was. I have been everywhere, but I still don't know where I am.

Young people wanted more control, but *not* complete control, over larger decisions and day to day events. They wanted more choice over where they lived:

> Social services never asked me where I thought the best place would be for me to live, where I could settle.

They wanted more control over the running of residential units:

> . . . if you live in a residential unit you should be allowed to help decide what goes on and what the rules are.

More specifically young people commented that they should have a say in the staff who were recruited to homes:

> . . . we should never come home to a stranger.

and also that they should be told why and when a room search will be done.

Underlying ideas of involvement and control is the requirement to recognise the competence of young people. The young people involved in the consultation exercise consistently felt the need to ask adults to respect them, to keep appointments and to listen to them. Effective participation demands a shift in power between adults and children, and this can only take place where the competence of young people is acknowledged.

Relationships

Young people also commented on relationships with professionals, friends and family. In connection with professionals they identified the sort of care worker they would like to have. Someone who is amongst other things:

> happy; a laugh; reliable; understanding; fair; generous; kind – and not a West Ham supporter.

They suggested that such a person would: care about them; trust them, believe in them; give sound advice; be available – you should be encouraged to contact them even if it's not an emergency. At the same time they would: have a 'small mouth, doesn't tell everyone what you talk about' be less defensive and bureaucratic; have a smaller case load; and they would not 'leave as soon as meet the young person'.

These comments make clear that the young people consulted have a deep understanding both of the significance of relationships with professionals, and also of what constitutes a warm and valuable relationship (except perhaps in connection to West Ham!) They wanted to live in a positive social environment (Sinclair and Gibbs, 1998) and to be trusted by care workers. They understood there had to be reciprocity, and they valued support from professionals. Social workers and foster carers should trust young people as they would their own children. Social workers should:

> Let them [young people] into your life as they are letting you into theirs, be open and honest.

> I have had a lot of social workers – a good social worker doesn't try and do everything for you. The social worker I have got now is good – she helps me help myself – helps me to learn to do things myself.

As these comments suggest young people wanted, and often had, supportive relationships with their social workers.

Young people also suggested that they valued the help of other professionals such as school nurses, lawyers and advocates. In addition they were enthusiastic about the idea of a special person to look out for them, someone chosen by the young person, who was not part of the care system, but who would give support for as long as the young person wanted them to, and who could give them advice on practical and emotional matters.

Beyond professional relationships, the comments made by young people about the value of relationships with their peers tie in with Emond's findings (see above). Again combining young people's views, they suggested:

> . . . a friend could help give you confidence and introduce you to other friends, and ask you how you are feeling.

> . . . a friend could take the place of social workers.

> . . . and friends made in children's homes should be treated as 'sisters' and have the opportunity to be placed together.

As other research has found (see for example Marsh, 1999) this last comment suggests that friendships are sufficiently significant to some young people that they blur the boundaries of 'family'.

Not all peer relationships are so positive, and this was recognised by comments which suggested that the bullying of young people in care should be taken very seriously. It was argued by several young people that there needs to be special attention paid to bullying, but young people should be asked how they want to deal with it. One way of dealing with it was the proposal that rules made by young people in children's homes would include no bullying, indicating that young people wanted a framework within which relationships could be made to work.

The comments made by young people about their family, indicated the importance that they attributed to family relationships. Most when asked who they cared about said that it was their family, especially mothers, siblings and other relatives. It was suggested that it should be made easier to see family and friends. For black young people birth families fulfil a particular role. Often they are the only 'gateway' to other black people and as such are vital to their sense of identity (for more details on the experience of black and minority ethnic young people in care please see the Blueprint Report (2004)).

Residential care suited some young people (see for example Emond, 2002). It reduced conflicting loyalties between care and birth family. As some young people said neither residential social workers nor foster carers should try to be your Mum.

Taken together all the views expressed make it clear that both participation and relationships are important to young people. More than being involved in discussions they want to feel that they are influencing events, they want some control over their situation where appropriate. Young people value positive relationships with professionals. They want to be trusted and feel cared for, requirements which must be considered central to any constructive relationship. It is probably only through such positive relationships where there is trust, that effective participation can be developed. At the same time young people rely on relationships with family, and with friends. Any attempt to develop child-centred residential care must take these ideas into account.

Creative thinking group on residential care

Nine representatives from English voluntary sector organisations involved in the provision and operation of residential care were invited to one in a series of creative thinking groups on aspects of the care system. The groups were described as *creative thinking groups* rather than focus groups or similar, because the aim was to provide a forum for innovation and new ideas. Those coming to the group on residential care were asked in advance to come prepared to talk about the nature of child-centred residential care, what it looks like and also what gets in the way. This section of the chapter directly reflects the views expressed by the group.

Once the group discussion got under way it was apparent that there was considerable consensus about what child-centred residential care would look like. Several key features were quickly identified including: continuity, predictability of placement, a sense of security within the home, an appropriate staffing ratio, targeted funding, and a participative culture. As one participant suggested:

> I think actually we do know quite a lot about what are the features of child centred residential care and even in its complexity I think we could put together a very useful model that's almost there anyway. It's more a question of what is the environment . . . in which this model is to be embedded . . .

The group discussed a variety of the environmental factors which get in the way of child-centred residential care, including social and policy factors, the skills and training of residential workers, and the lack of a positive supportive culture within residential care. Several interlinking themes recurred throughout this discussion and raise important issues for delivering child-centred residential care. Three in particular, risk and anxiety; the role of residential care; and residential culture, will be discussed below.

The notions of risk and anxiety were a *leitmotif* of the discussion. It was suggested that the policy debate was driven by the concern not to 'have another North Wales', a reference to the circumstances surrounding the inquiry by Sir Ronald Waterhouse into child abuse in children's homes in North Wales, which was completed in 2000. This concern fed through into the standards regime, which was seen as being less concerned with delivering quality than monitoring policies and procedures. 'It's just an audit', rather than a process with the capacity to address and learn from the complex task of working with children and young people. While the need for inspections was affirmed in the light of the 'terrible betrayals' in residential care, the participants suggested that the current regime was counter productive. Residential workers feel targeted and vulnerable; they are expected to spend time dealing with bureaucracy at the expense of time spent with the young people, there is no scope for creativity and individual initiative, residential workers themselves 'become institutionalised'. It was suggested that effective training could give workers the confidence to break through the disabling effects of anxiety and lack of trust (from management) in order to be 'stronger and more creative . . . for the children'.

The vulnerabilities and anxieties of residential workers were highlighted in a discussion of the problem of physical contact. It was suggested in the discussion that it is abnormal not to have contact, young people need to know that there can be good contact, but the anxieties raised are considerable. Indeed it was felt in the group that anxiety levels are so high, and the consequences so serious, that people may be silenced. Things are not worked through within a residential unit, and lessons learnt, rather it is *straight away to court* . . . Participants suggested that such high levels of anxiety can have a paralysing effect on residential workers, constraining effective work with young people and sidelining their anxieties:

. . . and believe you me, where there's acting out and places breaking down it's always where the anxiety of adults has dominated.

Such indications of poor morale amongst residential workers can be seen to run contrary to Mainey's findings (2003).

At the heart of the discussion was the question of the role of residential care within the care system. Linked again to ideas of risk there was a sense that in policy circles there was almost a wish that residential care would disappear. It was felt that residential care is undervalued, and the complexity of the task underestimated, a point reflected in the low skill level currently expected of residential workers. In the view of the group, the reasons for this approach to residential care seem to go beyond concerns for risk and scandal. It was suggested that group living, as distinct from the family, has been regarded for a good 15 years now in our society as at very best second best. There was almost a sense of frustration among participants that the value of group living that residential care can offer, is being disregarded among policy makers. There is always going to be a group of children who are in need of good solid skilled residential care; children with mental health problems; children from the secure estate; children labelled as un-fosterable. If this recognition was granted, and effective planning delivered (through mapping of needs and resources) then residential care could move from a deficit to a positive model.

Participants discussed what constituted a positive culture in residential care, one that supports a child-centred approach, including effective participation. It was argued that there had to be a physical and emotional culture in which all – children and workers – can invest. Residential workers needed better support and training to improve their confidence and thus avoid the tendency to tie up their self esteem with the maintenance of control, which can contribute to a negative culture within the unit. There had to be boundaries, but also the capacity for young people to negotiate them. Interestingly, participants varied in the level of participation that would be supported. It was said on the one hand that some children were unable to cope with full participation, or that children needed to have permission to be children, to learn to be as well as learning to cope within a group. Equally models involving fairly extensive participation and control for young people were referred to.

Crucially however, there was agreement that engagement and relationships with young people formed the basis of effective participation.

Participants in the English creative thinking group were agreed on the importance of child-centred care, and felt able to identify its constituent parts. However they raised serious concerns about the structural and political issues that get in the way of child-centred residential care.

European creative thinking groups

The English creative thinking groups had a relatively broad focus on what child centred care looks like, and what gets in the way. The European groups, which were similarly intended to provide fora for innovation and new ideas, involved representatives from 12 countries, and had a more specific focus. Two of the themes considered were those of participation and relationships in connection with children in care. Given the fact that the groups involved academics and practitioners from the residential care sector, discussions and comments were centred on this sector. Participants identified barriers and challenges to participation, well being and relationships in advance of the groups, which provided a basis for group discussions.

A variety of barriers to participation were identified by participants. Perhaps the most fundamental was – what does participation actually mean? It was suggested that in the United Kingdom at least there was a lack of clarity about what is being aimed for:

> *Most staff don't have a clear enough understanding of what participation could be and how it fits into the overall practice or philosophy of a unit.*
> (Scottish participant)

Equally it was also suggested that residential workers can feel threatened by ideas of participation, on a personal or a professional, we know best, level. This line of thought also fed into suggestions that there was a continuing failure to recognise young people's competence in society and within the care system, especially in the case of younger children.

In addition to problems several strategies for change were identified, including equipping young people with sufficient information and experience to make informed decisions, as well as the use of training as a way of changing culture within units. One proposal for training involved

joint training of young people and adults within a unit on a variety of topics including child rights. Such joint training would mean that adults and young people would be on the same level, no-one would be the 'expert', with a consequent shift in the balance of power between adults and young people.

There seemed to be general acceptance among participants of the importance of participation, and also that children needed to be accepted as competent and supported in participating. However two distinct understandings of participation could be identified amongst participants. Many participants were from countries with a social pedagogic tradition and this was reflected in their contributions to the discussion. They argued for a notion of participation that was learnt through daily activities, through this process children develop into social actors. The rationale behind social pedagogy is to support individuals to become members of society, an approach which demands that individuals understand how to interact, how to participate.

Other contributors expressed a slightly different approach to participation, focusing on competence and ensuring that children could directly influence decisions that affect them. It was argued that children should be supported in participating because they are competent, a competence that is often contested or ignored by the care system, and some contributors suggested that the consequences of this participation could be uncomfortable for the adults involved. From the group discussions, social pedagogy seems to imply both more and less than this understanding. On the one hand it is assumed that children will participate, from decisions over clothing onwards, and a degree of competence and participation is not within doubt in the social pedagogic system. On the other hand, it is also assumed that this participation will be guided and developed by an adult social pedagogue.

In connection with relationships, participants from different countries and traditions shared the view that professional relationships were crucial to children in state care. The range of comments made reflect the complexity of that relationship. Workers need to be qualified and well trained; they need to be able to understand and interpret young people's behaviour; they need to have the ability to develop a child's emotional capacity and potential; they need to be able to support emotional development on a day to day basis, by giving and receiving trust; they need to be available to young people; and most complex of all, they need to provide warmth and care while maintaining an appropriate balance in the relationship.

Some of the problems in developing positive relationships were identified as structural by participants, in general terms the difficulties of bureaucracy meeting individual needs – a point which echoes the concerns of young people themselves. Another major problem was the difficulty of working with children and families, a difficulty arising not from the children and families, but from the professionals themselves. For instance it was suggested that professionals expect young people to trust them, but are reluctant to trust young people. With regard to family relations it was felt that there could be a tendency to define them negatively:

> When young people get in residential care professionals tend to view their existing relationships and the environment of their origin only as a bad influence to their development. But to the young the existing relationships often mean something valuable . . .
> (German participant)

> This tendency of professionals to define relationships extends to friendships, which may be seen as good and bad – important and unimportant.
> (Belgian participant)

At the same time relationships were seen as crucial to child development. Children need to be taught about making relationships, supported in making friendships, and in resolving difficulties in previous relationships. As participants indicated, social pedagogy places particular stress on relationships:

> In this [social pedagogic] view relations with others is a core principle. Through relations you get involved in the cultural meanings of society, through relations you develop skills to promote your own motives and finally you will get your identity through relations with others.
> (Danish participant)

Perhaps because the focus within the European groups was specifically on relationships and participation, or perhaps because participants were away from their home context and encouraged to think creatively, fewer structural and concrete barriers to change were identified in the discussions, than in the English groups. Positive ideas were identified, particularly in relation to participation, and social pedagogic perspectives provided an alternative approach to the development of elements of child-centred residential care.

Discussion

The English creative thinking group identified a series of interconnected structural and political issues that have an impact on residential care. They suggested that the idea of living in groups was unpopular in policy circles, that guidance and standards were driven by the need to regulate residential units in the light of child care scandals, and that, contrary to Mainey (2003), residential workers were demoralised and lacking in scope and opportunity to work creatively with young people.

The research messages referred to above suggest that such a sense of disjunction between the residential sector and governmental expectations can have adverse effects. There needs to be cohesion between goals set out in legislation and guidance, local residential policy and the values of managers and residential workers (Sinclair and Gibbs, 1998). The discussion in the English creative thinking group suggests that such cohesion is limited. Equally the impact of high anxiety levels among residential workers, apparently produced by the standards regime, may challenge cohesion within the home, again identified as significant in producing a positive social environment. The implication of this line of thought is that there may need to be a rethink of role and value of residential care within England in order to support a sense of cohesion between all levels of policy and practice. The Choice Protects initiative may present just such an opportunity.

Part of any rethink may be the need to move from a deficit model of residential care – residential care as the last resort – to a more positive understanding. Many of the young people in the Blueprint consultation exercise, and in more formal studies (Sinclair and Gibbs, 1998; Emond, 2002) have suggested that they did not want to be in foster care. As suggested above any child-centred system must recognise and respect young people's priorities. Some young people make a positive choice to be in residential care, they are more than simply unfosterable.

The young people involved in Blueprint expressed clear ideas on the importance to them of participation and relationships. They recognised what constituted positive relationships with professionals – people who have time for them, people who care. The adult participants in the creative thinking groups also recognised the importance of relationships with young people, but identified several problems which get in the way. Bureaucracy reduces time available to be with young people (as the young people themselves understood). Professionalism could also be a constraint. It was recognised that it might be construed as unprofessional to express warmth in relationships with young people leading some workers to keep an emotional distance from the young people in their care, the very thing that young people find hardest to cope with. It is perhaps necessary to reconsider appropriate relationship boundaries, for all young people in care.

The tendency of professionals to know what is best and to define what relationships are good and bad on behalf of young people, was identified as a problem by some of the adult participants. This approach is incompatible with an acceptance of young people's priorities in their relationships. It is perhaps also this approach which reduces the capacity of some professionals to see that residential care is an appropriate choice for some young people who feel that foster care compromises family relationships.

Most of the adult participants in the creative thinking groups accepted that engaged positive relationships are significant to participation. However what participation actually means in practice may need to be defined. From a Blueprint perspective 'participation' means more than a process of consultation or involvement. It means recognising young people's competence and respecting their views. This failure to acknowledge young people's competence is demonstrated by much of existing research on group culture in residential care. It is notable that the discussion in *Caring for Children Away from Home* (DoH, 1998) concentrates on adult group culture within residential units. Where there is a focus on the resident group, as Emond suggests, it tends to concentrate on the adverse effects of group living. Unless young people are recognised as positive social actors, further developments in participation and child-centred care will be unlikely.

Social pedagogy was identified by some participants in the creative thinking groups as offering a useful model. It was for instance suggested that relationships are central to the pedagogic work, and it also that pedagogy offers an approach to participation, in which it is learnt through daily living, guided and controlled by adult workers. This distinctive approach to participation concurs with Petrie's (2001: 24) comment that 'pedagogy is not value free'. Young people are allowed to participate, but on specific terms and led by adults. Nonetheless, social pedagogy may provide useful insights that can contribute to practice development in the UK, as suggested by both Petrie and Higham (2001) (see research messages above).

Whatever approach to residential care is adopted, the Blueprint experience suggests that it needs to include the following components to support child-centred care:

- Clarity over the role and value of residential care.
- Acceptance that residential care may be a positive experience for some young people.
- The importance of supporting young people to maintain as far as possible warm and valuable relationships with workers, friends and family.
- The recognition of the competence of all young people, with or without support, to be effective social actors.

References

Allen, M. (2003) *Into the Mainstream: Care Leavers Entering Work, Education and Training*. York: Joseph Rowntree Foundation.

Brown, E., Bullock, R., Hobson, C. and Little, M. (1998) *Making Residential Care Work: Structure and Culture in Children's Homes*. Aldershot, Ashgate (cited in DoH, 1998).

DfES (2003) *Every Child Matters*. London: TSO.

DfES (2004a) *Choice Protects National Partnership in Placement Forum*. www.children.doh.gov.uk/choiceprotects

DfES (2004b) *Choice Protects Update Bulletin* No 5 February, www.children.doh.gov.uk/choiceprotects

DoH (1998) *Caring For Children Away From Home: Messages from Research*. Chichester: Wiley.

Emond, R. (2002) Understanding the Resident Group. *Scottish Journal of Residential Child Care*. 1: 30–40.

Farmer, E. and Pollock, S. (2003) Managing Sexually Abused or Abusing Children in Substitute Care. *Child and Family Social Work*. 8: 101–12.

Gibbs, I. and Sinclair, I. (2000) Bullying, Sexual Harassment and Happiness in Residential Children's Homes. *Child Abuse Review*. 9: 247–56.

Harker, R., Dobel-Obert, D., Lawrence, J., Berridge, D. and Sinclair, R. (2003) Who Takes Care of Education? Looked After Children's Perceptions of Support for Educational Progress. *Child and Family Social Work.* 8: 89–100.

Higham, P. (2001) Changing Practice and an Emerging Social Pedagogue Paradigm in England: The Role of the Personal Adviser. *Social Work in Europe.* 8: 1, 21–9.

Jackson, S., Ajayi, S. and Quigley, M. (2003) *By Degrees: The First Year. From Care to University.* The Frank Buttle Trust and National Children's Bureau.

Mainey, A. (2003) *Better Than You Think, Staff Morale, Qualifications and Retention in Residential Child Care.* Social Education Trust/National Children's Bureau.

Marsh, P. (1999) Leaving Care and Extended Families. *Adoption and Fostering.* 22: 4, 6–14.

Petrie, P. (2001) The Potential of Pedagogy/Education for Work in the Children's Sector in the UK. *Social Work in Europe.* 8: 3, 23–5.

Petrie, P. (2002) All Round Friends. *Community Care.* 1452, 34–5.

Sinclair, I. and Gibbs, I. (1998) *Children's Homes: A Study in Diversity.* Chichester: Wiley (cited in DoH, 1998).

Utting, W. Sir (1991) *Children in the Public Care: A Review of Residential Care.* DoH/HMSO.

Voice for the Child in Care and NCB (2004) *A Blueprint for Child Centred Care.* London. Voice for the Child in Care.

Whitaker, D., Archer, L. and Hicks, L. (1998) *Working in Children's Homes: Challenges and Complexities.* Chichester: Wiley (cited in DoH, 1998).

Chapter Nine

The Future Direction of Inspection

Roger Morgan

The Children's Rights Director is the 'Children's Auditor' for children living away from home in social care settings (children's homes, foster care, adoptive homes and residential family centres) or in residential education (boarding schools, residential special schools or further education colleges) for children receiving social services support of any kind from local councils, and for young people leaving or who have recently left care. He has personal statutory duties to ascertain and advocate children and young people's views about the services they are receiving, to audit how well the Commission for Social Care Inspection is carrying out its duty to safeguard and promote the rights and welfare of children, and to advise on inspection, standards, regulations and ministerial guidance.

Introduction

There are many ways in which the safety, rights and welfare of children living away from home can be safeguarded and promoted. Providing safe, good quality care for children is the duty of those taking on the task of looking after those children. Good front line care, good management, sound staff recruitment, training, supervision and support are all essential, as are good policies put into effective practice, sound records systems that are put to work to inform practice, and sound regular monitoring systems. Other factors in assuring sound care are effective outside inspection of how the children are being looked after, and regular and effective consultation with children themselves, by both those caring for them and at intervals by outside and independent people.

The purpose of this chapter is twofold – to set out and discuss some of the key developments in inspection from the child's point of view, and to present a number of key messages from children and young people themselves about both the inspection process and about how those who care for them should care for them.

Provision of services to children and the inspection of those services, are related issues. The value of inspection lies in robustly monitoring how far services for children are safe, appropriate and achieving the intended outcomes for children, and also to be a force stimulating continuing improvement in those services.

Inspection is not helpful if it only comments on inputs and arrangements, but fails to assess the twin issues of outcomes for children, and children's own personal experiences of those services. It also misses its opportunity if it fails to stimulate and help to guide improvements, alongside the contributions towards improvement of good management, training and self monitoring by services, or if inspection is done and reported in such a way as to engender defensiveness rather than improvement.

External inspection can offer an objective assessment, which can bring the insights of independence, the value of assessment in comparison with other similar or related services, and aggregated feedback on the evaluations children and staff will give to trusted outsiders but which they are constrained from giving to those in charge of them.

National drivers for the future of inspection

There are two key government drivers towards improving the provision of services to children, including those living away from home, and towards improving the inspection of those services. The first is the vision of the Green Paper *Every Child Matters*, based on the five key outcomes for children of staying safe, staying healthy, enjoying and achieving, contributing to society, and becoming economically productive. Broadly, children in my own consultations have agreed with these outcomes, with added emphasis on achieving happiness in life. The children's viewpoints given in this chapter come from consultations focusing on the 'Five Outcomes'.

The second national driver is the set of government principles for good inspection, which form the agenda for improving inspection of all types of services, by all inspectorates, as a way to contribute to the improvement of services (and alongside this, to focus resources so that inspection does not constitute a distraction or unnecessary burden).

In summary inspection should:

1. **Have the purpose of improvement** in the services inspected.
2. **Focus on outcomes** for those using services (here, children and young people).
3. **Take the perspective of those using services.**
4. **Be proportionate** to the levels of risk, or lack of risk, in the services concerned.
5. **Encourage self assessment** by those providing services.
6. **Assess by impartial evidence.**
7. **Disclose the criteria** being used for assessments.
8. **Encourage open processes** such as handling complaints and quality assurance.
9. **Work towards value for money** in both services and their inspection.
10. **Learn from experience** including the impact and outcomes of inspection.

My aim is to consider developments in inspection for children under a selection of these headings, exemplified from the work of the Commission for Social Care Inspection, and expanded by the key messages from my own consultations with children themselves, carried out statutorily under the Children's Rights Director Regulations.

The new Commission

In the spring of 2001, the previous system in which local social services councils carried out inspections of children's services such as children's homes, boarding schools and residential special schools was replaced in England by a national organisation, the National Care Standards Commission. That Commission amalgamated all the local inspection units into a single inspectorate, which at the same time began assessing homes and schools against a comprehensive set of National Minimum Standards, which remain in force and spell out what is expected in the practical delivery of welfare for children in each main type of children's social care and residential education service. At the same time, the new Commission took on additional inspection duties, in relation to all fostering and adoption services, residential further education colleges, and residential family centres. Other divisions of the same Commission

were responsible for the inspection of adult residential care services and private health care services.

The National Care Standards Commission was replaced in April 2002 by the current Commission for Social Care Inspection. This Commission amalgamated the adult and children's social care and residential education inspection functions of the National Care Standards Commission, with the work of the former Social Services Inspectorate of the central government Department of Health in inspecting and assessing the performance of local councils providing social services, and that part of the Audit Commission responsible for joint review work with local council social services departments. The new Commission did not inherit the inspection of private healthcare (that was transferred to the Health Care Commission) but for the first time became a single national inspectorate able to evaluate and speak upon the whole range of social care and residential education provision in England.

The Commission for Social Care Inspection came into being at a time of change in the concept of inspection itself, and has committed itself to modernising welfare inspection, focusing on outcomes for those using services it inspects, gearing inspection to improving rather than just commenting upon services, and taking and advocating the viewpoint of the individual child or adult for whom services are provided.

Cooperation

In line with the government objectives in *Every Child Matters* all inspectorates working with children's services are working towards a new objective – that of cooperation of services, and therefore their inspection, around the needs of individual children. A new major criterion by which inspectors will judge services in the future is how they work together to provide for children without gaps, unnecessary barriers and overlaps. In terms of inspection, it means that inspectorates themselves will work together, for example in single teams of 'united specialists' from different specialist inspectorates, and in carrying out single joint reviews of services for children in a given geographical (council-sized) area of the country.

The purpose of improvement

The commitment to improvement as the intention of inspection is a major change in both the working, and eventually the perception, of what inspection does. Those on the receiving end of inspection sometimes see the process as one of passing or failing, or of outsiders hunting for shortfalls, sometimes without a real understanding of what it is really like running the service on the ground.

Inspecting for improvement has become a key objective of inspectorates such as the Commission for Social Care Inspection. This inspectorate is revising its methods to identify not only shortfalls, but also good practice to recognise, commend and spread, plus the capacity of services themselves to improve, and their trends over time, rather than solely a current snapshot against the relevant standards. It is reviewing the method of reporting following inspections, aiming at a more useful document in improving the service (for those providing it) and in choosing between services (for those selecting a service), which is also readable by children.

As a concrete example of reporting capacity to improve – and encouraging improvement – rather than solely stating current positions and shortfalls – consider the performance of children's homes and residential special schools in two key areas of the national minimum standards that apply to both. These are their extent and use of consultation with children in running and developing their services, and how well they are doing in countering bullying.

The bald figures are that 78 per cent of children's homes and 87 per cent of residential special schools were in the latest inspection cycle assessed as meeting the national minimum standard for consulting children and taking their views into account, and that 74 per cent of children's homes and 76 per cent of residential special schools were assessed as meeting the required standard for dealing with bullying.

Inspection reports also however identify those homes and schools which are almost meeting the required standard, with only a minor shortfall. Such shortfalls are likely to be well within the capacity of the establishment to improve to eliminate. If this capacity to improve were to be converted into eliminating the minor shortfalls, then the improvement to the 'pass rate' figures would become impressive. 99 per cent of children's homes and 99 per cent of residential special schools would then meet the standard for consulting children, while 96 per cent of children's homes and 95 per cent of residential special schools would then meet the standard for countering bullying.

Clearly, identifying the capacity to improve, by focusing on those establishments with not a long way to go to reach the required standard, is more likely to encourage that improvement than is solely a league table of the raw figures.

Changes to inspection are however driven by national policy, not primarily by the wishes and views of children on the receiving end of services. It is part of my function to inject that driver also into any change of inspection towards helping to improve services.

Two processes are under way to ensure that the Commission for Social Care Inspection focuses on the improvements that children and young people themselves want from their services, and that children's views and wishes inform the improvements that inspection aims to encourage.

One of these processes currently being developed, is the 'ChildMark'. Once implemented, this will be an award for good quality care or welfare provision, either generally or in a particular aspect of the service, which a service is nominated to receive by children themselves in the course of inspection. At its core is a question to children asking whether they think their service does something in particular so well for children that the service deserves a prize – and if so, what that aspect of the service is. If enough children nominate the service, a ChildMark will be awarded.

When the ChildMark has been running long enough to publish a national overview, this will provide a national picture of what children themselves – independently of any adult-set standards – see as a good care and welfare service to them.

The other process for children directly to say and influence what service improvement means, for both service providers and inspectors, is the publication of reports on children's views of various aspects of social care and residential education. These result from the permanent consultation programme I and my team carry out under my statutory functions, and the children's views are published widely (e.g. through our children's website www.rights4me.org).

The children's agenda for service improvement

Children and young people have provided me with consistent views of what makes a good service, and a clear children's agenda of the issues for an improvement action plan for any service which is not seen as fully up to the mark by the children using or living in it.

The following ten key attributes are consistently identified by children as the keys to a good children's service:

1. **Treat us individually, not as children as a whole** – children and young people, as much as any other human age, wish to be treated as individual people, not as an age group. It is sometimes salutary to substitute the word 'adults' for the word 'children' in a sentence contained in a policy, to illustrate the assumptions of homogeneity that are often made when planning for children and young people.
2. **Even troublemakers may have a point to make and need to be protected.**
3. **We have a right not to be bullied** – and when dealing with bullying, please ask the bullied child and get it right so you don't make things worse.
4. **Treat our private worries confidentially** – they're not for chatting and joking about.
5. **Children have a right to privacy** – don't assume that privacy is less important for the very young; the wish for privacy emerges from consultations with children, as for other age groups. A sound test is to ask ourselves whether we would be happy with the levels of privacy we give other age groups, e.g. for washing and changing.
6. **Check for risks** – but balance fun (and other things) and risks.
7. **If you are placing us somewhere, give us a real choice of placement, keep checking we're OK there** – don't just place us and leave us, and have a back up alternative if the first placement doesn't work out for us.
8. **Understand where to draw the line** – in touching children, 1:1 contact with children, in coping with challenging behaviour, in what you can and cannot do to punish children.
9. **Know how to spot a child's 'crunch point'** – where they most need help.
10. **Beware untrained staff using restraint** – and anyone using restraint wrongly, dangerously, without children knowing that it can happen, using it to hurt, to punish, or to make someone do what they're told, or by holding you in a way that reminds you of being physically or sexually abused. Restraint needs skill, to be a limited last resort, and only

when it is the only way to stop someone injuring themselves or someone else, or seriously damaging property.

11. **Get police checks done properly to protect us after what happened at Soham.**

One particular issue of importance to children is the extent to which they are able to raise a concern or trigger an improvement to a service themselves. Services are nowadays expected to operate effective complaints procedures. Traditionally, such procedures have concentrated primarily on complaints – i.e. dissatisfactions when the individual believes something has gone wrong. That is an important element of such procedures. However, the procedures operated by councils for children under the Children Act 1989 (with all its amendments) is not only a complaints procedure, as it is often described, but a procedure for *representations*, including complaints.

The term *representation* is not a synonym for a complaint. It means, as well as a complaint about something going wrong, that the procedure is for children to use to make (and have formally considered and responded to as carefully as a formal complaint) any feedback or proposal they wish to make about the services they receive.

It is common for professionals to espouse the cause of enabling complaints as feedback and correctives to a service – it is salutary to accept that the law gives the same powers to children under Children Act procedures to make proposals, as to make complaints.

This merits greater publicity to children, and constitutes an important means for children to contribute to the processes of improvement that are currently the national policy objectives for both services and their inspection.

When speaking of how councils and others respond to complaints and representations, children want a resolution to a problem – but the outcome that many professionals are programmed to deliver is a written report forensically examining past events and recommending future actions. The children are more usually interested in the happening of change rather than the writing of a report. As one memorably put it: 'sort it; don't report it'.

Children have given us the following ten key messages on what makes a good representations and complaints system for children:

1. **When we make a complaint** – sort it, don't just report it.

2. **Don't always believe an adult over a child** – ask for the evidence then decide for yourself – it isn't true that adults always tell the straight truth without trying to defend themselves, while children don't.
3. **Deal with a complaint as quickly as possible, but without rushing and spoiling the job.**
4. **Keep us posted on how you are getting on with our complaint** – there is always a risk that if you don't deal with a complaint, a child or young person may take things into their own hands, which can get serious and damage people.
5. **Train our own staff to deal with complaints** – and make whoever we choose to hear our complaint have to consider it impartially – even if the complaint is against another member of staff.
6. **Let us make a complaint to any adult we know and trust** – including staff members of our choice.
7. **Give us the opportunity to discuss a problem informally with a trusted staff member or other adult first, to help us decide if we have a good reason for making a complaint or not** – it helps if we know the rules establishments and services are supposed to be following. (To help with this, the Office of the Children's Rights Director is writing a series of Young People's Guides to the various sets of National Minimum Standards, published by partner organisations. Web versions of these are being put, as each is finished, on the children's website www.rights4me.org).
8. **Remember that a troublemaker could just be right this time** – it is important to avoid the situation of the child who 'cried wolf' so often that he was not believed when there really was a dangerous problem.
9. **Older young people (however strong they may usually be in their views) may find it harder to raise certain things with you such as worries about abuse, while younger children may find it harder to make a complaint or to know what is and is not unacceptable** – take age into account, and have special opportunities for both younger and usually confident older children and young people to raise concerns.
10. **Make it possible for us to take something serious to the person at the top** – but beware not simply to refer a complaint back to the person we are complaining about to sort out. We are often afraid of you doing that. It puts us at risk and doesn't protect us.

Focus on outcomes

It is all too easy, whether one is providing a service, working in it, or inspecting it, to focus attention on what the service provides, rather than on what the outcomes and experience are for the children living in or using the service. Focusing on the provision, or inputs, only, has a number of flaws. It assumes that provision in practice does what it is expected to do; it fails to take account of how it is experienced by children themselves; it fails to take account of how the same provision can have different results for different children, even of the same age group; it fails to differentiate between the differing needs and wishes of individual children; and it fails to acknowledge that an otherwise good service may still fail those individual children who do not 'fit in' to the wider child group or service generally. What a service, school or home does to the child in the wrong placement must affect how we judge the outcome of that service – whether we provide it, place in it, or inspect it.

Outcomes are what happens to, and what are experienced, by individual children when receiving a service and once they have finished receiving it. They are the results achieved for children by a service. Assessing outcomes requires consideration of results against what was intended, together with feelings about how the results were achieved. Ends do not automatically justify means – a good result achieved unnecessarily unpleasantly may sometimes be efficient in terms of resources, but it is not a good outcome. Services need to achieve intended outcomes, efficiently, through acceptable means, assessed both objectively on results and subjectively on the experience and feelings of those – principally the children – concerned.

There is always a danger when applying standards, either as a blueprint for a provider, or as a yardstick as an inspector, that one can lose sight of the outcome while focusing on meeting the 'letter of the law'. On one inspection I conducted, the children did not receive the choice of main dish at each main meal that the standards stipulated. Therefore the establishment failed the letter of the standard. However, the establishment employed a retired restaurateur as its chef, who met the children every morning to agree the day's menus, making sure that he served meals that no-one disliked, and giving everyone a turn at having their favourite dish, sauce or side order. To quote one child, 'who needs choice when we've got Chef?' Outcome met, standard input not met. We always need to keep our eyes on the horizon of whether children are receiving and experiencing the intended outcome of our services, alongside the more routine consideration of what should be on the standard 'menu' of those services.

Outcome focus also requires both providers and their inspectors to focus on possible unintended consequences of the best intended actions or services. Children have told me about some of their experiences of unintended consequences. They have spoken volumes about how well-intentioned staff can make bullying worse by punishing the perpetrator without consulting the victim, triggering both revenge and better covering up. They have spoken about fears that provision of health care and social support for children within schools, while making these easier to access where children are, also run the risk of exposing children to their peers finding out all about their special needs and support. The child said it all when their teacher had said in front of the class that it was time for them to go to the special counselling room.

A major unintended outcome for many in children's homes and foster care has for years been that with the best of child protection intentions, staff or carers requiring that the children's friends' parents should be police checked before allowing children to visit there overnight, simply results in children looked after being unable to stay with friends, or have sleepovers which are attended by their school friends. Such was the spontaneous objection during our consultations to this unintended discrimination, that we secured a clarifying and corrective government circular spelling out the importance of young people in homes and foster care taking part in the same peer group activities as others living with their own parents, with staff and carers making the same balance of risk assessments as parents make in agreeing or refusing a sleepover.

Turning to inspection, the same considerations about outcomes for children apply. Children want inspections to give them opportunity to input their views and any concerns, and to take them fully into account in any improvements that may result from inspection. One of the steps to give life to this in the Commission for Social Care Inspection is the advent of Children's Audits, where a member of my team contacts or visits children in services that have just been inspected in order to ask their experience and evaluation of the inspection. That will be followed by a subsequent contact to ask about any changes that occurred in line with the inspection recommendations. Not an extension of, nor a follow up to, the inspection itself, but an audit by children of how inspection is doing in both its own process and its outcome for children. The first Audit report can be found on www.csci.org.uk

Taking the perspective of those using services

Both good inspection and *Every Child Matters* place the child at the centre of consideration. The intention is that services for children should focus on the needs and concerns of the individual child, and that services themselves should be individually tailored as far as is practicable to what is appropriate for each individual. Inspection must follow suit, and increasingly assess how good a service is at individualising to each child, and how good it is at responding to the wishes and concerns, as well as assessed needs, of each child.

This places great emphasis for those inspecting services (or monitoring them on behalf of a provider organisation) to speak directly to children whenever making their assessments, asking about the outcomes as they experience them (which may not be the same as the perception of either the adult service provider or observer).

There are a number of clear reasons for those inspecting or monitoring a service for children to ask children directly for their views, rather than either relying on what others say, children say to them, or on adult observations and interpretations of what children experience, want or do:

1. **There are legal duties to consult children being looked after by councils or living in residential settings** – the Children Act 1989 requires councils to ascertain, as far as is reasonably practicable, the wishes and feelings of children likely to be affected by a decision. The Children's Homes Regulations statutorily

require consultation, by those responsible for the home, with the children in monitoring the home's operation and improving its quality of care.

2. **Children and young people know things the adults around them don't know** – e.g. for a risk assessment, it is the children who have the first hand knowledge of risks from illicit (rather than 'licit') activities.

3. **Children are best placed to provide first hand commentary on the outcomes as they are experienced by children.**

4. **Evidence from children of how a service or establishment operates is evidence in its own right, and can corroborate evidence from other sources.**

5. **Perceptions about a service are as important as what is objectively happening or intended, and children need to be asked about their perceptions of a service.**

6. **The law requires children's feelings to be taken into account in decisions by councils affecting children** – inspectors and monitors need to ask children about their feelings, and about whether children believe their feelings are taken into account by their services.

7. **Children can interpret what goes on and identify unintended consequences for them.**

8. **Children's first hand experience can contribute ideas and recommendations for improvement.**

9. **Children can provide first hand evidence to validate – or invalidate – self assessments by senior staff managing their service.** It would be decidedly risky to accept self evaluations by staff without checking them against what children say about their own experiences of the service.

The inspector (or internal manager or monitor) of a children's service therefore needs to ask children directly what they actually experience and perceive. This can be compared with the objectives of the service, the perceptions of its managers and staff, the objective provision, and the assumptions of providers and commissioners of what the service delivers.

Whether we are an adult or a child, our daily experience of a service is what we perceive, not necessarily what is objectively occurring, and for a child that perception may be very different from what the adults involved intend and believe is happening. Inspectors need to assess recipient perception as well as provider intention, and to take into account that different children will have different perceptions of the same service.

We need to ask children what they wish and feel about a service, and about any concerns they have about it. Feelings may not always be rational, but they are nevertheless real. Considering children's feelings is not woolly – it can be an offence not to consider them. Children's feelings are a required factor in decision making under the Children Act 1989. Choice about services is nowadays given a high profile – but neither your choices nor mine are always either rational or logically justifiable. Children too make choices and evaluate services according to feelings rather than logic, and you do not have to justify your feelings.

Being proportionate

Inspection should not become a burden on those providing services. Further, children should not be asked their views so often that they become over-consulted, suffer from 'consultation fatigue', and reluctant to participate. This is likely if they are asked often, receive little or no feedback of what the asker concluded or recommended, and then see nothing positive as a result of what they said.

Inspection and monitoring processes need to count each time they are done. There is in essence a 'burden balance sheet' of asking and finding out, as against resultant improvement assisted or achieved. Feeding back conclusions and what happened as a result of consultation – even if views could not be acted upon for good reasons – help avoid excessive drain on that balance sheet.

Modern inspection is increasingly becoming proportionate to risks and concerns, rather than following a routine 'one size of inspection fits all' approach. Worrying services should get inspected more, good services and services with good capacity to improve on their own (and to take appropriate corrective action when something goes wrong) get less outside inspection. How good a service is at self monitoring can also affect how much external inspection is needed.

It is too simple to think only in terms of the frequency of inspections. Proportionate inspection can mean more frequent but shorter visits, focused on specific core issues or follow up. Children have said they would rather more frequent, unannounced, spot check visits, including follow up checks on recommended changes, which are centred upon talking directly to them as the people experiencing the service. That is not achieved by simply doing a big standard visit less often.

Asking and listening to children is not the easiest part of inspection or monitoring, but is essential to secure a valid assessment of a service or establishment. It is therefore the one aspect of inspection that cannot be omitted in any lightening of the burdens and resource use of inspection or internal monitoring.

Usefully however, asking the children for their views and any concerns is a valuable starting point or preparation for a visit. This can boil down to asking children what is going well for them, what is not going well for them, and what improvements they would wish to see. What children tell us can then be used in 'funnelling' our attention and resources proportionately, onto issues raised.

Alongside what children say, there are other vital sources of issues to focus upon. These include what we already know of the provision, any complaints we have received, previous inspection and monitoring findings and recommendations, and 'core checks' on bits of infrastructure that are vital to children's safety and welfare, but which they are unlikely to be aware of. One of these identified by children themselves is the conduct of Criminal Records Bureau checks.

The following ten messages for inspectors and service monitors come from children and young people:

1. **Come more often, for short unannounced spot checks rather than big inspection visits, and concentrate on asking and listening to what the children and young people say about what it is like for them.**
2. **Go into detail on safety issues, and look out for small signs that show good or bad practice.**
3. **Always check with children and young people about bullying.**
4. **If your visit is expected, expect that things will just have been improved specially for you to see – don't be taken in and think that you are seeing things as they usually are.**
5. **Listen to what children tell you; use what children tell you** – 'listen to children like they matter and so you believe it'. Speak to children without staff present – they will say different things to inspectors than to their

usual staff, or in front of their usual staff. Pay attention and talk seriously to children, taking what they say seriously. Ask children directly about their lives, what is going well, their concerns and the services they receive – don't just ask staff what the children think. Choose the children to see for yourself, don't only see those the staff choose for you to see. Be open and don't put children off telling you how it is by the way you react to them.
6. **Don't walk around in a suit like a penguin** – mix with children.
7. **Don't take things at face value** – be questioning, cross check things, think of different explanations for what you see and hear.
8. **Ask yourself 'if I were a child or young person, would this be acceptable to me?' Or 'would I send my own child here?'**
9. **Ask and listen to the quiet children too – not just the confident spokespersons who usually speak for everyone.** Give all children and young people the opportunity of a say to you, but the choice to say no.
10. **Always follow up the recommendations you make. Don't just make them and leave it.**

Self assessment

A service which does not assess itself how it is doing, and relies on infrequent external inspectors or monitors to tell it how it is doing and how it should improve its service, is not a safe and good service for children.

External inspection acts rather like a speed camera for a motorist. Seeing it ahead triggers awareness of what one is doing, and corrective action if necessary. Self assessment achieves more continuous assessment of what one is doing, with more frequent triggering of corrective action if necessary, but without the approaching external scrutiny.

Self assessment cannot fully substitute for external inspection or monitoring. There is the obvious conflict of interest that arises from evaluating that which you are also responsible for running. It is also sobering to consider that in children's services, a very few of those working with children and carrying out self evaluations of how they are doing for children, might be paedophiles. Children need the route of raising worries with external inspectors.

Self evaluation does however afford a service a means of triggering and maintaining its own improvement. The role of outside inspection is then to validate.

The uses of self assessment can be summarised as:

- A basis for selecting issues on which to focus other inspection activity.
- Corroborating other evidence received by inspectors.
- Enabling independent inspection verification of the robustness of an establishment's continuing self evaluation.
- Enabling an establishment to produce its own action plan for consideration by inspectors in the light of other inspection evidence.
- Identifying current and planned changes.
- Enabling the establishment or service to identify issues on which it needs inspection assessment, recommendations or advice.
- The context for the establishment itself securing and acting upon evaluations and concerns from children and parents.

My job is to listen to children and young people, and to advocate their views. I will therefore end with two exhortations from children, which are important for all of us working in any capacity with children.

The first summarises how we should respond to the right of children (under the United Nations Convention on the Rights of the Child) – 'Take what a child says as seriously as what an adult says'.

The second exhorts us to think of the child as an individual, not as an adult in waiting, and to pay attention to that individual's enjoyment and fulfilment now, as well as the business of developing and learning for the future: 'they think we're there to become adults – you're only a child because you can't be born as an adult.'

Part Four:
Group Care Theory and Practice

Chapter Ten

Resilience and Residential Care for Children and Young People

Robbie Gilligan

This chapter examines how resilience can be used as a key organising concept in thinking about residential care practice. Resilience is about doing better than expected when bad things happen. In the case of children in care, to whom bad things have usually happened, it is about their doing better than expected. Some young people in care may do badly, but where they do well against the odds, that young person may be said to show resilience. And they may only do well – or show such resilience – in certain parts of their lives, possibly, for example, in school. The fact that some young people in care can do well, or better than we might reasonably expect, prompts us to consider how other young people in care might be helped to do well and what carers and other concerned adults can do to assist that process.

The paper seeks to explore how the application of resilience ideas may help contribute to an essential sense of common purpose among care staff in a residential unit. But hopefully this may also come to be shared with the young person, the young person's family and professional and other stakeholders in the young person's destiny. The paper aims to give concrete ideas as to how professional workers in the residential care of children can help to promote resilience enhancing opportunities for the children in their care. By extension, the paper will also explore how workers can help to reduce two of the most striking care related adversities that may affect children in care. These are the risk of experiencing *stigma* because of the low social status often associated with being in care, and the risk of experiencing *isolation*, both from people who are close to them outside the care system and from normal social opportunities. Residential care in many countries is based today on much more enlightened thinking than in the past and offers more positive opportunities for the young people who live within it. But it is also important to acknowledge that some of the previous negative features of residential care (e.g. excessively routinised practices) are surprisingly enduring and difficult to eradicate.

The paper will consider firstly what experiences in residential care may enhance the potential resilience of a young person and secondly what elements in the approach of the care worker can help promote such resilience. What can care staff do to promote resilience enhancing opportunities in the *inner* and *outer* worlds of the care setting, the inner world being the world 'inside', and the outer world being the world 'outside'? The paper will draw on examples from the care experiences of children in residential care, as well as of those in foster care, where it is felt that such examples from fostering may also be relevant to practice in residential care.

It should be noted that while the concept of 'promoting resilience' can provide one valuable organising frame for thinking about the role of the carer in residential care, it is also important not to ask too much of the concept. It cannot provide or underpin a comprehensive or all encompassing theory of residential care practice. (That is it cannot tell us everything that is to be said or done about residential care for children.) At the same time, however, it can reasonably lay claim to being an essential element of such a theory. It is also important to say that resilience is not a fixed trait possessed in some mysterious way by some fortunate young people, nor is it some kind of mysterious 'magic bullet' that can be used to 'zap' the intractable problems that may have accumulated in the life of a young person in care, nor is it a substitute for humane social policies that guarantee decent living conditions and opportunities for people.

Resilience is enhanced not by some 'high tech' specialist practice. It is enhanced, where this proves possible, by attention to some of the fundamentals of good care – close relationships, purposeful engagement in valued tasks, opportunities for enriching social and educational experiences. The issue then is how care workers can make their contribution in this regard.

It should also be noted that the term 'residential care' covers a very broad span of provision. It may include comparatively large institutions with education on the premises; relatively closed institutions, some of which may be secure (locked) smaller units where total staff numbers may exceed the number of young residents; right down to an emerging trend in certain places of single child provision in cases of what are deemed hard-to-serve children. The risk of stigma or isolation facing a child varies not just by type of setting, but also by the culture and practices enacted in each particular setting. The challenge of offering normalising and resilience enhancing opportunities may be greater in larger or more secure settings, but even in smaller settings children's opportunities may be constrained in subtle ways. It is the attitudes and practices of residential workers that will play a major part in nurturing any potential for resilience and in promoting resilience enhancing opportunities for young people in their care. These attitudes and practices will be influenced in turn, of course, by organisational and wider societal factors that impinge on the world of care.

Care staff managing the inner world and the outer world of care setting for the young person

In their work with resident children and young people, care staff are helping to manage the child's life and relationships within the centre *and* in the world outside.

In the centre, care staff are managing the physical and psycho-social environments within which the centre's inner world relationships unfold. These relationships include the child's relationships with other resident children, at an individual, small group or whole group level. They also include relationships with adults who work in the centre or whose presence in the centre somehow impinges on the child's daily life within the centre. Focusing on life within the centre and the child's part in it is a necessary – but not sufficient – part of the role of the carer staff in residential work. Care staff must also attend to the world outside the centre and the child's part in that. In particular, staff need to be concerned with the child's relationships with family – or former carers who merit consideration as quasi-family, as well as with the child's experiences and relationships within the orbit of school.

Within the world of the care setting, care staff strive to promote social and emotional learning through the daily experiences and relationships afforded by the group setting. In effect, the care setting offers multiple layers of group relationships and experiences that interact in complex ways. There is the child-world as represented, firstly, by the whole child-group, the inner workings of which may operate well below the gaze of the adults. There are then, also, smaller sub-groups of children, separate or overlapping (and likely to be ever shifting in composition) that structure or mediate much of the daily experience of the children in the setting. Most people familiar with residential settings are aware that there is an undercurrent of dynamics within the resident-world that remain at least partly hidden from those who manage the centre. Emond reminds us that in the young residents' group there is a world beyond the adults' view where much happens; information is exchanged, support is offered, power plays are managed, humour is enjoyed. Children and young people retain a strong sense of agency and autonomy, even in the highly constrained and structured world of a residential setting.

There is also, of course, the whole staff group whose workings may not be fully accessible or visible to the children. As with the staff in the children's case, the children in the case of the staff group may have a sense of some of the emotional climate that permeates the world of the staff. As in the case of the children, there are sub-groups of staff – enduring or transient – that are structured by choice or by, for example, the exigencies of the roster, that may become important conduits for child-staff relations. Structural or serendipitous influences on staff rosters may prove to have effects on events or morale in the child group. Finally, of course, important relationships and learning opportunities may occur in one to one relationship that emerge between particular children and particular adults.

In terms of the outside world, a healthy residential setting may be said to be, in many senses, open to the outside world – open to what the outside world brings in, open to what it may offer. Boundaries between the inside world and the outside world should feel real to those who cross them. But they should also be boundaries that can be crossed without too much difficulty or 'palaver'. Considerations of privacy and protection must be observed, but not at the price of hermetically sealed isolation. Visitors may bring fresh air, fresh eyes, fresh ideas all of which may be protective and stimulating. The young person cut off from outside influence faces a shrinking social network whose members may be confined to other adults and young people belonging to the setting or to the 'care' world.

One young person had spent many years in care and was attending a leaving care party in her honour. She was very appreciative of all the care and attention she had received along the way and the benefit she felt. But she also observed, not necessarily in a consciously critical way that 'all my friends are adults', and she meant essentially adults in the care system, social workers or carers. Similarly, an Australian who had aged out of the care system some years earlier observed somewhat less sympathetically that one legacy of life in care for him was that although he would like to get married to his girl friend he would have 'no-one to invite to the wedding' (Maunders et al., 1999). It is clear from various research evidence, that family and friends are important sources of social support in adult life (Gardner, 2003). One of the key tasks in residential care is to preserve *actively* ties to family and friends where these might be the source of ongoing support in later life, a point to be touched on further below.

But it is not just visitors who may bring the outside world into the world of the unit. One such example is of a male care worker who was also an accomplished sportsman. He was a hurler, that is someone who plays the game of hurling (a free flowing native Irish version of hockey). He brought his hurley (the stick with which the game is played) to work with him one day to provide some diversion for the residents. As it happened one of the most disaffected residents proved to be a 'natural' in terms of the skills required, and this chance discovery led on to the young person playing at club and representative levels and to a transformation in his self-image.

Good care practice is about managing not only the inner world of the centre but also about how that world connects with the world outside.

Historically, however, it can be argued that much of residential care has turned away from the world outside. Residential care has often been provided on the premise that residents had to be rescued and protected from the malign influences of the outside world. Think for example of how residential institutions were used to rescue aboriginal children from their families and culture in Australia, Canada and the USA; or of how remote rural institutions were often conceived as healthy antidotes to the malign

influences of urban poverty. One of the key challenges today for residential care providers is to avoid such unhelpful 'splitting' in thinking-bad outside/good inside, bad past/good present, bad home/good care, bad parent/good carer. While good practice today recognises the need to avoid such splitting, it still may emerge at times despite formal policy and at quite a subtle or unconscious level. Where this happens, its effects may be discerned, for example, in possible degrees of resistance to contact with family, or to providing facilities for visitors, or at least to providing facilities that are genuinely inviting or welcoming, or to facilitating wholeheartedly the young person's engagement with opportunities presented by the world outside. This attempt, in some senses, to erase the outside may seem tempting because the outside world may be said to introduce challenge and ambiguity. The complexity of what it introduces will be harder to manage, since it reduces the comparative simplicity and fuller control apparently available internally in a setting that, metaphorically at least, may in some ways turn its back on the world outside.

Another challenge is for care staff to remember that the task is to equip the young person to survive and thrive – not in the setting itself, but in the 'real world' beyond the setting. The care setting is itself, of course part of this real world but it is generally a much more sheltered and partial version of what the young person may face when making the transition out of full-time care. This may be particularly an issue when residential care is delivered in more closed types of settings. Creating a sterile environment free of malign influences may seem a tempting project but, in fact, youngsters need controlled exposure to problem forces in their lives, if they are ever to acquire the means of coping with such pressures.

As in the world of medicine, in the social world, children may be said to acquire immunity to toxic elements by controlled exposure to those same elements. In terms of handling risk, the implication of this view is that the urge to reduce risk should be tempered by the contrasting need to nurture opportunities for development. Coping with a certain level of risk may actually help development and render the young person stronger and better able to resist increasing levels of risk. Excessive closing down of risk (or exposure for the agency) may stymie precious developmental opportunities for the child or young person. As Rutter (2000) puts it, resilience is enhanced by 'successful coping with life's challenges'. In fact he asserts that 'attempts to shield children completely from stress may be damaging as well as futile'.

Clearly residential care must have a focus on the present; but not just on what goes on in the inner world of the care setting. The focus on the present must also include the child's wider world beyond the care setting. But the caring agenda in residential care must, in addition, embrace, in an appropriately measured way, the child's past and future. It is no longer possible for residential care to operate as before, as if the past is erased and the future remote or irrelevant.

For good or ill, the child's destiny lies in the world outside. Residential care may offer respite, even asylum, from the stresses of the world outside. But ultimately the task is to prepare and equip the child to operate in the fuller world outside. Decisions about even the minutest detail of daily care must be judged by the test of whether a decision enhances or diminishes the resource base the child can call upon in that outside world. Good residential care is about building that resource base, about nurturing both social skills and self-belief in the child, and social connections on which the child can draw in the daily challenges of life 'on the outside'. Good practice today recognises these points, but traces of the old thinking can stubbornly linger. Think of how difficult it may be to secure permission for a child in care to 'sleep over' in a friend's family home. A whole host of reasons may be offered but essentially such bureaucratic hesitancy to allow a child in care such a normal experience serves to underline the sense of being different that is so easily the lot of the child in care. In fairness too, this is a burden that may also face children in foster care.

The task of residential care is to provide emotional and practical 'scaffolding' to support each young person as they build their future, to borrow a great concept from the Russian psychologist Vygotsky. As in building a physical structure, scaffolding may be needed in different places at different points, and it should only be in place as long as it is needed, although of course it may need to be put back in place to investigate and make repairs when something goes wrong.

In many senses, residential care is about helping preserve old connections to key people, and also building new connections that extend beyond the inner world of care. Good care is also about helping a child to appreciate such connections, and perhaps working to enhance their understanding of what may have gone wrong, and why, in such connections in the past. It is about helping organise, facilitate and maintain connections, or at least connections from which, on balance, positive energy flows. It is also about building the child's capacity to think positively about and 'work' those connections. 'Working' those connections will entail the young person having an understanding how they and their connections all fit together. Good care is about helping young people to have a story that in some way holds the connections – and their life – together. It is not the care staff's responsibility to specify the story, although they may play a key role in prompting those who can tell parts of the story to do so and, as with all good stories, they can help ensure that it is a story with many opportunities to be re-told and refined. Good practice may help to assemble or preserve such stories. One such example is that of a social worker who persuaded very estranged and mutually antagonistic parents, very much against their better judgement, to stand together with their child in care in a photograph at a landmark religious service in the child's development. The photograph did not re-write the family's history, nor erase the pain felt by its members, but it did perhaps offer some kind of symbolic coherence to the child and a precious memento for the future that may prompt many tellings of aspects of the child's story.

Valuing what the outside world may bring to the unit

Sometimes, an adult from outside the unit may appear who proves able to play a long term mentoring role in helping the young person to develop a skill or interest – if the unit's culture and operating procedures are open to such opportunities. One example of this involves a grandfather, who had been a French polisher (skilled polishing of quality furniture). He began to teach his skills to his grandson who was an adolescent living in a children's home. The head of home allowed the youngster to use 'a shed out the back' to practise his new-found skill. He was able to get some work from staff and neighbours.

This was an example of the professional – the head of home – using his influence to release positive energy in the grandfather – grandson relationship and add a resource which assisted the fullest exploitation (in the best sense) of what the grandfather had to offer. Lending the shed reflected practice of a very high standard, a practice sensitive to the layers of meaning in the grandfather's generosity to his grandson.

This transmission of a skill was not only giving the young person a social niche, a meaningful role, a means of enhancing self esteem and self efficacy. It was also helping the youngster to connect with traditions in his family of origin and thereby assisting his sense of belonging and identity as part of that family grouping. It was also helping the boy ease into the world of work. He ultimately found a niche as a French polisher in adulthood.

The following is another example of how contact with grandparents may offer an important legacy to children in care as they grow up into adulthood. A set of six siblings were placed in care as pairs in three separate placements. Each pair in turn visited the same set of grandparents each weekend. The grandparents thus served as keepers of their identity and communicated key family news and information between the youngsters. Years later, it emerged through a reunion of a larger group of adults formerly in care that these six siblings were still in touch with each other, probably thanks to the earlier efforts of the grandparents. Good care practice is about supporting such grandparental concern and initiative.

Contact with roots may also gradually encourage greater realism and understanding in terms of the young person's appreciation of why they are in care. Again, carers may play an important role in this as they step beyond the care setting, as this story from foster care illustrates. A foster child whose parents were out of touch wanted to re-connect with his own roots and visit the neighbourhood from where he came. The carers brought him on a visit to the area. Everything seemed smaller than he had remembered. And the problems of the area were fairly obvious. The whole visit helped him to begin to process emotionally some of the issues around why he was in care.

This story reminds us that contact does not have to follow some dull dreary format involving tedious, stilted and predictable sessions in often ill-suited locations. Instead these sessions can be organised around activities of mutual interest to parent and child. Andersson (1999) gives examples of activity based contact between fathers and their sons in care: BMX biking; going to football matches together; a boy practising

football moves with the help of his father; another boy building a go cart together with his father. In another case an aunt was the only relative in contact with a child in care. The aunt was a line-dancing enthusiast and her contact with the child was sustained by their sharing line-dancing as an activity. While the young person can benefit from contact and relationships with key adults in their family network, it is important to acknowledge that the young person is also a source of energy and capacity in building their lives and their supports.

Recognising the agency of the child and other players

In a recent workshop I ran, a professional told a very moving story that strongly underlines the point that children can have a strong sense of purpose, responsibility and agency even in difficult circumstances and even when adults are unaware. The woman spoke of how she is a lone parent and a couple of years ago she received a diagnosis of cancer. Her three children were obviously shocked but they put on a brave face. But what she didn't know, until six months later when the news about her condition was much brighter, was that the children had indeed been very worried. But they had judged it best to shield her from that worry. With better news about the cancer, they were now able to admit to her that they had talked a lot amongst themselves and with best friends about their concerns and fears. They had also discussed at length about who would mind them after she died. These three children were aged between seven and eleven. The woman who told this story said she had learned deep lessons about how much is going in children's minds beyond what adults can see, and how resourceful children can be. It is a challenge for us as adults to respect the child's capacity and to try to anticipate the impact of stress on the child's inner world.

Supporting the young person's educational progress

Education presents a challenge for the residential care worker in finding the right approach. Workers must strive to avoid being either too intrusive or neglectful in relation to the young person's educational progress. A stance of clear interest and appropriate engagement seems to be what is required. These can be demonstrated in various forms of support in the home for the child's educational progress in terms of physical conditions (dedicated quiet space for study or homework, practical guidance and advice with homework, positive expectations, interest and support from staff, staff liaison with school teachers, availability of books and other educational 'props'). This is not just a question of having books for school, important though that clearly is. It may be more about the presence of books in the home generally as a way of fostering a climate supportive of reading and learning as natural, worthwhile and enjoyable activities in themselves. Staff who value learning themselves would seem more likely to give off messages about the value of learning. In many senses, children may be said to absorb our enthusiasms.

Staff will also be alive to the school not just as a setting for educational progress, but also as a critical and pervasive space for the child's social interaction and development. As Rutter (2000) puts it 'social and pedagogic experiences at school have an important role to play' in enhancing a child's potential for resilience. It seems developmentally normal in Western culture for young people to be somewhat reticent about relating the 'nitty-gritty' of everyday life in school to their parents or carers. It seems that it is a developmentally healthy and normal part of their emerging autonomy (even if seeming to fly in the face of good practice educationally!) for adolescents to have a strict and unwavering view of school as a 'parent- or carer-free zone'. It is important, however, that the level of trust and engagement between the child and, at least, some care staff members helps to overcome this developmentally normal reticence. While it is right that children, including children in care, can shelter parts of their life from the gaze of carer adults, even if for certain periods, it is also important that the child has a sense of whom and what to tell, whenever they may feel the need. Children with stable lives and secure relationships with parents are generally likely to have a strong intuitive sense of this. For young people in residential care, the position may be a little more ambiguous. Levels of trust, comfort and familiarity with the possibly shifting set of adults in caring roles may be an issue. Nurturing this sense of there being potentially rewarding opportunities to reflect with an adult about school experiences seems important. This may not be helped by over-anxious 'hovering' or 'prodding' by adults, both of which behaviours

are likely to be counter-productive. It is well to avoid a daily set-piece of what may seem to the child as a recurring inquisition. Being around at the right moments, and for long enough, and having a fundamentally sound relationship are probably the key ingredients of good and prudent practice in this regard. One foster carer related to me how, sensitive to these issues, he tried to make it his business to 'be around' to make and have a cup of tea in the late evening after his teenage foster children had finished a spell of study. This was a very low-key but reassuringly regular sign of interest at a moment when school-related chat and reflection might arise naturally.

The experienced worker will also know that children may 'leak' concerns and worries not so much through early or prompted verbal disclosures but more through changes in disposition or behaviour which may be a signal of some turbulence in their life. Although, every presumption of such sources of turbulence should be tested against the possibility that they are merely signs of the developmentally normal occasional grumpiness or 'bolshiness' of the adolescent. It is also important to tailor the approach to the needs of the individual, as the following example suggests. Two siblings in care in the same residential setting proved to have very different views about the desirability of contact between their carers and their school. One seemed to appreciate the value of such contact, whereas the other seemed to regard it as an intrusion into a private part of her world that was going well. The second girl was well integrated in a low-key way into the social and academic rhythm of the school. For her, contact with the school risked drawing unprecedented and unwelcome attention to herself, and her status difference, that previously had never been an issue in the school setting.

Young people may have many motivations for doing well in school. They may see it as a way of proving others wrong, as a way of subverting the low expectations that others hold of them, as a form of asylum and resistance in the face of overbearing pain in other contexts of their life. One survivor of horrific child abuse in Ireland explained that she had been 'just as military about [her] study as my father was about his abuse'. School and education had provided vital respite for her and helped her to maintain a strong sense of her own autonomy and agency (Sophia McColgan in McKay, 1998: 104).

Other youngsters may regard school performance as a way of earning or repaying the pride of adults whose esteem they value. One young adult care-leaver at a conference about education and young people in care spoke about how she saw her effort and ultimately success in education as her way of honouring the memory of her deceased mother, who had died when she was a young teenager. This mother had sown the seeds of valuing education and had set the young woman on the road to educational success. Other carers besides parents may also exert influence. In her research about what young people in residential care saw as influences, Emond (2002a: 33) recounts how much it meant to the young people to know that a care staff member felt pride in their progress.

Teachers too may play a crucial role. They may help to inspire and motivate a commitment to learning. They may nurture fundamental self-belief. They may help to release latent talent. They may help to carry the young person through dark times. Their relationship with the young person may literally prove a turning point in the young person's life. Debra Fearn, now a university academic, reflects on the help she received from a teacher as she coped with life in care.

> ... the intervention of my English teacher has helped shape the person I am today.
>
> She became a 'surrogate' mother to me in many ways, with very little effort it seemed at the time. However looking back, she put in time and energy over and above what could be expected. She saw a 'spark' in me and for the next seven years, ensured that the spark became a flame that did not extinguish itself. She believed in me, and gave me courage and a belief in my self that could have easily been lost along the way.
>
> When I failed Maths and French at 'O' Level, she ensured that I received extra tuition after school, and she gave me the belief that I would be successful the second time around. In addition, she gave me extra handwriting lessons, and these were crucial in helping me to pass French especially. My handwriting was neat but very, very small, so these extra lessons made a vital difference.
>
> What makes her stand out in my mind is that she cared for me and she liked me. She was my friend, so even though she did not teach me for two years, she had regular informal chats with me, and kept an eye on my progress. Other teachers were an important influence on me, too, and they played their part in making school an enjoyable experience, but Mrs Hoole walked the extra mile that made the difference.
>
> (Debra Fearn (2002))

Challenging though it may seem in some ways, helping young people to do well in school, or as well as possible in the circumstances is likely to bring a good pay-off in terms of their overall development and progress. And 'doing well' need not just be in the academic sphere. A major New Zealand study of adult women who were victims of childhood sexual abuse found that positive school experiences in the academic, sporting or social spheres were among the influences which helped those women who had largely recovered from the experience (Romans et al., 1995). This study suggests that recovery from other kinds of adversity may also be linked to positive experiences in school, whether in the classroom, or in social or sporting activities.

What might be the ingredients of care practice that may enhance resilience?

The child has brought their past in some sense with them into the present and will merge both as they bring them to their future. In a sense, the caring task involves helping the child deal with the past, cope with the present and prepare for the future. Residential workers need have a strong developmental perspective. They need to play their part among the adults who must serve as custodians of the long term interests of the child. They can help to do this in a number of ways by:

- Sustaining and building social connections for the child in the two worlds to which the child belongs.
- Showing tolerance for any ambivalence in the child's relationships in, and between, the two worlds.
- Appreciating that such ambivalence is almost bound to be the 'natural state' for children in care, since in some senses a child in care risks being a double exile.
- Helping the child to have and hold a story about their unfolding life that brings coherence and meaning.
- Avoiding working in any way that erases from memory or contact any parts of the child's past.
- Avoiding sanctions that may in some way obstruct or jeopardise a child's positive social connections.
- Ensuring that care planning attends to maximising positive educational and recreational opportunities for children in residential care, opportunities that may prove

to be precious sources of resilience for these youngsters.

- Remaining open to chance positive opportunities that may present themselves for a young person.

In terms of building the child's capacity, good residential care practice is about helping young people to widen their set of social role identities, well beyond the master identity of 'young-person-in-care', to that of friend, club member, skilled exponent of a given hobby, competent student etc. Good practice is also about finding and reinforcing any positive turning points in the child's pathway of development. These turning points may occur in the different social contexts in which the child lives out their life – school, social network, leisure time pursuits, care setting, place of worship and so on. Specifically care workers can build capacity by planning and working pro-actively to:

- Support the child's educational and social progress (reading, social skills etc.).
- Value and support the young person's participation in any structured spare time activities in or out of school.
- Help the child develop relationships in the different domains in which they play out their life (friendships with peers, ties with family, connections to adults with mentoring role in the child's life).
- Helping young people in care to find positive role models of young people formerly in care who have 'done well' in some way.

These contributions may be especially important in larger or more closed settings.

Two final thoughts

Helping young people escape the ghetto of care

Care is important for young people and greatly valued by most of them. But it is important that the price of receiving care is not in isolation from the rest of the world in which the only social contacts or friendships one has are with other young people in care or with adults working in the system. One way of reducing such isolation is to help the young person to widen their repertoire of social roles or social identities. Each social role, student, part-time worker, sportswoman, musician and so on bring forth

relationships and relationships may bring forth support and a reduction of isolation.

A lone foster carer sized up the prospects for her older teenage foster son. She figured that he needed to come under the influence of older and reasonably wise male role models and also that he needed to learn to drink alcohol in circles where there was some element of restraint. She decided that rugby offered structured use of spare time that tapped into the boy's sporting potential, male role models that most of the time would be positive and that it also offered some degree of inter-generational and therefore supervised drinking. The boy thrived as a rugby player and as a young man generally and he now plays representative professional rugby at the highest level. This woman's canny decision to try to steer this boy towards rugby has helped to achieve many developmental gains not least of which is escape from the ghetto of care.

Respecting and liking the young people

It is significant that Debra Fearn mentions Mrs Hoole, the influential teacher liked her. It seems very probable that this was a key ingredient in sustaining their relationship and its positive influence. Influence, unsurprisingly, seems connected to respect and affection. Key to working well with young people and having a positive impact on them seems to be the issue of actually enjoying their company. Joe was a retired business man, who did some part-time bus driving to help out a friend who ran a small local bus company and as a way of counteracting boredom. He ended up driving a local school bus that a more established driver had refused to drive any more, after many 'runs-in' with what he saw as a very unruly group of young passengers. The whole contract for the young people's carriage between home and school was on the point of breakdown. Joe took on the task, and got on really well with the young people – fundamentally he enjoyed their company and respected them. The day he finally retired from his second career as a bus driver, the children managed secretly to get early access to the bus, decorated it inside and had a surprise thank-you party for him. These were the same children who had been previously seen as out of control. This story highlights the point that one person's 'difficult' may be another person's 'easy'. 'Difficult' does not necessarily reside in the person seen as such, it resides as much in the eye of the beholder. Because someone has the power to apply a label does not mean their perception is accurate, the label may say as much about the person applying the label as the person to whom it is applied. An important ingredient of care practice that may promote resilience is 'expecting well' – expecting well of the young person and expecting well of the social environment in which the young person is growing up. In each of their ways, Mrs Hoole, the teacher, Joe, the bus driver, and the lone foster carer who encouraged her foster son to take up rugby all demonstrate the power of relationships, support and 'expecting well'.

Promoting resilience enhancing opportunities for young people in residential care is about being alive to such opportunities – inside *and* outside the care setting, proactively striving for such opportunities, and recognising and facilitating them whenever they emerge.

References

Andersson, G. (1999) Children in Residential and Foster Care: A Swedish Example. *International Journal Social Welfare*. 8: 4, 253–66.

Emond, R. (2003) Putting the Care into Residential Care. *Journal of Social Work*. 3: 3, 321–38.

Emond, R. (2002a) *Learning From Their Lessons. A Study of Young People in Residential Care and Their Experiences of Education*. Dublin: The Children's Research Centre.

Emond, R. (2002b) Understanding the Resident Group. *Scottish Journal of Residential Child Care*. Aug. 30–40.

Fearn, D. (2002) Protective Factors for a Childhood in Care, in *Enriching Education for Children in Care: Resilience, Potential and Attainment*. Report of Conference held by Hertfordshire Council Nov. 8th.

Gardner, R. (2003) Support Networks in the Community. In *Supporting Families – Child Protection in the Community*. Chichester: John Wiley.

Kendrick, A. and Smith, M. (2002) Close Enough? Professional Closeness and Safe Caring. *Scottish Journal of Residential Child Care*. Aug. 46–54.

Knorth, E. (2002) Residential Child and Youth Care in the Netherlands: Developments and Challenges. *International Journal of Child and Family Welfare*. 5: 3, 84–95.

Maunders, D., Liddell, M. and Green, S. (1999) *Young People Leaving Care and Protection*. Hobart: Australian Clearinghouse for Youth Studies.

McKay, S. (1998) *Sophia's Story*. Dublin: Gill and Macmillan.

Romans, S., Martin, J., Anderson, J., O'Shea M. and Mullen, P. (1995) Factors that Mediate Between Child Sexual Abuse and Adult Psychological Outcome. *Psychological Medicine*. 25, 127–42.

Rutter, M. (2000) in Shonkoff, J. and Meichels, S. (Eds.) *Handbook of Early Childhood Intervention*. 2nd edn. Cambridge: Cambridge University Press.

Vygotsky, L. (1978) *Mind in Society – The Development of higher Psychological Processes*. (Version edited by Cole, M., John-Steiner, V., Scribner, S., Souberman, E.). Cambridge, Mass: Harvard University Press.

Chapter Eleven

Rethinking Residential Child Care: A Child and Youth Care Approach

Mark Smith

This chapter on occasion uses the word 'kids' to describe children and young people. Its use is deliberate as it reflects the language people use about their own children and that used by most staff in residential child care settings. It introduces, in my opinion, an appropriate informality and warmth into our discussions about children.

Introduction

The way in which we think about the purpose and task of residential child care depends on the lens we view it through. In the UK we have come to consider it through the lens of professional social work. Many of the beliefs we have and the assumptions we make about it derive from that tradition of practice. This can lead us to believe that certain practices or ways of working are self-evidently good or bad. Examples of this might be assumptions in some quarters that smaller units are preferable to large ones, that staying in residential child care for an extended period of time is undesirable, or that demonstrations of affection from adults to children are somehow unprofessional. Very often, such assumptions are merely expressions of dominant professional value preferences, as much as they are grounded or evaluative statements about the actual quality or experience of care.

The UK in fact stands apart from other traditions of practice in locating residential child care professionally within social work. This chapter gives a brief outline as to how this has come about and identifies some of the implications. It is suggested that understandings gained from other traditions of practice offer practitioners' powerful ways through which they might reconsider their work. The chapter goes on to describe a child and youth care (CYC) approach to practice, which is the dominant model in Canada, parts of the United States and increasingly in countries such as South Africa. It is argued that the theoretical orientations that

frame a CYC approach capture the essence of residential child care in a way that most social work frameworks fail to do. As such, they provide a way through which we might rethink the discipline.

Residential child care in social work

The professional location of residential child care within social work is of fairly recent origin. Until around 30 years ago it was provided under the umbrella of the education service (residential schools) or within discrete children's departments (children's homes run by the local authority or voluntary organisations). In Scotland in particular there was a tradition of considering care within a broadly educational frame (Smith, 2003). The Kilbrandon Committee review of juvenile justice (1964) drew upon some of these strands of a particularly Scottish approach. It proposed that child care services be delivered through new *social education* departments, prescribing education 'in its widest sense' as the preferred societal response to children; both those who offended and those deemed to be in need of care and protection. However, an increasingly powerful social work lobby captured some of the social optimism that characterised the 1960s, holding out the hope that a whole range of social problems might be addressed through a unitary social work department which would provide cradle to grave welfare provision. The White Paper, Social Work and the Community (1966) claimed some of Kilbrandon's ideas and proposed that child care functions be subsumed within the emerging social work profession. The Social Work (Scotland) Act 1968 which followed heralded the birth of professional social work in Scotland. The new profession adopted generic models of practice. A similar pattern of professionalisation occurred in England following the Seebohm Report and the subsequent Local Authority Social Services Act 1971.

In the wake of these developments, the newly established Central Council for Education and

Training of Social Workers (CCETSW) asserted that residential child care was social work (1973). However, there was an underlying ambivalence and some fundamental ideological tensions around the place of residential work in the new profession (Milligan, 1998; Smith, 2003), and from the beginning there were demands for 'parity of esteem' (and qualifications) from the residential side. This issue has never been resolved and persists. It continues to manifest itself in consistently lower status and poorer levels of qualifications amongst staff in residential child care. At another level, because of the way residential child care is taught, or in many cases isn't taught, in colleges and universities, staff who work in the field often struggle to articulate what they actually do in a way they think sounds 'professional'. They can try using social work terminology and constructs but it rarely sounds completely convincing because when residential care workers talk the language of other professionals the resulting 'jargon' is dissonant (Phelan, 2001).

At various points along the past thirty years or so, there have been attempts to claim a place for residential child care within social work. Ainsworth and Fulcher (1981) and Fulcher and Ainsworth (1985) proposed the concept of group care. This was distinguished from dominant fieldwork models of social work by the idea of groups of residents being looked after by teams of staff within a defined physical space, with the inevitable dynamics this entails. Ward (1993) further developed thinking on group care, introducing the concept of *opportunity-led work*, which essentially sees the professional intervention encapsulated within the kind of everyday situations and opportunities that arise in the moment in such settings.

However although CCETSW continued to make statements that residential work was 'central to social work' (1992) developments in social work over the past decade or so have not proved conducive to attempts to claim a space for residential child care within it. Over the course of the 1990s social casework gave way to case management, where the emphasis of the social work role shifted from undertaking direct work with clients to one of accessing services. Practitioner autonomy has been subsumed beneath managerial imperatives and targets (Parton, 1999). Target setting and outcome-focused social work models do not accommodate the complex, organic nature of residential care

settings, rendering them beyond the understanding of a managerial mindset. A model of practice which has any utility or credibility with practitioners in residential child care needs to reflect what they actually do. It needs to foreground notions of process and relationships and the way in which social work practice is developing increasingly fails to do so.

There has been periodic recognition of the dis-junction between social work and residential practice and dissatisfaction with social work as the model of practice for residential child care. Warner (1992) questioned its appropriateness. In Scotland, Kent (1997) toyed with the idea of social pedagogy, the preferred European model of practice, pulling back from it, not for educational or professional reasons but because he felt the die had been cast in favour of training within a social work frame. Social pedagogy has resonances with Kilbrandon's idea of social education. It is education in its widest sense, incorporating a holistic notion of 'upbringing'. The focus in pedagogical training, which is one of the most popular professional disciplines in Northern Europe, is on relationships and reflection. The applicability of social pedagogical models of practice to a UK context is currently being considered in compelling ways by staff at the Thomas Coram Institute in The University of London (Moss and Petrie, 2002; Brannan and Moss, 2003). It does however suffer in not having a literature that is accessible to most English speakers. Some of the ideas of the CYC tradition are similar to those of social pedagogy. However, they have the advantage of an accessible and growing body of practice knowledge and literature. The remainder of this chapter focuses on a CYC approach and the possibilities it holds out for re-thinking and professionalising residential child care in the UK. It will give a brief history of the approach, will consider the therapeutic environment or milieu, the nature of the CYC relationship and intervention. From this discussion some underpinning values and principles of practice are identified. It is argued that together these provide a coherent and discrete model of practice for work with children and youth in residential settings.

Central to the CYC tradition is the concept of 'lifespace'. This is a term some practitioners may be aware of through Cornell University's Therapeutic Crisis Intervention (TCI) model of crisis management. In that context they may associate it with dealing with difficult behaviour or restraint situations. The term in fact has a far wider applicability, essentially encapsulating everything that goes on in residential child care settings.

What is lifespace?

Residential child care is a unique environment in which 'practitioners take as the theatre for their work the actual living situations as shared with and experienced by the child' (Ainsworth, 1981: 234). They share the lifespace. A lifespace orientation to practice can be described as 'the therapeutic use of daily life events in residential settings' (Murphy and Graham, 2002). It means that every action or intervention in the here and now of the living situation is replete with opportunities to enhance or detract from the developmental and learning experiences of children and youth. Practitioners therefore need to realise that everything they say and do in their interactions with children and youth has significance. The task is to consider more consciously how to maximise the opportunities provided by these engagements. This way of working can be lost on practitioners and certainly on students who often think that 'real' social work involves doing things like group work or anger management programmes or individual counselling in planned and structured ways.

> *Lifespace work is neither individual casework nor group work, nor even individual casework conducted in a group context, but a therapeutic discipline of its own.*
>   (Keenan, 2002: 221)

A history of the lifespace intervention
With the rise of child psychology and psychiatry from around the 1930s, *treatment* was conceived as being distinct from *care* in work with children and young people. Those encountering particular emotional or behavioural difficulties would receive counselling from outside experts such as psychologists, psychiatrists or child guidance social workers. The job of residential workers was to provide everyday care, a task that was viewed as essentially a parenting or more particularly a mothering one. As such it was not professionally valued.

Bruno Bettleheim (1950) who established the Orthogenic School in Chicago, challenged this separation of care from treatment. Bettleheim, a survivor of the concentration camps, believed that the difficulties experienced by the children in his care were so extreme that they required a

round the clock psychotherapeutic environment or 'milieu'. Bettleheim's ideas can be subject to some criticism nowadays on account of their overly clinical, psychoanalytic orientation. This can make it difficult for most workers to practice within the rarefied theoretical base demanded by his approach. However, many of his ideas and writings provide insights into residential child care that remain relevant today.

The idea of treatment happening alongside care was further developed by Redl and Wineman in *Children Who Hate* (1951) and *Controls from Within* (1957). Redl in particular was interested in the potential of the group as a medium for changing delinquent behaviour. The theoretical underpinnings and much of the terminology, which are part and parcel of TCI, stem directly from Redl and Wineman's work.

The Other 23 Hours

The classic text on the lifespace is *The Other 23 Hours* (Trieschman, Whittaker and Brendtro, 1969). The title of the book conveys the relative importance of what happens in the hours of the day when children and youth are not involved in formal therapy or treatment. The use of the term treatment derives from a North American tradition and reflects the pre-eminence in those cultures of medical models of practice. In a Scottish or UK context, rather than think about treatment we might consider things like review meetings, keyworker meetings or, increasingly perhaps, the time spent in some settings on individual or groupwork programmes, around particular behavioural difficulties. While such planned interventions may have their place, they are not the only times that we are 'working' with young people. Lifespace theory suggests that everyday life events or experiences, from getting children up in the morning to putting them to bed at night offer opportunities to enhance children's growth and learning that are at least as powerful as more formal interventions.

Developmental care

A defining contribution to the development of CYC is Henry Maier's paper *The Core of Care* (1979). Maier asserts that child care and child development need to be seen as two sides of the same coin. We need to have some knowledge of how children grow and learn in order to properly care for them. In this respect, the residential child care environment offers potent opportunities to understand how children *do* grow in relation to those they live alongside. *The Core of Care* offers a framework within which we might conceptualise the relational basis of care. It introduces seven components essential to the provision of developmental care. Maier says that we need to start by ensuring **bodily comfort**, the provision of good basic care. This needs to take into account the differences or **differentiations**, that exist between children. Maier describes some kids as human radars, others as go-go kids. We can imagine the difference; the first are the active scanners, the second, those kids who only make sense of their world once they've bumped into it. Interventions that might suit one character trait are unlikely to suit the other. In stating this fairly obvious point, Maier challenges that old residential child care rallying call for 'consistency', which he says is neither possible nor desirable.

In building relationships with kids, workers need to take into account the individual differences between them and to enter into a **rhythmic interaction** with them. This is essentially about getting onto a similar wavelength. The process might be helped through involvement in some common interest or activity that allows worker and youth to find a level and a comfortable way of being together. Out of the experience of rhythmicity, comes a level of **predictability**, where youth can anticipate the responses of a worker in a situation. Once they have reached this stage they can begin to experience **dependency**. Notions of dependency can be frowned upon in a social work discourse. Maier argues however, that it is only through the experience of a healthy dependency that youth can move on to achieve meaningful independence, or interdependence. Moreover, he claims that the strength of appropriately dependent and reciprocal relationships becomes the basis for **personalised behaviour training**. In such a model, acceptable behaviour does not come from sets of house rules or contracts, but through the developing personal relationship.

The final element in The Core of Care is **care for the caregiver**. Just as parents need support in bringing up children, so too do care workers need to feel safe and supported in the task if they are to provide an appropriate quality of care for young people. At one level this can be provided by organisational structures such as supervision frameworks, but more important is an organisational culture in which they feel safe and valued at a personal level.

The milieu

The milieu is the medium or environment of a residential home. It encapsulates what a place 'feels' like. The term is not particularly tangible. It has been described as the 'particles in the air' (EUROARC, 2002). However anyone who has set foot in a group care centre picks up very quickly on its atmosphere; whether there is a tension or a 'buzz' or a sense of calm. The 'feel' of a centre is fundamental to how good it is. This will impact profoundly on the experiences of the children and youth placed there.

Practitioners need to reflect on the milieu and identify some of the elements that go towards shaping it in order that they can influence it to enhance the opportunities for learning and growth of the children and youth who live there. A range of variables impact on the milieu. Readers might consider the following; the use of time, space and activity (Maier, 1982).

Use of time

The use of time in a centre is largely determined by the staff rota. The way the rota is structured is a bone of contention in all residential units. The trouble is, the kind of discussions that occur in staff meetings across the land generally proceed from a basis of staff preferences and taken-for -granted assumptions of what a 'good rota' is. They rarely include any consideration of how the rota might actually support the developmental goals of a centre. There is no such thing as the perfect rota. The priorities of young, single staff will differ from those with young children. Some of the assumptions that serve to maintain the standard 'late onto early' shift pattern don't hold much water. The defence offered for such systems is that they ensure that the staff who put kids to bed at nights will also get them up in the mornings. But of course, taking that line of argument forward, those who get kids up in the morning will not be those who put them to bed that night. Besides, the early/late shift pattern requires staff changeovers in the middle of the day. This may be appropriate during school days but can easily get in the way of day trips or other out of centre activities at week ends and holidays. Accepting that there is no perfect rota, those charged with constructing rotas might do well to bear in mind some basic principles.

Essentially, the rota should be based around a unit's programme. It ought to support and reinforce the development of teamwork practices and consistency of relationships. As we have already seen, good quality care demands predictability. The rota should as far as possible model this. Anyone who has worked in residential care will be familiar with the 'Who's on the back-shift' refrain from young people. And the follow up, 'Aw naw' or 'Sound'. 'Who's on' allows young people to know what to expect. Staff too need to experience some predictability in the rota. They should know when they are on and off to allow them to plan their lives outside of work. Rotas that chop and change all the time don't allow normalising opportunities away from work.

Use of space

The importance of the physical environment is highlighted by Henry Maier (1982) who tells us that 'The space we create controls us'. The physical environment impacts fundamentally on the personal interactions and processes of a centre, determining those activities that are possible and those which aren't. Maier suggests that attention needs to be given to what constitutes public and private space, and the balance between the two. Public space, according to Redl and Wineman (1957: 6) should be 'an area which smiles, with props that invite, and space which allows'. To achieve this staff and young people need to feel an investment and an involvement in the layout and appearance of a centre. Everyone who lives and works there should share in everyday chores and should consider ways in which to introduce small ways in which they might contribute to the 'feel' of a centre. I recall working with one domestic who stamped her mark on the home by ensuring that there was a small vase of flowers on the dining tables. Such small and simple gestures convey a powerful message of care to young people and to staff and visitors alike.

Activity

The way in which activities in a centre are organised again influences the milieu. These should be structured to ensure changes of pace through the course of the day. Opportunities should be built in for physical activity, for social interaction and for moments of quiet reflection.

Consideration should be given to the kind of rhythms of the day, to ensure, for instance, a sense of purpose in the mornings when kids are getting ready to go out to school and a sense of winding down as it gets nearer to bedtime. The importance of mealtimes as a focus of community life is fundamental, and of course patterns will vary with the age and stage of the children or young people. The evening programme might involve offering an activity or a choice of activities after tea, then an opportunity for kids to get bathed or showered or otherwise ready for bed, followed by supper and some time with staff watching the television or playing quiet games or just chatting, before it's time to go to bed.

The main determinant of the milieu of a centre however, is likely to be the attitudes and expectations of the staff group. 'At the heart of a positive milieu is the message conveyed to young people that they are cared for and valued by the staff who look after them' (EUROARC, 2002).

Rhythms and rituals

The concepts of rhythm and ritual have become central to child and youth care practice (Maier, 1979). Rhythm is the process through which worker and young person find a common and comfortable way of being together. We all find a sense of comfort from being 'in tune' with the environment around us, but even more so in experiencing the sense of safety and intimacy that comes with being on the same wavelength as someone else and being comfortable in their presence. When that happens, it says something about the 'fit' between an individual and their environment. There are ways that staff might influence the rhythms of a centre. A colleague tells how, when he was on duty, he would tune into a classical music station on the radio. Playing classical music set a particular, relaxed rhythm in a centre. It also became associated with him and with particular ways of being when he was on duty. I recall myself, getting into the habit of sitting down with the newspaper after tea. I did this with little hope of concentrating sufficiently to take anything in it, but to give the impression that I wanted to slow down and relax and to give the cue that I expected the boys I worked with to do likewise. Whilst I sat with the newspaper in front of me, eyes scanning and ears picking up what was going on around me, they generally sat quietly in front of the telly until it was time for the evening's activities.

The idea of rhythm might also be applied at an organisational level, to convey the sense of order and predictability in the patterns of daily living in a home. Rhythm is less rigid or prescribed than the kind of routine that might (or might not), emerge from procedural attempts to impose order. When appropriate rhythms are established in a centre, things can seem to run like clockwork. Rules and expectations become implicit rather than needing to be continually re-enforced. New residents pick up on the rhythms of a home and readily fit into them. However, it is worth maintaining an awareness of the rhythms of a centre lest they become too embedded and routinised. Staff may consider introducing a bit of variety to established rhythms to ensure that they don't become stale. They might decide for instance to dispense with cooking on a particular night and get everyone a takeaway meal. Or they might allow kids to stay up past their bedtimes to watch a particular programme on the television, making popcorn and hot-chocolate long after the normal supper-time. Such deviations from established routine can threaten the need some staff have for order. However, rather than compromising any sense of order in a centre, these deviations from the norm, so long as they're properly thought through, actually contribute to a sense of order. They also avoid kids becoming overly institutionalised, by introducing an element of flexibility into their lives in safe and managed ways.

Rituals are those practices that become embedded in the fabric of a place and which have a significance and special meaning to the workers and youth who engage in them. Examples of the kind of rituals that can develop between them might be things like 'high fives'. I recall one lad I worked with. Somehow or other, we got into the habit of gently nudging each other as we passed one another by. Often the nudge was barely perceptible to anyone other than the two of us. Nevertheless, that simple and seemingly mundane ritual was a powerful means by which two emotionally inarticulate Scottish males could say to one another, 'Hey, I like you'. At another level, workers may be able to think of what they consider to be foibles in particular young people, which they might in practice try and ignore or cut across. Particular ways and sequences of settling at bedtime for instance might appear only as irritating habits to workers trying to get off shift, but they may carry a particular significance and sense of meaning for the child concerned. This

was brought home to me with my own kids. One in particular insisted on lining up his soft toys along the top of his bed with a military precision. As parents eager to engage in our own ritual of sitting down in front of the television with a glass of something, his insistence on this particular order could be frustrating, especially when one of the soft toys was posted missing. However, we came to realise that this ritual meant something to him and he wouldn't settle without everything in its proper place. Appreciation of the seemingly simple rituals in the everyday lives of those we work with speak of a connection and a sense of care.

Groups too have rituals and ways of making meaning, as is evident in Emond's chapter in this volume. We would do well to consider the composition and social structures of resident groups and to take into account rituals of encounter (how we make initial contacts and facilitate entry into the group); rituals of initiation (how we mark events that are significant to individuals or to the group) and rituals of transition (how we support and provide some continuity for those who move on from a group).

The idea of programme

The notion of programme has been around for a long while in the CYC literature. In the North American tradition, a centre's programme is likely to refer to its overall purpose and theoretical orientation. In the UK, the idea of programme is historically underdeveloped. We have tended to react with some suspicion (and very often a lack of understanding), to attempts to locate care within any conceptual or theoretical frame.

More recently however, the notion of programme has been introduced to residential child care (particularly secure accommodation and residential school settings), to refer to specific forms of intervention to target offending behaviour. A recent report for instance, recommends the development and accreditation of a range of programmes based around 'What Works' principles, to address problems of youth offending (Audit Scotland, 2002).

Child and youth care workers would do well to be wary of any definition of programme that restricts its usage to such a specific context. As Steckley points out elsewhere in this volume, the notion of programme can be conceived of in far broader and less stigmatising ways, such as considering the school football team as being central to its overall programme. And seductive though they may be to the managerial mindset, evidence for the efficacy of programmes geared specifically at tackling youth offending is either unexplored (Audit Scotland 2002) or distinctly questionable (Pitts, 2001). Workers might consider Scott's (1999) reflection:

> *Is it possibly a sign of our own tendency to expect the worst that we offer all these cliché skills to troubled children – conflict resolution, problem solving, anger management, self-defense ...? I wonder how necessary these things would be if we offered them experience of sailing, vegetable growing, soccer, playing bongo drums or fixing bikes.*
>
> (cited in Phelan, 2001: 1)

The foregoing section is not to suggest that CYC workers can just ignore the notion of programme altogether. A well developed programme, which articulates what a centre sets out to do and how, is invaluable in providing a focus and a sense of purpose in a staff group. Indeed, the ability of a manager to articulate and carry through a particular way of working is crucial in determining effective outcomes of care (DoH, 1998). In the absence of a theoretically and practically grounded programme, staff teams may resort to ways of thinking and intervening that reflect their disparate and often very personally rooted views of children and how to bring them up. A well articulated programme provides a unifying framework within which staff can make sense of and against which they can be required to justify their interventions with youth. 'Get with the programme' is a common refrain in North American centres. Workers in CYC need to reclaim programmes and locate them within a lifespace context, rather than hiving them off to a new breed of 'programme worker'. The programme itself may include interventions aimed at particular areas of a child's life but the focus needs to remain on the whole child and the opportunities to effect change that are offered in the course of daily living.

The personal relationship

Irrespective of how well conceived a centre's programme might be, we are confronted in CYC with an essential truth; that ultimately it's 'the singer and not the song' that's going to make a difference to the lives of the kids we work with. Any programme is only as good as the workers who

enact it. This is a message that's beginning to get through in the criminal justice field (Batchelor and McNeill (2004). The relationship established between worker and youth is the cornerstone of any intervention. Unlike other professional contacts, where the relationship between worker and client is primarily instrumental (e.g. a doctor performs a particular function when they prescribe antibiotics – we may prefer that they engage us personally in the process, but ultimately this isn't essential) the CYC contact is essentially and perhaps inevitably affective and relationally centred. The most powerful moments are when a personal connection is made between a worker and youth. One of the most commonly referred to quotes in CYC practice is that 'every kid needs at least one adult who's crazy about him' (Bronfenbrenner, 1977). And while it might be hard to admit, in this climate, with its heightened awareness of child protection, that we're crazy about any kid, the reality is that there are those who will touch all sorts of powerful and personal emotions in us. It isn't unprofessional to acknowledge this. Indeed, it's central to our professional task. It's going to determine how we use our relationship with them to bring about change.

Whilst fundamental, relationships cannot afford to be indiscriminate. Fewster (1990: 26) has suggested that 'the personalised relationship continues to be the greatest challenge in professional child and youth care'. He refers to the difficulty that child and youth care workers sometimes seem to have in developing a relationship with a young person in which the experience of intimacy and connectedness can be present, while appropriate boundaries are maintained. However, he goes on to say that in the absence of relationship, the child and youth care worker's ability to affect a youth's values, beliefs, attitudes, or behaviours is seen as extremely limited.

To maximise the impact of the personal relationship in the care experience, workers need to be supported to examine how aspects of their own experiences and ways of being might enhance or detract from their ability to intervene effectively with children and youth. This calls for open and supportive team cultures and systems of supervision. More than that however it requires self aware individuals who are able to reflect on what is going on for them in a particular situation or relationship. That is a task requiring ongoing personal reflection and constantly finding out new things about oneself.

The lifespace intervention

Traditional social work approaches might conceive of intervention in terms of a package put together to cater for the needs identified in the assessment process in any particular case. Child and youth care workers can get caught up in thinking about interventions along similar lines. Consider a review meeting where everyone sits around discussing what to do with Johnny. At the end of this, the various professionals involved might come up with a plan that involves Johnny being required to join a group to look at anger management and to join another group to address his offending. The meeting might also consider referral to a specialist resource to work on issues of previous sexual abuse. His keyworker might even be accorded a role in this whole intervention, which involves sitting down with Johnny on a weekly basis to discuss his performance at school.

These specific pieces of work might be important in the overall care plan. However, how often does such a plan take into account 'the other 23 hours'? How often do we consider that issues of anger management, for example, might be most productively addressed at the point where Johnny 'blows up' over a request to help with the dishes, or when he's put out of class for throwing his jotter at the teacher for the umpteenth time? Do we make connections at all between the plans we make for kids in a formal meeting and what we actually do in the here and now of living alongside them? Or do we take Johnny's behaviour as confirmation that he's well placed on the anger management programme and make a mental note to pass on the details of his latest eruption to the programmes worker? When we take this latter approach we fundamentally undersell our role as child and youth care workers through passing on to those on whom we confer some 'expert' status, responsibility for the care and management of the children we live and work with. We also undersell the very real skills of staff who intervene in these situations.

We might at this point pause to consider how we learned to behave when we were growing up. Or how our own children do. We learned of course through the constant guidance and reinforcement of the caring adults around us. Why should we expect that children in our care should learn differently? Now of course the children and youth we work with can rarely count on the kind of consistent and generally benign experiences of care that most of us hopefully enjoyed. That isn't to say that they need an altogether different approach to their care, merely a more intensive, focussed and compensatory one.

The 'interventive moment'

In CYC settings, interventions happen every minute of every day. Every engagement we have with young people has the potential to enhance or detract from their experience of care and to reinforce, for better or worse, their attitudes and the meaning they make out of events and situations. We need then to reframe our understandings of intervention, away from ones based around what happens in a review meeting to include and perhaps foreground, what happens in what Garfat (1999) calls the 'interventive moment'. We need to try and deconstruct what is going on in this moment and whether what we do within it is likely to advance the broader care plan and developmental goals of a particular child.

In practice, many of our day by day, minute by minute interventions may appear so mundane that we don't even think about them. And in many respects that's a place we want to get to, for good workers generally do get their interventions right, without necessarily over-analysing what they've done. However, they also reflect on what went right and what went wrong in a situation, and incorporate some of that thinking, with various degrees of consciousness, into subsequent interventions. At a very simple level, and again this is linked to lifespace notions of rhythm and 'fit', good workers instinctively learn how particular kids respond to everyday events, such as how best to get them up in the morning. Small things, like whether we give their shoulder a gentle shake or whether we open the curtains first (if indeed we're allowed to do either in this risk averse climate), become second nature. In situations that are potentially more difficult, where feelings are running high and conflict of some sort may be just round the corner, it is a good idea for a worker to try and buy themselves a bit of time, to get a sense of the bigger picture. If they don't, they risk responding to their own issues and feelings rather than those of the young person. In such cases they might if possible (and it isn't always) consider the following advice:

... before we can move from one challenging encounter into a second or a third, we need to get centred, to 're-collect' ourselves. In the naughty old days we might have wanted (gasp!) a quick cigarette; today we can take a walk down the drive and back, eat an apple or have a short conversation with the cat ... anything to help us enter our next one-on-one at our best, with a fresh mind and a warm heart.

(cyc-net.org October, 2003)

Counselling within a CYC approach

A CYC approach to practice allows us to reframe the way we think about activities like counselling. When we hear that term it probably throws up a picture in our head of a planned and private one-to-one encounter. Fritz Redl, on the other hand, talks about 'therapy on the hoof', the kind of intervention that happens in a spontaneous way in response to everyday life events. This may happen in the aftermath of a difficult situation; it may happen at bedtime or during a car journey, for it is at these times that kids are at their most receptive to our interventions. We need to be ready to respond with the kind of reassurance or guidance kids are looking for at these moments rather than fobbing them off with responses such as 'Wait until you're keyworker's next in', or 'Have you told your social worker this?'

Phelan (1999) goes further and suggests that 'child and youth care work is not about verbal counselling strategies, therapeutic conversations in an office or insight into past experience'. This approach often serves to 'stick' children and youth in the past, retelling the same stories that have contributed to their current difficulties. Phelan suggests that CYC workers need to become 'experience arrangers', using activities in such a way as to allow youth to experience their worlds in different ways and to open up to them the possibility of telling their stories in new, more positive ways.

Self in action – characteristics of the effective child and youth care intervention

Developing themes from the CYC literature, Garfat (1998) explored worker's and youth's views of what was meaningful in their experience of particular interventions. In this study he brings together the importance of the personal characteristics of the worker in the process of intervention. He identifies several themes of what constitutes an effective intervention. These include adults having a high degree of care for and commitment to the young people they work with, high levels of self-confidence and responsibility, and a general and immediate awareness of themselves.

Good workers also possess an awareness of the wider context, an understanding of the individual young person with whom they are intervening, and an intimate familiarity with the issues or situations facing that young person. The latter in particular seems to be promoted by the ongoing process of sharing and working together in the lifespace. The ability of a worker to prepare for an intervention and connect with the individual young person in a manner that 'fits' was also identified as important. Effective interventions were related to the immediate circumstance and experience of each young person; they enabled them to see their responsibility related to their situations, and challenged their perceptions and expectations. A young person's experience of continuity in the relationship with the worker emerged as a final theme in the study.

Values underpinning a CYC approach

It will be evident from the foregoing description of the CYC approach that caring for children and youth is not a technical or rational task, but a relational and reflective one. It involves human beings connecting with one another in what are often fairly raw and intimate ways. These connections need to be rooted in a deeper consideration of questions around what we think about children and what kind of relationships we want to have with them (Moss and Petrie, 2002). We can be encouraged in the prevailing managerial climate to think of care as a commodity, like any other service we might contract to. Such an orientation according to Brannan and Moss (2003):

... calls for individualism, instrumental rationality, flexibility, short-term engagement, deregulation and the dissolution of established relationships and practices.

By contrast, they argue:

... caring relationships ... are predicated upon an expressive rather than instrumental relationship to others. They are based on trust, commitment over time and a degree of predictability.

A CYC approach to practice embraces these qualities. It is predicated upon particular beliefs about how children and youth grow and change. Essentially, youth don't change because we wag our finger at them, warning them of the consequences of continuing to offend. Nor do they change when we bombard them with educational literature appraising them of the dangers of smoking or unsafe sexual activity. People change through what might be called a 'social method'. Jane Addams, founder of the settlement movement, from which grew a significant strand of American social work theory and practice, explained the purpose of the settlement houses as being 'to express the meaning of life, in terms of life itself, in forms of activity' (Addams, 1899, cited in Magnuson, 2003). Growth and change happen through everyday living, through 'being with' others, so that different understandings and new forms of behaviour can emerge. A CYC approach starts from the premise that:

> *Development and growth is a mysterious, asynchronous, nonlinear process . . . All child and youth care work aims to further growth and change, yet its pedagogy is not interventionist and direct. Youthwork practice is indirect, cooperative, collaborative, and invitational.*
>
> (Magnuson, 2003)

Such understandings challenge the ways we have become accustomed to working, where we often assume or look for some linear connection between what we do and how people change. Yet practice experience tells us that that we often can't put our finger on what it is that makes youth change. We need to learn to live with the mystery of that dynamic, trusting that somewhere along the way we have done something right, to help support the change. A CYC approach demands that we put 'the primacy of the person before behaviours and performance' (Magnuson, 2003). Garfat (1999) encapsulates such values in a catchy way when he describes the job as being one of 'hanging out and hanging in' – of 'being with' youth as they live their lives and hanging in with them when things get tough. He also speaks of 'doing with, not to or for youth', of entering into reciprocal relationships with youth.

Philosophically, such principles resonate with a strengths perspective in social work. They eschew what Saleebey (1992) views as a professional 'obsession with problems, pathologies and defects', which he argues isn't productive in 'helping clients grow, develop, change directions, or revise their personal meanings accounts and narratives'. A CYC approach acknowledges clients' strengths and experiences, requiring

workers to operate collaboratively alongside them to effect change, all the time acknowledging their dignity and our own capacity to learn from them.

Conclusion

This chapter has sought to introduce readers to a Child and Youth Care (CYC) perspective on practice in residential child care. It is argued that such a theoretical orientation captures the realities of the field better than the casework or case-management approaches that are privileged within social work models of practice. A CYC approach begins at where it's at for staff and for youth, which is about being thrown together in a particular place and time. Practitioners need to understand the dynamics that result from this and to use these to help children and young people learn and grow. Such an approach is inevitably relationally based and as any approach that foregrounds human relationships and connections should be, it is framed by a set of values that set out some beliefs and assumptions around the nature of care. A CYC approach may offer practitioners in the UK a framework that allows them to rethink what their work is all about.

Endnote: The Child and Youth Care Network International, www.cyc-net.org provides an excellent internet resource for those wanting to read more on child and youth care.

References

Ainsworth, F. (1981) The Training of Personnel for Group Care With Children, in Ainsworth, F. and Fulcher, L. (Eds.) (1981) *Group Care for Children: Concept and Issues.* New York: Tavistock.

Ainsworth, F. and Fulcher, L. (1981) *Group Care for Children: Concept and Issues.* New York: Tavistock.

Anglin, J. (2001) Child and Youth Care: A Unique Profession. cyc-online Issue 35 Dec.

Audit Scotland (2002) *Dealing With Offending by Young People.* www.audit-scotland.gov.uk/publicationspdf/02pf06eag.pdf Auditor General Accounts Commission.

Batchelor, S. and McNeill, F. (2004) The Young Person-Worker Relationship, in Bateman, T. and Pitts, J. (Eds.) *The Russell House Companion to Youth Justice.* Lyme Regis: Russell House Publishing.

Bettleheim, B. (1950) *Love is Not Enough: The Treatment of Emotionally Disturbed Children*. New York: The Free Press.

Brannan, J. and Moss, P. (Eds.) (2003) *Rethinking Children's Care*. Buckingham: Open University Press.

Bronfenbrenner, U. (1977) The Fracturing of the American Family. *Washington University Daily*, Oct. 5 5.

CCETSW (1973) *Residential Work is Social Work. Improvements 1*. London: CCETSW.

CCETSW (1992) *Residential Child Care in the Diploma in Social Work*. Improvement 15. London: CCETSW.

DoH (1998) *Caring for Children Away from Home: Messages for Research*. Chichester: Wiley.

EUROARC (2002) Ready Steady Care: A Recipe Book for Child and Youth Care. www.euroarc.net

Fewster, G. (1990) *Being in Child Care: A journey Into Self*. New York: Haworth.

Fulcher, L. and Ainsworth, F. (1985) *Group Care Practice with Children*. London: Tavistock.

Garfat, T. (1998) The Effective Child and Youth Care Intervention: A Phenomenological Inquiry. *Journal of Child and Youth Care*. 12: 1–2.

Garfat, T. (1999) On Hanging out (and Hanging in). CYC-online editorial No 8 Sep.

Keenan, C. (2002) Working Within the Life-Space, in Lishman, J. (Ed.) *Handbook of Theory for Practice Teachers in Social Work*. London: Jessica Kingsley.

Kent, R. (1997) *Children's Safeguards Review – Kent Report*. Edinburgh: HMSO.

Kilbrandon Report (1964) www.scotland.gov.uk/library5/education/krcy-00.asp retrieved 28th Oct.

Magnuson, D. (2003) Preface in Garfat (Ed.) *A Child and Youth Care Approach to Working with Families*. New York: Haworth Press.

Maier, H. (1979) The Core of Care: Essential Ingredients For the Development of Children at Home and Away From Home. *Child Care Quarterly*. 8: 4, 161–73.

Maier, H. (1982) The Space We Create Controls Us. *Residential Group Care and Treatment*. 1: 1.

Milligan, I. (1998) Residential Work is not Social Work! *Social Work Education*. 17: 3, 275–85

Moss, P. and Petrie, P. (2002) *From Children's Services to Children's Spaces*. London: Routledge/Falmer.

Murphy, Z. and Graham, G. (2002) *Life Space Intervention Training Video and Manual for Residential Care*. Dublin Institute of Technology.

Parton, N. (1999) Reconfiguring Child Welfare Practices: Risk, Advanced Liberalism and the Government of Freedom, in Chambon, A.S., Irving, A. and Epstein, L. (Eds.) *Reading Foucault for Social Work*. New York: Columbia University Press.

Phelan, J. (1999) Experiments with Experience. *Journal of Child and Youth Care Work*. 14, 25–8.

Phelan, J. (2001) Another Look at Activities. *Journal of Child and Youth Care*. 14: 2.

Pitts, J. (2001) Youth Justice. *Community Care Research Matters*, 11, 50–2.

Redl, F. and Wineman, D. (1951) *Children who Hate*. Glencoe, IL: Free Press.

Redl, F. and Wineman, D. (1957) *Controls From Within: Techniques For Treatment of the Aggressive Child*. New York: Free Press.

Saleebey, D. (1992) *The Strengths Perspective in Social Work Practice*. New York: Longman.

Smith, M. (2003) Towards a Professional Identity and Knowledge Base: Is Residential Child Care Still Social Work? *Journal of Social Work*. 3: 2, 235–52.

Trieschman, A., Whittaker, J. and Brendtro, L. (1969) *The Other Twenty Three Hours*. New York: Aldine.

Ward, A. (1993) *Working in Group Care: Social Work in Residential and Day Care Settings*. Birmingham: Venture Press.

Warner, N. (1992) *Choosing with Care; the Report of the Committee of Inquiry into the Selection, Development and Management of Staff in Children's Homes*. London: HMSO.

Chapter Twelve

An Outsider's View of the Inside

Ruth Emond

Introduction

The research on which this chapter is based, explored the experience of group living from the perspective of young people. It sought to gain insight not only into what it was like to live alongside others, but also to examine how these resident groups were organised and controlled by the young people themselves. What resulted was a conceptual framework which identified the behaviours and beliefs that young people valued in their fellow residents. These valued responses contributed to the structure and management of the group (Emond, 2000).

In the three years following the completion of this research I have had a number of opportunities to talk to researchers, practitioners and policy makers both in the UK and abroad. The response to this has been fascinating. Whilst there has been interest in the key findings in relation to group structure and management, questions at the end of presentations have been dominated by requests for me to explain 'what it was like'. Having had time to reflect on this, I would suggest that this fascination with my experience of living in the children's homes has been motivated by a number of factors. Firstly, for those not familiar with residential care for children, there may be a perception that this type of provision is dangerous and risky for an adult to enter. For others, there is a methodological curiosity about the process of getting access to the residential group. However, for the majority I would argue that there is an implicit interest concerning my own learning as an adult in this environment or more precisely, as a residential social worker viewing the world of care from the 'other side'. It is this latter point that provides the focus for this chapter.

Research context

Residential care for children has been regarded as a somewhat under researched area of social care/social work practice, social policy and sociology. It may be argued that one of the reasons for this apparent 'neglect' of residential research is that studies have tended to be as disparate as the provision itself. There have been those which have tackled the whole milieu. In so doing, they have sought to map out this form of provision. Such work has provided insight into the types of care provided, the young people who are placed in residential care, the staff who work within it and the organisation and structures which underpin it (see for example Skinner, 1992; Berridge and Brodie, 1998).

Further research has sought to focus in on particular aspects of residential life. Fascinating work has been done in the field of 'looked after' young people and education (Borland et al., 1998; Jackson, 2001). This has gone some way to identify the impact of care on educational attainment and outcomes. It has also contributed to broader research on the experiences of young people leaving care, the role that care provision and systems play in supporting (or not) young people into 'independence' and the outcome for such young people as they move into adulthood (Biehal et al., 1992; Cheung and Heath, 1994).

More recently, there has been growing interest in problematising the residential milieu and in identifying the dynamic of residential life. Such research has emphasised the cultural elements of residential life and in particular, the interplay between the culture of the staff groups and those of the residents (see for example Brown et al., 1998). The focus on staff experiences has illustrated the complexity of the residential task and the range of ways that approaches to caring for young people impacts on the process and outcome for them. Indeed, staffing has been a central concern of much of the research which has taken place over recent times. The training and qualifications of workers, as well as the methods and interventions that they embrace, has been regarded as central to the experiences young people have of the service (Heron and Chakrabarti, 2003)

There also exists a literature which has young people at its core. The increasing profile of young people's views and perspectives has been facilitated by changing discourses of children and young people. Recent research under the umbrella of the sociology of childhood, has argued that children are not passive recipients of socialisation or indeed of services but are active social agents and consumers, who require the best service possible to meet their needs (James, Jenks and Prout, 1998). Such an approach is to some extent embodied by recent legislation, such as the Children (Scotland) Act 1995. Here, the views of children and young people about their care are required to be not only sought but listened and responded to.

Coinciding with, or perhaps as a result of, the growing body of research and social policy on residential provision has been the increasingly individualised approach to care. The concern to move away from the 'batch handling' of some forms of institutional provision has resulted in a belief that care should be tailored to the individual needs of the young person. Whilst this can only be seen as a positive step forward, there is a danger that the value of residential care, the group living aspect, becomes redundant.

Indeed, the group in group care is perhaps the most under researched aspect of residential life. Hudson (1986) argues that at the turn of the century, young people played a significant role in the care of their fellow residents. It may be proposed that the loss of this collective consciousness and group experience detracts from the aim of care; to help young people make sense of the relationships they have experienced prior to admission, to prepare them to be active social participants in adulthood, to make positive relationships with others and to participate positively in society.

Methodology

This chapter draws on a piece of research conducted in two children's homes in the North East of Scotland. The research was concerned with exploring the group experiences of young people in residential care and, in particular, the meaning they attributed to the group and its organisation and management. Originally I had planned to undertake interviews with a number of young people in residential care across Scotland. I gained access to two children's homes to pilot these interviews and afterward gathered the young people together to reflect on the method used. During the course of this discussion, the young people made clear that my approach would only provide a snap shot

account of views which they regarded as ever changing. They also argued that the group experience was difficult to explain or to conceptualise. Feeling pretty helpless and hopeless at this point, I asked them what they thought would be the best thing for me to do. In reply I was informed that the only way I could get the data that I sought was to move in.

After much soul searching and negotiation with the local authority, staff and young people, I moved in to one of the units (Strathmore) for a period of six months. This was followed by a further six months of five day/four night blocks in Strathmore and the second unit, Brunswick. The methodological approach of ethnography, and in particular participant observation has been shown to be successful in a number of studies of children and young people. Many of these studies have had as their focus young people's experiences of particular phenomena. For example, in recent times, ethnography has been successfully used in the study of dance culture (Thornton, 1995), of drug culture (Taylor, 1993) and of education (Burgess, 1985).

Ethnographic approaches allow the researcher to gain insight into the lived experience of those under study. In simple terms it is underpinned by the belief that to best understand the world of those being researched, one has to observe them at first hand, operating within their own 'natural' environment. As such, it requires the researcher to become immersed in that 'other' world and to have the time available to allow the acceptance and inclusion in the group to take place.

Originally, I had followed 'classic' participant observation approaches, in that I spent time with the young people attempting to remember their verbal and non verbal interactions. I would then leave the shared space to write up my recollections and also my thoughts on what had taken place. However, it quickly became apparent that such a method was interrupting the young people's 'natural' behaviour and was also preventing me from participating in any meaningful way. As a result, I renegotiated with the young people and agreed to use a tape recorder which they then controlled. To supplement this, I took brief notes recording who was present each time the recorder was switched on, the time and the location. What was of note was that as the fieldwork progressed, the tape recorder was left on for longer periods until by the last months of the project it was on almost constantly.

Getting admitted is not getting in

Despite being invited to move in to the units to conduct fieldwork, I quickly realised that getting into the building was not the same as getting into or accepted by the group. It was vital in those first weeks in residence to make clear to young people and staff that I was there in a research capacity and was therefore different from the other adults in the house. I was not responsible for the care of the young people nor could I intervene as a member of staff. I felt that I could not spend time alone with staff (this would be confusing to everyone including myself) rather I wanted to be with the young people. However, I quickly discovered that this was not my choice to make, I had to wait to be invited. Thus, my initial few weeks were marked by both fear and loneliness but also made me acutely aware of the importance young people have in the process of admission.

Young people made the route to group acceptance apparent to me in direct and indirect ways. The young women in particular gave me clear messages that I had to wait for an invitation to join the group and to be respectful of their view that the unit was home to many of the residents. Others gave more indirect, but equally as clear messages, in that as I walked into the room the conversation would either stop or everyone would leave!

This initial rejection served to increase my anxiety as well as my desire to get in at any cost. The view that young people had of me began to take on immense importance and I found myself judging my own behaviours and responses on the reaction that I received from those around me. Whilst the staff went out of their way to make me feel welcome, it was to the young people's group that I wanted to belong. It was this group that I realised was the key element of home life, the staff came and went but the young people remained.

I quickly became aware that my commitment to them as a group was being tested, the attitudes I held of them and the potential risks and benefits that I represented. It became very apparent that whilst young people could not control *who* they lived with they could control *how* they lived with them.

Well, its like people come here for lots of things. Maybe they were badly treated by their parents or they couldn't look after them or they've done something bad, sometimes really bad. It's that you've got to look out for.
(Allie, Bedroom, Strathmore)

The testing period that I experienced was mirrored in the way in which the group dealt with subsequent new admissions. They appeared to be concerned as to how the young person would impact on their group and on the way in which this group was seen within and outwith the children's home. It appeared that the collective identity of 'in care' was one that was negatively regarded by those in the community and the behaviour of all the individuals in the group could influence the degree to which this negativity was contained and expressed.

See some of the folk that come in here it's like they think that they have to be hard or something . . . sometimes, if its like lassies, they'll pal aboot wi a the slappers at the school. Well, I dinnae think that's right. It's bad enough what folk think about us that's in here wi'out all that.
(Anna, Bedroom, Brunswick)

Despite these initial challenges to acceptance, there were a number of what appeared to be small, insignificant actions undertaken by group members which supported me in this process of admission. The young women in particular helped me to begin to feel 'at home' in a range of practical and emotional ways. For example, they recognised how bare and unwelcoming my bedroom was and leant me posters and pictures to decorate my wall. Similarly, they helped me to understand the routine and structure to the day. Young people told me all about the staff; who was 'good to talk to', who was 'good fun', who was 'strict', who could be trusted and who was 'in it for the money'.

Whilst I was clearly not a new admission and could never describe my situation as like that of a young person, I did see a lot of the same behaviours, instructions and tests being undertaken with young people who were admitted once the fieldwork began. As a practitioner, this experience made me aware of the importance of being accepted and included in the group and how isolating the group care experience is without this. It also highlighted the central role that young people play in the admission process.

As a 'resident' in the group, I shared the sense of anxiety at the prospect of new admissions. Whilst as a practitioner I had been aware that new admissions unsettled the group, I had not really acknowledged the impact of sharing a living space with a 'stranger'. At such times, the young people with whom I lived made every effort to seek out information about new residents and more often than not these attempts were blocked by staff. To compensate, the group would turn to informal networks of relatives or friends or make the most of the scraps of information they had been able to glean. What resulted was often the creation of a false picture of the (about to be admitted) young person. Significantly, 'new admissions' were coming with an often distorted image of residential care (the prison, the orphanage etc.) and were being met by a resident group who had constructed a distorted image of them as individuals. This mis-match often took some time to resolve and was left to the group and its members to process. Such an experience made me rethink the balance between protecting an individual's privacy and at the same time providing an honest account to the group of the new person sharing their home. Similarly, the emotional process of admission is one which needs to be supported both at an individual and group level by residential staff.

Routine and rhythms of daily life

Ward (1993) in his framework for analysing residential and day care settings, states that routine 'consists of the whole patterns of arrangements for daily living, including both formal and informal activity' (Ward, 1993: 38). He argues that one way of understanding routine as it operates in practice, is to divide it into distinct elements. These he identifies as 'set-pieces', 'in-between times' and 'critical incidents'.

Ward argues that 'set pieces' consist of central and regularly occurring events. Such events are in the main designed to involve and include the residents but do also incorporate activities which involve staff members only, such as staff meetings or administrative tasks. The ways in which these events are scheduled and allocated time serves as the framework of the unit's routine as a whole. 'In-between times', by contrast, are those periods which fall between the scheduled 'set pieces'. Time here is less formally structured both for the residents and the staff. In 'good residential practice' Ward argues that the scheduling or controlling of these 'in-between times' should be monitored and reviewed and, if necessary, filled with planned activities or interventions if the needs of the clients warrant it. Such intervention prevents the development of the 'empty hours' (Oswin, 1973) during which residents are left unattended and unstimulated to pass 'great oceans of unplanned time'. Finally, Ward

presents the argument that within residential life not all events can be planned or expected. These he regards as 'critical incidents', critical in that they present to the worker an unplanned situation where intervention and decision making is required.

Ward's framework is useful in that it presents to the reader the notion that residential life is multi-layered and that despite there being a formalised or planned 'routine' there are many different patterns of behaviours or events occurring. From a practitioner's perspective, this framework gives insight into the ways in which workers shape and define time to residents. The distinction made between planned and unplanned time is a useful one.

The formal routines that were enacted in Strathmore and Brunswick ordered and shaped the day for the young people living in both the units studied. 'Routine' in this context suggests a systematic, planned control of time and relates to what Ward defines as 'set pieces'. It encompassed the regularly occurring events that gave understanding, and set expectations of behaviour on the part of both the young people and the staff. Indeed, many of these 'key moments' were devised by the adults as a means of regularising and normalising young people's behaviour.

Unlike Ward, I found that time was not divided into such distinct and separate segments as that of 'set pieces' and 'in between times' rather these merged and intertwined. These I thought of as the rhythms of residential life. Such rhythms differed from routines as they were unwritten and often unspoken patterns of behaviour that were, in the case of the young people, created by the young people themselves. As such they were more likely to be subject to change and evolution without requiring consultation through any formalised process. Many of the rhythms that existed did not stand as distinct from more formalised 'routines' but wove between or on top of the routine behaviours that were set up by staff. For example young people habitually left the dining table after a meal to smoke. The young people created such patterning of behaviour themselves.

During my time at Strathmore the ways in which such a 'rhythm' was enacted varied. There was a period during fieldwork when young people would leave the table immediately after eating their food. By contrast there was also a time where young people would linger after the meal was finished to chat with each other and staff. The ordering and timing of the smoking event was therefore shaped by the young people's actions and desire rather than imposed by staff members. The habitual activities displayed by young people did however have to take account of the formal routines that existed within the units. As a result such behaviours occurred around the control of time as laid down by the institutions. The routines and rhythms of residential life set the stage for the organisation of the young people's resident group.

As a residential worker, my experience of residential life was marked by particular routine moments in each shift. My day would begin with a changeover meeting, it was then punctuated by meal time, supper time and bed time. The end of the day was spent writing up case notes and would begin again with getting young people up, breakfast and off to school or work. Again, the morning was shaped by the times when those in the house would come together, morning tea, lunch and changeover.

In many ways this rhythm of residential life was replicated in the resident group. There appeared to be a split between time alone, usually only through the night, time all together (meal times) and time with the group. These group times reminded me of the 'staff' times I had shared as a worker. I remembered almost a sense of relief that a 'shared' moment, like meal times had gone well or indeed the need to process and make sense of the event that had passed. Young people appeared to use this time in a similar way and would talk about a staff or resident group member's behaviour. They would wonder about the agendas the staff were working from, what plans were afoot, what might happen next etc. There were moments when this group time was interrupted by the staff. Often this was for the purpose of meeting individual care needs for example contact with family or one to one work. At others, young people were encouraged to make a direct contribution to the group care experience. More often than not, this was done in the form of 'chores'.

All young people had to do a 'chore' in the evening and those out of education or employment were expected to perform similar chores during the day. These chores consisted of household tasks such as setting the table for tea or washing up the pots. Chores were avoided as much as possible and throughout my six months of living in the unit I did not witness a young person volunteering to do their chore. Staff were required to seek out the young people to encourage and cajole them into undertaking it. Young people 'coped' with chores using a range of strategies.

Avoidance strategies were used in attempts not to undertake the task that had been allocated to them. Unlike familial groups, young people were not afforded the opportunity to cajole or 'bully' young siblings into doing this work for them (Punch, 1999). Staff would not tolerate the chore being undertaken by anyone other than the appointed young person. On occasion young people would ask for permission to 'swap' chores. This was rarely entertained as it was regarded as 'tougher' young people trying to get 'weaker' young people to do a harder job. As Beth (staff) explains:

> *Everyone has different jobs to do here, staff and young people. They don't like having to do it. Just like any kids . . . the thing is we can't bend the rules because the bigger ones would just bully the wee ones into doing all the hard work while they got the easy jobs . . . not that I think any of them are particularly hard. We're hardly getting them to chop logs.*
>
> (Beth, Kitchen, Strathmore)

It was therefore an **individual** 'problem' to be dealt with by **individual** young people and, as such, strategies often relied on physical responses to avoid doing the task. These included leaving the building to visit family or friends during chore time or pretending to start the chore and then leaving as soon as the staff's gaze was averted. Young people would pretend not to have heard the request to undertake the task and would dash off before this request could be repeated. Occasionally young people would refuse outright to do what they were being asked. Staff would advise them of the consequences of their choice and often attempt to use humour to cajole them into changing their minds. It was rare for the issue of chores to be allowed to escalate into a major incident. It was argued by the staff that it was easy to get into a power based discussion where one of the parties had to be seen to 'win' and that this was not 'good practice'. Rather the young people had to learn that there were expectations of behaviour and responsibility to the unit.

The request to undertake chores was however seen by the young people as a source of conflict. They felt that staff 'harassed' them into undertaking work at the time that staff decreed rather than allowing the young people the freedom to choose when the work would be undertaken. The following extract from field notes demonstrates this:

There was real tension after tea tonight. Neil and I were chatting in the quiet room when Ian came in and asked Neil to do his chore (clean kitchen floor). Neil replied that he would go and do it after he had finished his conversation with me. Moments later Fiona came in and asked Neil to do his chore. He replied that he would be 'through in a minute'. We returned to our conversation and no sooner had we commenced Vernon asked Neil to go to the kitchen. Neil responded angrily saying that he was on his way. Vernon looked surprised and advised him to calm down. As he left the room Neil stated that he was sick of being harassed and that he was going to go and do it now. As he stood up Ian came into the room and said 'Neil, I've told you already, come on and get your chore done'. At this Neil started shouting, saying that everyone was 'on his back' and that he was coming to do it now. He stormed out of the room. Ian looked puzzled and commented that it was 'unlike Neil to over react'. I asked him if he had known that both Fiona and Vernon had also asked Neil to do his chore. Ian said he hadn't known and that he would go and apologise.

(Field notes, Strathmore)

Young people also relied on coping strategies to deal with the responsibility and monotony of undertaking household tasks. One of the most commonly used coping strategies was the expression of dissatisfaction at having to undertake this work. Such expressions centred around the position of the young people as 'looked after' and would include statements such as the following:

It's not fair. What do we have a cleaner for? She doesnae do nothing that woman . . . we have to do it all. It should be her washing the kitchen floor nae me. See the staff here, they do my head in. It's them that gets paid to look after us no the other way aboot.

(Sharon, Quiet Room, Strathmore)

It's hellish that . . . Bloody Dave he thinks he's it. I hate (washing) the pots. See that . . . I never had to dae stuff like that at hame. I dinnae ken onybody that has tae dae all this sort of work at hame. Their mams do it for them.

(Fraser, Kitchen, Strathmore)

A further strategy could arise out of such outburst. By complaining or shouting enough young people attempted to get other young people or staff members to help them with their chore. They would argue with staff that this was a 'compromise' or would promise other young people that they would help them with their chore. During the period of fieldwork I found that staff were more likely to assist young people

than their fellow residents. Young people were more likely to support each other by providing company and therefore entertainment whilst the job was being done. This in itself was a coping strategy, it made the task less monotonous and prevented the young people from feeling that they were 'missing out' on the activities of the resident group. It was also a very obvious use of the group to meet the needs of the individual. This behaviour was rarely encouraged by staff.

It may be argued that the experience of doing chores, the conflict that surrounded it and the strategies used by young people were no different from those being undertaken in family homes. It should be noted however that these enforced activities were one of the few tasks that young people undertook which had the notion of the 'collective' underpinning it. Young people were told that they had to do their share for the house and the group, to make a contribution, to have responsibility for others etc. As a practitioner, I have often had this conversation myself with young people but as a researcher, I was struck by how little the 'group' takes on a positive meaning. The majority of guidance and instruction about behaviour, responses and feelings was directed at the individual; 'to get ahead' 'to get pocket money' 'to be allowed to the disco' etc. It may be argued that by using 'chores' (which were the site of conflict and of playing out the power dynamic) to be the vehicle to discuss shared responsibility and collectivism exacerbated the negative view of the 'group' and its function.

Routines in both Brunswick and Strathmore served to structure time and manage resident's daily lives. Central to these routines were notions of 'care' and 'protection'. There appeared to be an underlying belief, held by the staff group, in the benefit of regular, habitual activity; indeed the point was made that routine 'was good for the young people'. Such a discourse has at its foundation the belief that children and young peoples lives need to be given order by 'caring' adults and that without such controls young peoples' lives would spiral into chaos. As such, meal times were created to provide regular access both to food and to social contact with staff and other young people. Times allocated to wake up and to go to sleep ensured that young people had enough rest to maintain physical and emotional health. Times to return to the unit made certain that young people were in the unit and 'safe'. An underlying principle to all of these routines was the belief that by placing such boundaries and expectations on young people they were provided with an opportunity to form trusting relationships and to manage responsibility. Whilst the young people in both units were regularly reminded of the reasons for these routines, this was often done when these 'rules' were being broken or challenged. The following example highlights this:

> *I hate it having to come in at 10pm. It's totally embarrassing. All my pals are out 'til 11pm. The staff here are just lazy. They want their beds so they have to have all of us home.*

(Allie, Quiet Room, Strathmore)

The rhythms of residential life (the patterning of time constructed by the young people) were much harder to identify and establish. It initially appeared that there was no pattern to the behaviours of the young people aside from the routine events that were set up by the staff. As the fieldwork progressed however it became apparent that young people did structure and habitualise their own behaviour both away from and in front of the staff. This was much more apparent at Strathmore. The 'outside' appeared to have greater influence on time for those at Brunswick. Young people spent little time, beyond that dictated by the routines, in the building. Often they were out with friends or each other or were attending school or work. The result of this appeared to be that young people established patterns of behaviour which overlapped that of the routines. They created their own timetable and expectations of behaviour that stood alongside that of the staff.

The social environment within Strathmore however allowed for longer periods when the young people spent time together as a group. Like Brunswick there was diversity in how this time was spent although, in the main, many behaviours or events occurred within the building itself. The rhythms of daily life at Strathmore centred around this notion of group belonging, the importance of collective time and 'filling time' (Roy, 1960; Cohen and Taylor, 1972). The majority of the young people in both units established patterns of behaviour which incorporated such rituals as smoking and challenging staff-established routines. There was habitual smoking behaviour occurring pre and post staff-defined events such as meal times, chore times and bedtimes. These key moments created a sense of structure to daily life,

particularly at Strathmore, and were solely devised by the young people themselves. This 'counter' behaviour extended to the challenge toward staff routine and would include avoidance of chores, staying up late or sleeping in. Young people devised strategies to deal with such events which became habitualised and patterned in similar ways to the routines that they sought to counteract.

The separation of front and back stage behaviour (Goffman, 1959) was far more apparent at Strathmore than at Brunswick. Not only were young people (because of their older ages) at Strathmore more likely to spend the majority of their time within the unit, they had been allocated a room which was set aside for their use and control. The number of young people in residence and the ever changing population created a stronger sense of a cohesive group which had functions separate from that of the staff group. This sense of solidarity was enhanced by the awareness of young people around notions of safety and protection from other young people both within and outwith the unit.

I would argue that the lack of ownership or indeed recognition by the staff of the group resulted in it being solely claimed by the young people themselves. As mentioned, the responsibility to the group was used as a means of levering young people to undertake tasks rather than being seen as the site for healing or change. I remember as a practitioner having an implicit fear of the group and its potential to 'overthrow' the control of the staff. In retrospect, this avoidance of the group as an entity and of considering it only in terms of negative power, was a missed opportunity. During the research fieldwork, it became apparent to me that the group was powerful, the experience of group membership provided a sense of solidarity and belonging that many of these young people had had lacking in their lives beforehand, yet it remained an untapped resource for staff.

Staff in both units made some acknowledgement of the collective experience of residential care in their use of house meetings. More often than not, these had a primarily administrative function; to inform the group of changes, to hear of 'collective' concerns about the running of the house or to use the will of the group to create change. Again, this latter function was in response to 'negative' behaviours e.g. if there had been a theft all would be punished until the culprit owned up. I became increasingly aware that whilst this was an appropriate use of the group it again relied on a 'negative' catalyst. The group were not gathered together to prepare to welcome a new admission, to praise and reward positive group behaviours, to process and manage transition etc. This was despite the very positive role that the group played in one another's lives.

Not just the boy in the next room

The final significant piece of learning for me as a practitioner was the role that young people played in caring for one another. As mentioned earlier in this chapter, Hudson (1986) identified the role that young people played in the formal and informal provision of care provided by young people in the large 'children's communities' and institutions that existed in the first half of the last century. During the course of the fieldwork it became apparent that the young people in my study offered a similar but unrecognised degree of support. Support within this context was delivered in both practical and emotional terms.

Young people, as highlighted in the consideration of accessing the resident group played a key role in the admission process. They helped fellow residents understand and learn the structure and dynamic of residential life. They assisted in welcoming the young person to the unit and to some degree controlling their access to the resident group. Young women in particular offered material goods to assist with this process and shared their own admission experiences, sense of loss and confusion as a means to provide the new admission with the knowledge that their responses were 'normal' and accepted by the group.

Young people were often the sounding board that residents chose to 'practice' or rehearse the concerns or disclosures that they would later make to adult staff. It appeared easier in the first instance, to speak of the worries that these young people carried to their fellow residents. At times, this had much to do with language and embarrassment, particularly if the information to be shared had a sexual or deeply personal content. However, young people also chose fellow residents to sound out their beliefs about their care, their contact with family etc. This served to allow them the opportunity to explore their beliefs and to get some measure of how these beliefs may be heard or accepted. At times,

they acted as advocates for one another, accompanying fellow residents to talk to staff or indeed to talk on their behalf.

Much of this support went unseen and unacknowledged by staff members. It was in the main conducted out of the gaze of the adults during times when young people were alone together. At times of crisis however, the young people's role was more visible and caused greater concern to those adults caring for them. Young people were often asked by staff to leave whilst their fellow residents were distressed or angry. Similarly the role that they had taken in preparing one another was not acknowledged and was at times seen as 'meddling' or 'making things worse'. A further discourse around the protection of young people from distress and harm was also used to remove them from 'critical incidents'. More often than not, this caused the young person in crisis greater alarm and made the resident group angry and frustrated.

Conclusion

This chapter has attempted to highlight some of the key areas of learning for me as a residential social worker having had the opportunity to view the care experience from the 'inside'. The research project on which the chapter was based illustrated for me the tension between the researcher and the practitioner, or perhaps the tension between 'the worlds of the field and academia' (Fook, 1996). Whilst undertaking the fieldwork I had little choice but to have the researcher role as dominant, however the experience forced me to reflect on my own practice and indeed on many of the mistakes that I have made in relation to how I viewed the residential group and the young people themselves.

As a practitioner, I had not been cognisant of the importance to young people of feeling included or indeed 'claimed' by the resident group. This dominated my admission process and shaped many of my responses to the social world of the children's home, the staff and my fellow residents. I had also been unaware of the informal role that young people took in facilitating this admission process. Such 'intervention' extended from sharing information and knowledge concerning the micro and macro systems of care to offering their own stories and experiences pre and post admission. I was struck by how re-assuring this shared knowledge was and how much it helped me to understand what I was both feeling and doing at this time. As a practitioner I had also been unaware of the extent to which young people 'tested' out new admissions and what underpinned such practice. The sense that young people had of wanting to protect their group as well as the need to control the image this group had in the community was made explicit to me during this time of my own 'admission' as well as being evident in the admission practices which surrounded those who came to live in the units after I had arrived.

I had been aware of the routine of residential life and the extent to which this created group time, time with staff and time alone. Again, I had been less attuned to the way in which the resident group patterned their behaviours around this. These rhythms of daily life influenced much of what individuals did within the setting. The use of time, how it was structured and controlled often became a collective rather than an individual decision. Young people adapted to the control of time that routine provided and created their own ordered behaviours which served as an adjunct or addition to this.

It was interesting for me to experience the range of ways that staff managed routines and the ways in which young people responded. If tensions were building in the house it was often the routinised activities which became the sites of conflict both between young people and staff and between the young people's group. This was particularly the case in the negotiation of chores. Often 'chores' became the trigger for young people to resist controls, to remember familial home life, to negotiate and to conform.

I was similarly struck by how anxiety provoking many of the shared activities could be. This was particularly the case during the initial months of fieldwork. I found meal times to be points in the day that I looked forward to and at the same time dreaded. It was at these collective moments where I felt most exposed. Many of the young people appeared to share this anxiety and acknowledged that it took time to get used to eating and talking in front of so many people in such a formal way. Interestingly, in the latter stages of fieldwork, meal times became the highlight of the day.

The last section of this chapter illustrated some of the ways in which young people supported one another. Again, whilst I was aware that such support existed between some of the young people that I have worked with I was unaware as to the extent of the support, the skill that young people have and the knowledge of the system that is held. What was particularly interesting for me was that young people encouraged one another to talk to staff members and would support one another in so doing. Equally, I was struck by the impact that adult recognition of young people's support had on perpetuating and strengthening such 'positive' behaviour. Young people gained a lot both individually and collectively from being praised for their capacity to care for one another and for giving 'good' advice. By contrast, at times where their help was dismissed or unacknowledged, residents were left feeling angry and frustrated.

The research on which this chapter is based did not seek to evaluate staff practices neither in relation to individual young people nor in terms of the group. Rather, it sought to gain insight into the experience of living in a group and how such a group was managed by the young people themselves. However, I would argue that the culture of the resident group cannot be seen in isolation from that of the staff group. In both units I was, like all residents, treated with care and compassion. I witnessed staff groups who worked sensitively not only with young people but also with each other. The nurturing behaviours demonstrated by staff both to each other and to the young people in their care provided a context for the resident group to value and mirror such behaviours. Throughout my year in residence, I felt safe, supported and respected. I very much felt 'looked after'.

However, perhaps the greatest piece of learning that occurred during my year long period in residence was one that does not fit so easily into the headings that have structured this chapter. The opportunity to conduct research, to listen, to observe and interact without having to problem solve or intervene showed me the restricted level of engagement with young people that I consider I have undertaken in the past. As workers, it is very difficult to resist the pressure to act quickly and 'solve' the dilemma which has been presented. Residential staff have the difficult job of balancing not only the needs of the individual young person but also those of the resident group. I am now aware of what it feels like to listen and to be listened to and the necessity of this. This continues to be something that I strive for in my practice. Similarly, I hope that this experience has taught me to value and encourage not only the individual's resources to achieve growth and change but also the significant resources of the resident group. As a practitioner, I would hope to not only develop a greater understanding of the group with whom I am working in terms of how it is functioning and the behaviours and beliefs that it values in its members but also that I would use the group as a resource.

It is important to note that I can not in any way claim that I know what it feels like to be a young person living in residential care. I moved in to the units with a clear knowledge of why I was there, how long I was staying and an awareness that I could leave at any point. Furthermore, I did not have to come to terms with enforced separations and memories and experiences of trauma. However, I would argue that the journey that I made in terms of admission, making relationships and moving on was punctuated by a number of experiences that were shared by the young people with whom I lived. Indeed, without them I believe the journey would have been far more difficult.

References

Berridge, D. and Brodie, I. (1998) *Children's Homes Revisited*. London: Jessica Kingsley.

Biehal, N., Clayden, J., Stein, M. and Wade, J. (1992) *Prepared for Living?* London: NCB.

Borland, M., Pearson, C., Hill, M., Tisdall, K. and Bloomfield, I. (1998) *Education and Care away from Home: A Review of Research, Policy and Practice*. Edinburgh: The Scottish Council for Research in Education.

Brown, E., Bullock, R., Hobson, C. and Little, M. (1998) *Making Residential Care Work: Structure and Culture in Children's Homes*. London: Ashgate.

Burgess, R.G. (Ed.) (1985) *Issues in Educational Research: Qualitative Methods*. London: Falmer.

Cheung, S.Y. and Heath, A. (1994) After Care: The Education and Occupation of Adults Who Have Been in Care. *Oxford Review of Education*. 20, 3.

Cohen, S. and Taylor, I. (1972) *Psychological Survival: The Experience of Long Term Imprisonment*. Harmondsworth: Penguin.

Emond, R. (2000) *Survival of the Skilful: An Ethnographic Study of Two Groups of Young People in Residential Care*. unpublished PhD, University of Stirling.

Emond, R. (2002) Understanding the Resident Group. *Scottish Journal of Residential Child Care*. 1: 30–40.

Emond, R. (2003) Putting the Care into Residential Care: The Role of Young People. *Journal of Social Work*. 3: 3, 321–37.

Fook, J. (Ed.) (1996) *The Reflective Researcher: Social Workers' Theories of Practice Research*. Australia: Allen and Unwin.

Goffman, E. (1959) *The Presentation of Self in Everyday Life*. New York: Doubleday.

Heron, G. and Chakrabarti, M. (2003) Exploring the Perceptions of Staff Towards Children and Young People Living in Community-based Children's Homes. *Journal of Social Work*. 3: 1, 81–98.

Hudson, J. (1986) *Peer Groups: A Neglected Resource*. Paper presented at Realities and Dreams: International Conference on Residential Child Care, 3–6 Sep. Glasgow.

Jackson, S. (2001) The Education of Children in Care, in Jackson, S. (Ed.) *Nobody Ever Told us School Mattered: Raising the Educational Attainments of Children in Public Care*. London: BAAF.

James, A., Jenks, C. and Prout, A. (1998) *Theorizing Childhood*. Cambridge: Polity Press.

Oswin, M. (1973) *The Empty Hours: A study of the Weekend Life of Handicapped Children in Institutions*. London: Penguin.

Punch, S. (1999) *Negotiating Independence: Children and Young People Growing Up in Rural Bolivia*. unpublished PhD Thesis, University of Leeds.

Roy, D.F. (1960) Banana Time: Job Satisfaction and Informal Interaction. *Human Organization*. 18: 4, 158–68.

Skinner, A. (1992) *Another Kind of Home: A Review of Residential Child Care*. Edinburgh: The Scottish Office.

Taylor, A. (1993) *Women Drug Users: An Ethnography of a Female Injecting Community*. Oxford: Oxford University Press.

Thornton, S. (1995) *Club Cultures: Music, Media and Subcultural Capital*. Oxford: Polity Press.

Ward, A. (1993) *Working in Group Care*. London: Venture Press.

Chapter Thirteen

Just a Game? The Therapeutic Potential of Football

Laura Steckley

Introduction

On a crisp autumn day in late November, I found myself running down the steps of the local leisure centre, feeling a sense of excited anticipation, almost what could be described as glee, rise within me as I approached the pitch to watch my residential school's football team play. I could see similar feelings reflected in the faces of the boys as I watched them warming up. I also felt a bit guilty, as if I was 'skiving' or avoiding *real* work, in favour of an 'easy afternoon'. As it turned out, nothing could have been further from the truth. During the game, one of our boys was thrown into crisis when he was directed to take two minutes off the pitch for repeated, abusive swearing. He had such difficulty coping with this event that he refused to return to the school. It took a good bit of time and a lot of support from a trusted and capable member of staff for this young man to get himself back to a place where he did not hate the world and everyone in it. In fact, during the subsequent discussion in the changing room, he was able to identify and acknowledge his anger and disappointment in himself and his own conduct on the pitch. This was a significant and difficult step forward for this young man – one that required strength and courage. So upon further reflection, it was clear to me that the *real work* of residential child care was well encapsulated within the processes that occurred that afternoon.

This chapter will explore the potential and actual benefits of involvement in a school football team for young people in residential care, and will draw, at times, from my experiences at a residential school in Scotland. This school participates in a league comprised of football teams from other schools catering for young people with emotional and behavioural difficulties, and most of them are residential as well. While the benefit of involvement in organised sports has been examined and discussed in other settings, such discussion in a residential child care context is scarce. Yet, its use as a vehicle for promoting pro-social values, enhancing resiliency and acknowledging culture fits well within the child and youth care perspective of utilising the lifespace, and everyday events within that lifespace, to provide healing and developmentally enhancing environments for young people.

On the use of the word '*programme*'

During the course of this chapter, I will use the word *programme* to encapsulate all the activities that are associated with the boys' football team. This word seems to be used in the UK to describe particular treatment packages aimed at reducing or extinguishing specific problematic behaviour (e.g. anger management programmes, programmes for sexually aggressive young people, or cognitive behavioural therapy programmes). While a school football team is not consistent with this current notion of programme, my reasons for choosing to use the term anyway are twofold: one, because it is congruent with my professional background. In the United States, the concept of *programme* has a much broader base. The entire residential milieu, including the various activities, therapeutic groups, treatment strategies, education provision and daily activities of living constituted the *residential programme*, and at times, young people (or even staff) were encouraged to 'get with the programme' (meaning 'invest in these processes and how they can help you to get yourself sorted, improve your life, tackle your problems, etc.'). Additionally, there were programmes within *the programme*. Examples of these included the recreation or education programme, and further sub-programmes also existed (e.g. the Tae Kwondo programme). While the overuse of a word can render it meaningless, in this case and in retrospect, it seems that the broad use of the word conveyed the importance of a multitude of processes in providing compensatory and developmentally enhancing experiences that assisted young people to heal and take positive control of their lives.

The second reason for this decision is closely related to the first. It seems that the current use of the word programme has potentially damaging consequences in terms of narrowing our understanding of what constitutes therapeutic process, focussing our efforts solely on problematic behaviour. This direction has a dangerous potential towards categorising and therefore reducing young people to their difficulties and/or dysfunction. This also resonates, unfortunately, with my professional background, as there can all too often be a preoccupation in the United States with labelling and pathologising those on the receiving end of services. While I have witnessed greater insight and commitment to avoiding this approach in Scotland, this possible trend towards exclusively problem-focussed programmes designed to 'fix' young people is concerning and familiar. Using the notion of programme more broadly is a deliberate response to this narrowing of focus.

What the research tells us

While research is equivocal regarding the impact of sport on children and young people, there is a widely held belief about its benefits. Research in Canada found that 92 per cent of those polled believe that involvement in sport at a community level positively influences the personal and moral development of young people. In the minds of these Canadians, such involvement promotes values of teamwork, commitment, hard work, striving for excellence, fair play, courage to try new things, respect for others and honesty (CCES, 2002). In a longitudinal study based on interviews in the same country, researchers found a direct relationship between children and teenagers' participation in organised, extracurricular activities, and their performance in school, their ability to get along with others, and their self-esteem. Conversely, those who rarely or never participated in such activities, or who had participated during the early years of the study but had subsequently stopped, were more likely to report having lower self-esteem and difficulty with friends. The researchers, however, were not able to draw any cause-and-effect conclusions, noting that the complexity of the relationship is difficult to measure. One example is the chicken-and-egg-type question of whether sports and activities help to develop the positive qualities in young people, or whether it is those children and youth who already have these qualities who are drawn to sports (Thompson, 2001). Other studies have shown

similar connections between ongoing involvement in extracurricular activities in high school and later academic achievement and pro-social behaviours (Zaff et al., 2003) and an inverse relationship between organised sports and substance use (Duncan et al., 2002).

Closer to home, the Scottish Office commissioned a study to explore the role of sport in regenerating urban areas and countering social exclusion (Coalter, Allison and Taylor, 2000). While the researchers found a strong theoretical basis for the part sports can play in positively impacting a range of social issues, systematic monitoring and evaluation of sport-type projects was lacking. This was attributed to the complexity of defining and measuring outcomes, limited time frames and/or funding, and a lack of expertise. In the section devoted to sport, young people and education, the inability to establish a causal relationship, this time between physical activity and academic performance, was again apparent. The researchers did find evidence that the *salience* of sport, rather than the physical aspects of it, was likely to have an indirect, positive impact on cognitive and emotional development. Examples included social acceptance through being good at something of value to peers, or even interest in or knowledge about sports promoting peer acceptance. As part of the *Playing for Success* programme, Leeds United Football Club provides a range of academic activities during after school hours to pupils who are underachieving and demonstrating evidence of poor self-esteem. This programme has been effective in attracting students and substantially improving educational progress (measured by pre- and post-testing in certain core subjects). Whether the positive impact has been more strongly influenced by factors such as high staff to pupil ratios and greater access to computers, or the power of the Leeds United name and the resulting increase in positive identity and confidence is unclear. It seems unlikely that either one would be an insignificant factor. What is interesting is that parental feedback did reflect a perception that their children had experienced improved confidence, and in some cases, a wider circle of friends (Coalter, Allison and Taylor, 2000).

Coalter (1996: 15) advises against generalised statements related to the 'inherent therapeutic properties of sport', again pointing to the lack of systematic evaluation, and explaining that:

. . . proposals for the use of sport in the prevention of, or rehabilitation from, 'anti-social behaviour' must acknowledge the heterogeneous nature of this term and the multiplicity of causes.

Instead, he argues that claims must be measured and limited, and concludes that to be wholly effective in addressing issues of antisocial behaviour, sport must be part of a broader programme of intervention. Coalter outlines a variety of theories as to the benefits of sports for delinquent youth, and discusses relevant studies. Findings were similar to some of those previously mentioned; participation in sport alleviated boredom (a preventative or diversionary measure) and appeared to help with the development of social skills, self-confidence, and self-esteem, especially for those deemed socially inadequate, damaged or having a drug problem. In addition to the more peer-based component of camaraderie, the presence of a caring, adult role model was also identified as being an important factor. Other findings indicated that young people who exhibited delinquent behaviour tended to prefer games that were exciting, non-competitive, individual, and that required fewer rules and less conformity.

Shifting to a residential child care focus

Tapping into the potential of football makes perfect sense in the context of utilising everyday events as opportunities for therapeutic benefit of young people (Garfat, 2002; Ward, 2000). Henry Maier (1975: 408–9) articulates so well the 'critical strategic moments when child and worker are engaged with each other in everyday tasks', and how these 'joint experiences constitute the essence of development and of treatment'. These daily events of wake-up and bedtime routines, of shared meals, chores and recreation, and the inevitable crises they often bring, all provide rich opportunities for bonding, strengthening attachments, working through fears or resentments, and developing a sense of competence and basic worth. At my school, not a day went by without one or more requests to go to the games hall or pitch for a kick about. For a majority of the boys, football was a daily focus, both in terms of its general desirability for fun and energy release, and as an ongoing investment in developing skills for performance on the team.

Activities have long been an integral component of the therapeutic milieu (Maier, 1981; Trieschman, Whittaker, and Brendtro, 1969). They have been regarded on the one hand as time fillers, separate from therapeutic processes and goals, and on the other as vehicles through which young people interact with each other, staff and their environment in a manner that promotes change and development (Pratt, 1990). Activities have no rival in terms of a sense of mastery and self-esteem, and can prevent the all too often adversarial climate that can develop between staff and young people (VanderVen, 1985).

At times, planning or fulfilling the boys' requests for various activities seemed like playing the part of entertainer, and it felt draining and unsatisfying. Admittedly, during periods of exhaustion or laziness, my lack of responsiveness in this area inevitably yielded boredom and almost always a more difficult and demanding shift. In retrospect, I think this reflected an occasional perception of activities as a chore or a way to get through an evening. Conversely, it felt good when participating *with* young people while having fun, witnessing development and enjoying the fruits of our labour as we promoted experiences of belonging and enhanced self-esteem. I often remember feeling amazed that I was being paid for this. In actuality, the skills, knowledge and energy to consistently and effectively work from the latter perspective is not adequately understood or valued.

Lennhoff and Lampen (2000) discuss the importance of activities (particularly sports) in residential settings in helping young people develop self-discipline. The challenges of sharing and co-operating, contributing to the team, persevering when tired, and controlling (and appropriately channelling) aggressive impulses are more demanding than some youth can manage, especially early in their placement. While this observation is in keeping with the preceding findings related to delinquent young people preferring games that were individual, non-competitive, and required few rules (Coalter, 1996) it points to a strength of residential child care; a young person who would otherwise shy away from a community-based sport might be more inclined (or more supported and empowered over time) to participate, and therefore reap the benefits, in the therapeutic environment of a residential child care setting – especially those 'socially inadequate, damaged, or drug misusing' young people (ibid) who stand to gain the most.

The young man mentioned in the beginning of this chapter exemplifies the struggle to meet the demands related to playing for the football team, and there have been times he has refused to participate due to his fear of lack of self-control. His involvement provides a shared developmental focus, one that sometimes has been painful, but also one to which he has been willing to dedicate a sustained investment (as opposed to learning to use manners at the table, for example). It has been difficult and exciting to be a part of his growth process in this way.

Care workers as 'experience arrangers'

Phelan (2001: 2) describes a model of activity programming that is based on the notion that many of the people with whom we work are so stuck in a negative personal story that they have little or no hope of being able to change. Their associated beliefs are based upon past experiences, are reinforced time and again by what has often been referred to as 'self fulfilling prophecy', and continually colour their view of the future. With requisite safety and trust, care workers can provide activities that serve to create a *free place*, where young people encounter an *experience gap* – a place where they can be in the present moment with 'minimal interference from these self-defeating messages, so that new experiences can happen and be acknowledged'. Within these new experiences, young people can experience themselves in a new way, one that begins to weave together a personal story that includes competence, trustworthiness, happiness, and probably most importantly, hope. Communication occurs through the senses and through the experience, rather than just through words. The care worker must utilise skills of presence, relationship, doing *with*, understanding each young person and their personal story, and awareness of activities as a strategy for change in order to be effective 'experience arrangers'.

While Phelan argues against the use of competitive, win-lose activities with those people who have a particularly hopeless or self-defeating personal story, the football programme seems to work quite well in helping many of the boys 're-write' their personal stories. One young man in particular springs to mind when I think about its transformative potential.

Ewan

When Ewan first came to us, he appeared to possess little or no confidence and seemed to see himself as capable of very little. A saving grace, in terms of him being able to invest in his placement with us, was the popularity of football as a nightly activity in the games hall. To say he loved football would be an understatement; this kid lived, ate and breathed it. He was not content unless every moment of his free time was dedicated to kicking the ball in the games hall, and he often struggled when this request was not quickly met. However, he would not play for the school team. In fact, if memory serves, he initially would not even participate in team training sessions. Because these took place in the games hall once or twice weekly, he soon opted into these rather than miss out on his regular football fix.

For weeks on end, Ewan was selected for the team but chose not to play. Staff consistently encouraged him to take the risk, and tried to help him develop a less self-defeating perspective as to what would happen if he did not play well. Still, he refused. Finally, another young person raised the issue in a unit meeting, and with a bit of adult facilitation, the entire group of boys were able to communicate to this young man that the taking part was the most important thing, and that as long as he did his best, he would not be letting the team down. He attended a match to watch, and the following week played his first.

During the years that followed, it was amazing to watch Ewan develop a stronger sense of competency – not just on the football pitch but in other areas as well. Even his posture and eye contact began to communicate increasing levels of confidence. He began to engage in banter with staff and young people, and was even able to sometimes laugh at himself in a good-natured way. The most extraordinary part of this process was that this young man played goalkeeper, a position that requires tremendous confidence, composure and courage. And what a fantastic keeper he was.

It would neither be accurate nor fair to assert that the football programme was wholly responsible for Ewan's hugely positive development. By the same token, it is not only clear to me that it was a vital component, but that without the supportive, inclusive environment that the residential school provided, he would not have joined (let alone sustained involvement with) a community based team. I strongly suspect that the experience of being capable, liked and valued by fellow team mates was a new one.

Resilience

A sense of competence or experiences of mastery have long been considered important in promoting positive development, and more recently resilience (Brendtro, Brokenleg and Van Bockern, 1998; Daniel, Wassell and Gilligan, 1999; Fahlberg, 1991). The concept of enhancing and promoting resiliency in young people who have encountered adversity seems to be one of the most salient and likely to endure over the long road ahead of furthering our understanding and effectiveness in working with young people in residential child care. Resilience has been defined by Gilligan (1997: 12) as:

> ... *qualities which cushion a vulnerable child from the worst effects of adversity ... and which may help a child or young person to cope, survive and even thrive in the face of great hurt and disadvantage.*

He asserts that influences on resilience are multi-faceted, only some of which can be influenced by practitioners or policy makers (1997). Daniel, Wassell and Gilligan (1999) discuss six domains that have been associated with resilience, and how they might be integrated into practice with accommodated children. In the most relevant domain to this discussion, that of talent and interests, they argue the potent potential of participation in valued activities (valued to the young person) in building a sense of self-efficacy, competence and success. The aforementioned (in addition to being of benefit in terms of helping young people to 're-write their personal stories') are vital components in building self-esteem, a fundamental building block of resiliency.

In a more detailed examination of the value of mentoring young people's talents and interests, Gilligan asserts that children and young people may indeed benefit more in therapeutic terms from their involvement in 'mainstream' activities that are within their social network or community because of the absence of the stigma that is often associated with more clinical approaches to intervening. While involvement in activities seems to be more within the realm of influence of direct care workers than family stability, for instance, it can often be an overlooked, undervalued, or completely untapped possibility.

Gilligan also points out that activities provide an avenue through which young people can access supportive relationships. The divergence from more clinical approaches (which involve talk), as well as the importance of relationship as a context within which a young person can gain the most benefit from involvement in hobbies or activities resonates well with Phelan's emphasis on communication occurring through the senses and the experience, rather than through words. This also rings bells for me. For anyone who knows me would readily agree that I am a *talker*, and looking back, I think this was often difficult for some of the boys who related quite differently. Playing football together gave us a way to connect that worked for them (and for me).

In terms of how notions of resiliency relate to the football team, it is clear that for most of the boys who participate on the school team, this is an opportunity in the week (maybe the only one), where they feel like they are *good* at something, that something is of significant value in *their* world, and they are a part of something successful (when the team wins or plays well, anyway). Football seems to be one of the only areas in these boys' lives where they experience what might be called *progressive achievement* in an area of value to them. While many children take for granted the private dance classes, music lessons or involvement in a school or community based sport, children and young people in residential care often do not have such opportunities or are not emotionally capable of managing them. Aside from football (and Tae Kwondo in a previous residential school), the activities provided in all of my residential work places have either been one-off, progressed over a very short time span, or have been repeated but did not provide observable signs of progress coupled with formal, public recognition of that progress (i.e. regular kick abouts in the games hall, excursions to the swimming pool or snooker club versus dance performances, music grades, or league standings and end of season awards).

The notable exception would be the progressive gains young people make during various activities as part of their education. However, because so many of our young people have had such negative experiences of school, they often automatically devalue (to some degree) gains made that they associate with education. The lack of opportunities for progressive achievement has not been for lack of trying, it must be said, for on many occasions the school has attempted to support a young person in pursuing an interest in the local community. To my knowledge, however, in each case the young person did not continue the pursuit over time. I suspect for many of the boys, their feelings of not fitting in, of worrying about how to answer other young people's questions about where they go to school, or fears about how other adults might deal with their struggles with impulse control must have been contributing factors to their lack of persistence, and many of their comments confirmed this. Additionally, it would be fair to say that many of them do not see themselves as someone who 'sees things through' and does not quit in the face of adversity. It then makes sense that the potentially supportive, nurturing environment of a residential school can provide a sense of safety, belonging, and the opportunity to see themselves as capable of accomplishment in spite of difficulties.

Promotion of pro-social values

One of the hopes many of us working with young people hold is that they are able to find their place in this world in a manner that, at the very least, is not at the expense of other people. On an intuitive level, it is not simply about a general concern for society and its members, but a notion that thinking and behaving in an anti-social manner not only hurts the victims of such behaviour, but also the one behaving in such a way (whether or not that person is caught and held accountable). While these notions might reflect religious or spiritual beliefs, pro-social tendencies have been identified as good predictors of social adjustment. Some research shows that even in early childhood, a higher degree of pro-social behaviour indicates a greater ability to overcome behavioural problems. Conversely, children who demonstrate lower levels of pro-social behaviours are more likely 'to be rejected by peers and to adopt antisocial roles' (Durkin, 1995: 435).

In addressing the value of interests and activities in enhancing resiliency, Gilligan (1999) also identifies their facilitative properties in re-awakening or nurturing natural pro-social tendencies in children. He points to particular behaviour exhibited by parents or carers associated with pro-social behaviour. These include clear communication about rules, principles, and expected behaviour, as well as messages about the inherent goodness of the child.

Trotter (1999) offers a model for working with people who are resistant or even openly antagonistic toward the services they are being offered (or more likely, services they are required to work with). He asserts that skilled use of pro-social modelling and reinforcement (a component of his model) is shown in research to be effective, and in his own study, was the most influential worker skill. It would be fair to say that, at the time of being placed in residential care, the vast majority of young people do not want to be there, though some might concede that it is preferable to any other option they might have. In my own experience, 'antagonistic' would be an understatement in describing how many demonstrate their desire not to be 'in placement', and the question of how to work effectively with especially resistant young people has consistently been a challenge.

Trotter outlines a four-part approach in promoting pro-social outcomes:

1. **Identify pro-social comments or actions.**
   This includes clear-cut pro-social comments or behaviours as well as acknowledgement of harm done or remorseful feelings for anti-social words or deeds.
2. **Reward those comments and actions wherever possible.**
   Praise is identified as being the most frequent and powerful of reinforcers available to workers, but is only effective if it is genuine and directed at the pro-social comments and behaviours of the clients. The use of other rewards must be explicitly linked to desired behaviour, and the promise of a reward is less effective than simply providing it as a result of the pro-social act.
3. **Model pro-social comments and actions.**
   This not only includes modelling the behaviours the worker wants to foster in the client, but also *coping modelling*, or acknowledging vulnerability and difficulty in consistently conducting oneself in a pro-social manner.
4. **Challenge anti-social comments and actions.**
   This includes clear-cut anti-social comments or behaviours, as well as rationalisations for such comments or behaviours. Negative reinforcers include expressions of disapproval, ignoring of behaviour or simply pointing out that a comment is a rationalisation for an unacceptable behaviour. This aspect of the approach, however, must be used with

caution, as studies indicate that greater emphasis on positives (with sparing use of negatives) is more effective.

This approach seems well suited to residential work for a number of reasons. The strength of praise, modelling or disapproval can be directly related to the strength of relationship between worker and young person. The time residential care workers spend with their 'clients' is of greater quantity, intensity and longevity, thus providing fertile ground for deep, strong relationships. It must also be said that this can be a double-edged sword, in that uninformed, unskilled or unscrupulous use of positive or negative reinforcers can cause hurt to the tender hearts hiding behind angry, aggressive facades.

When applied to the football programme, this approach appears even more strongly suited. While the relationship may be an important factor in the effectiveness of the four parts of the approach, the context is significant as well. Praise or disapproval carries greater weight when it is related to something of value to the recipient. I am certain that complimenting a young football player on his sportsmanship for how he managed the aggressive conduct of an opponent has a much greater impact than complimenting him on his table manners. Additionally, because a member of staff plays within the team for each match (for both teams), the boys get to witness pro-social modelling of behaviours in an area in which they have an investment. This can be quite demanding for that member of staff, but the power of their example, especially when they are demonstrating 'coping modelling' on the pitch, should not be underestimated.

The game of football also provides a structure that young people can accept, including those young people who struggle with structure in other aspects of their lives. A coach's clear communication of expectations for conduct, as well as the rules and principles of the game, can reflect the same pro-social parental qualities identified by Gilligan (1999). It would also be difficult to see how the experiences of belonging, teamwork, self-control, appropriate expressions of physical aggression, working toward a greater good, respecting of one's opponent, accepting authority (referee/coach), and supporting one's team mates do not also contribute to the development of pro-social values.

One final point related to the promotion of pro-social values; it could be said that each young person needs his 'moment in the sun' when he stands out from the rest of his classmates, and football provides the opportunity for him to do so in a pro-social manner. Gilligan identifies recognition for performance in activities to also enhance resiliency (1999), and it seemed to me that the boys I worked with were continually searching for recognition, though they often were not fussy about whether it was positive or negative. I can remember on more than one occasion kicking myself for making a positive comment about a young person's table manners, only to realise, as a result of his radical change in behaviour, that this was a grave error. It seems that I keep picking on table manners, and the truth of the matter is that I believe young people need to develop and maintain basic skills related to how to behave and interact while eating. In addition to the issues young people bring to the table, meal times can be difficult due to the opportunity they provide for negatively showing off to peers. It is the consistent time of the day when all the young people in the unit come together, and sometimes being seen as conducting oneself in a way that is desirable to adults can be a social 'kiss of death', depending on the mindset of that young person, the other young people he wants to impress, and the general state of the milieu at that time. It has been my experience that the more opportunities young people have for pro-social recognition in areas of value *to them*, the less efforts I see towards anti-social recognition, both for individuals and in terms of group norms.

Rhythms and rituals

Have you noticed that when people jog, dance or throw a Frisbee in rhythm with each other, they seem to experience momentary bonding and a sense of unity? . . . In fact, it is almost impossible to dislike a person while being rhythmically in 'sync'. Rhythmic interactions forge people together. Rhythmicity provides a glue for establishing human connections.

(Maier cited by Krueger, 1994: 50))

Maier (1981) identifies the central importance of rhythms for promoting a sense of permanency and predictability in early childhood, and points out that they continue to be an essential component in effective interpersonal relationships throughout life. Krueger (1994) contends that our efforts to manage behaviour and promote growth in young people only work when we are present and attuned to their rhythms for trusting and growing. Without such qualities, we are more likely to do things to them rather than with them.

In the materials used for tutorial sessions at the Camphill Community in Aberdeen, a residential school for children with special needs, rhythm is espoused for its healing, harmonising and calming qualities, and its ability to provide a sense of safety and security. While the notions of rhythm here are more oriented around daily, weekly, monthly and yearly rhythms, its place of importance in providing compensatory environments for pupils suffering from 'rhythm disturbance' is noteworthy (Unpublished Camphill Community Training Materials).

The obvious rhythms of staff and young people kicking a ball back and forth should not overshadow the rhythms shared between young people, either during kick abouts, training drills, or actual matches. I wonder how many times some of these boys have experienced the level of harmony and connectedness that occurs during elevated levels of play – those moments of synchronicity where players are so attuned to one another their anticipation and movement related to passing transcends everyday experience. The rhythms around weekly training and matches are also of great value, and many young people have commented that looking forward to a game has gotten them through some of their most difficult times.

Rituals embody psychological rhythmicity, bring about a great sense of togetherness (Maier, 1981) and can convey a sense of cultural safety (Fulcher, 2003). The rituals referred to here are not the basic routines that provide order and smooth functioning in a shift, but those repeated practices, often initiated by young people, which have special significance for them (ibid). Playing for the school team can be bound up in rituals, from cleaning and polishing boots the night before a match, to the personal and group practices in pre-game dressing rooms and warm ups. For young people who so badly just want to be 'normal', these rituals can bring about a seemingly contradictory mix of comfort, connection, excitement, specialness and normalcy.

Culture

Acknowledging the culture of young people is one area of practice in residential child care receiving attention. Fulcher (1998: 333) discusses the importance of providing cultural safety, which he defines as:

> . . . that state of being in which the child knows emotionally that her/his personal wellbeing, as well as social and cultural frames of reference, are acknowledged – even if not fully understood.

He claims that rituals of encounter between staff and young people are grounded in a variety of manifestations of culture, including the child's culture of origin and/or experiences of gang or drug cultures. Green (1999: 87) describes *cultural competence* as being able to work:

> . . . in a way that is congruent with the behaviour and expectations normative for a given community and that are adapted to suit the specific needs of individuals and families from that community.

When I started work at my school, I had only been in this country a matter of months and it could be said I was culturally incompetent. I was highly aware of this, though not necessarily in those terms, and I found that playing football was one area where the boys' and my cultures overlapped. In a broader sense, the clashes experienced when many of our boys reject the middle class values espoused by 'the establishment' (and those of us that comprise it) contain a distinctly cultural component. When on the pitch or in the games hall, however, that gap diminishes for a while. Football provides an area of familiarity, comfort and a previously held value for many of our boys, and might be the one time of the week that they do not feel that we are trying to change who (they think) they are. Hugh McIlvanney's (1997: 138) citing of Arthur Hopcraft in describing the central place of football in the cultural experience of working class Britons clarified for me the power of this game:

> The point about football in Britain is that it is not just a sport people take to, like cricket or tennis or running long distances. It is inherent in the people. It is built into the urban psyche, as much a common experience to our children as are uncles and school. It is not a phenomenon; it is an everyday matter . . . It has more significance in the national character than theatre has.

While McIlvanney acknowledges the decrease in numbers and intensity as far as avid following of football is concerned (compared with when the above was written), it remains a vital part of many boys' identity.

In examining the Scottish context, Finn and Giulianotti (1998) argue that football has carried the burden for the expression of Scottish identity due to limited alternatives, with Scottish international supporters representing Scotland even to a greater degree than the Scotland Team itself. Bradley (2002) points out the importance of various regions or localities in comprising a more diverse notion of how Scottish identity manifests through football. These views support my experience of many young people's identity being intimately tied up with which football team they support. While Rangers and Celtic dominate the list of favoured teams and it would be fair to say that a percentage of boys align themselves with one or the other merely to fit in, a larger percentage invest heavily (in terms of time, money and emotion), often because of where they come from. One of my earliest related lessons occurred when a scared and resistant young man was being shown around on a pre-placement visit and the duty manager enquired, 'Where do you come fae?' The conversation quickly turned to which football team each of them supported, and a good-natured banter emerged.

> *The place that a child learns to call* **home** *and* **my people** *has a particular history, with a political, economic and social legacy.*
>
> (Fulcher, 2003: 21)

The school has infrequently had young people admitted who were of a different race or ethnicity (simply due to lack of referrals) but it does receive boys from all over the country. I wonder how often we missed the mark of acknowledging and holding as valid those subtle differences based on what could be termed 'sub-cultures', cultural norms based on region, socio-economic status, and even based on youth (i.e. youth culture). Football seems to provide an avenue through which a strand of many young people's cultural history can be validated and strengthened. By the same token, it also provides a place to enjoy a shared culture.

Not all milk and honey

Despite all of the riches the football programme has to offer, it also can be the source of difficulties. Over the past several years, it has been one or more members of the care staff who has taken on the role of team managers. While that person has always started off enthusiastic and aspirational, it has not taken long before these qualities have faded and been replaced by feelings of frustration and defeat. The added time

investment, responsibilities and occasional tantrums from boys that come with the job seem more than outweighed by the rewards of being a part of many of the aforementioned gains, and this view has been supported by former managers. However, the area of team selection – who gets picked for this week's match, who does not, and why – has consistently been a source of friction. One team manager described having his judgement challenged by someone or another *every* week while running the team. This not only impacted his motivation to continue in the role of football manager, but was also bleeding into his feelings about his post as care worker.

The complexity of decision-making surrounding team selection is a primary factor contributing to this ongoing problem, and it seems highly likely that other establishments struggle with it as well. In working with young people with emotional and behavioural difficulties, deciding which boys get to play each week is more complicated than simple factors of who has attended training and performed well on the pitch. Issues of *earn* and *deserve* appear in staff discussions, as well as the question, 'what message are we sending the boys by selecting this one over that one?'

There have been times in the past when one might have heard an adult fall back on the worn-out 'that'll be you not playing football this week if you don't get yourself back to class', in an attempt to manage a young person's acting out behaviour. While I felt we progressed beyond this more flagrant display of power and control (as opposed to attending to the issue at hand with the young person), it is much more difficult to fully move beyond the thinking behind it. It is a struggle to avoid the tendency to want to use what matters to young people as leverage to control them, or to extinguish the less than noble urge to 'show who's boss', or 'teach 'em a lesson'.

At the same time, a residential setting must hold its young people accountable for their actions if it is to provide a safe environment and promote the development of self-control. How this is done effectively, especially with young people who have not previously experienced boundaries and accountability in a safe and consistent manner (if at all), is extremely complex. The first step, it seems to me, is to acknowledge its complexity and importance, and commit to work together to meet it. Doing so requires stepping back, thinking critically and asking some more fundamental questions: 'What is our image of how *our* young people should be?', 'What are our ideas of what they should become?', 'How do we envision this happening, and what should the process look like?', and finally, 'What is it we're trying to accomplish through the use of the football team and how does this fit in with the preceding questions?' Such an approach might seem too complicated and abstract to some. Yet, whether consciously or unconsciously, we all carry around individual beliefs related to these questions, and our practice is strongly influenced by them. Reflective discussion about how and why young people are held accountable, combined with an openness about related inner struggles that sometimes impede effective practice, can be useful in helping staff teams more effectively manage the aforementioned complexity. Such focus on accountability also needs to be tempered with an understanding of resilience, 'experience arranging', promotion of pro-social values, rhythms, rituals and culture in maximising the therapeutic value of participation in the football team.

A side note

I am cognisant of this chapter's overriding male focus. While this is obviously a result of examining the therapeutic value of a boys' football team within a boys' residential school, it must be said that experiences of sport can have just as much importance in the lives of girls. Research indicates that girls who participate in sports are less likely to experience unintended teen pregnancy, smoke cigarettes, use recreational drugs or engage in other high-risk behaviours (Lopiano, 2002). At the same time, there is less opportunity and cultural support for girls to access these benefits. It may be an even greater challenge to provide girls in residential care opportunities to engage in organised sport, but one that should be embraced with equal enthusiasm and commitment.

Conclusion

One of the challenges residential child care faces is the tendency to devalue the seemingly mundane, day to day processes that, upon closer analysis, have the greatest ability to promote and restore well being. This tendency is often demonstrated by the uninformed outside the field, but it is sometimes fair to say we either overlook the potential of our daily actions or that

we fail to 'blow our own trumpet' as to their importance. This chapter has attempted to 'blow the football trumpet', locating it within existing theories as to what young people need in order to overcome adversity and thrive, and supporting it with evidence – both from research and from practice. It is also hoped that the reader will either come away with an enhanced sense of potential and pride for their own direct care efforts, or with a more vibrant image in their mind's eye as to what might occur within residential establishments.

What this chapter has not tried to do is assert that football can stand alone. It must be part of an integrated, holistic approach to working with young people. It can do nothing for those who are not athletically inclined – either due to lack of interest or ability. It cannot single-handedly provide opportunities for enhancing resilience, promoting connectedness or acknowledging culture. Moreover, the potential and actual benefits it brings to young people and staff cannot overcome poor practice, either directly related to its implementation or more generally to child care practice. For it can be used as a weapon against youngsters, either as leverage to force compliance or as expressions of inappropriate 'macho culture'.

The potential and actual difficulties, however, are more than outweighed by football's riches. As I think back on the feelings rising in me as I approached the pitch that crisp autumn day, I wonder how many times in a given day, week or month young people in care experience similar feelings. Dick Prouty, Executive Director of Project Adventure, Inc., eloquently captures the restorative power of such experiences:

In play, time itself often stood still while everyone became a little braver, stronger and more whole. Laughter flowed.
(Rohnke, 1984: 6)

References

Bradley, J.M. (2002) The Patriot Game: Football's Famous 'Tartan Army'. *International Review for the Sociology of Sport.* 37: 2, 177–97.

Brendtro, L.K., Brokenleg, M. and Van Bockern, S. (1998) *Reclaiming Youth at Risk.* Bloomington: IA: National Educational Service.

CCES (2002) *National Survey Reveals That the Power of Community Sport Remains Unfulfilled.* Retrieved Jan., 2003, from http://www.newswire.ca/releases/july2002/18/c5923.html.

Coalter, F. (1996) *Sport and Anti-Social Behaviour: A Policy-Related Review*. Edinburgh: The Scottish Sports Council.

Coalter, F., Allison, M. and Taylor, J. (2000) *The Role of Sport in Regenerating Deprived Areas*. Edinburgh: The Scottish Executive Central Research.

Daniel, B., Wassell, S. and Gilligan, R. (1999) It's just common sense isn't it? Exploring ways of putting the theory of resilience into action. *Adoption and Fostering*. 23: 3, 6–15.

Duncan, S.C., Duncan, T.E., Strycker, L.A. and Chaumeton, N.R. (2002) Relations Between Youth Antisocial and Prosocial Activities. *Journal of Behavioural Medicine*. 25: 5, 425–8.

Durkin, K. (1995) *Developmental Social Psychology: From Infancy to Old Age*. Malden, MA: Blackwell.

Fahlberg, V. (1991) *A Child's Journey Through Placement*. Indianapolis, IN: Perspectives Press.

Finn, G.P. and Giulianotti, R. (1998) Scottish Fans, Not English Hooligans!, in Brown, A. (Ed.) *Fanatics!: Power, Identity and Fandom In Football*. London: Routledge.

Fulcher, L.C. (1998) Acknowledging Culture in Child and Youth Care Practice. *Social Work Education*. 17: 3, 321–38.

Fulcher, L.C. (2003) Rituals of Encounter That Guarantee Cultural Safety. *Relational Child and Youth Care Practice*. 16: 3, 20–7.

Garfat, T. (2002) *The Use of Everyday Events in Child and Youth Work*. Retrieved 19 Nov. from http://www.cyc-net.org/cyc-online/cycol-0402-garfat.html

Gilligan, R. (1997) Beyond Permanence? The Importance of Resilience in Child Placement Practice and Planning. *Adoption and Fostering*. 21: 1, 12–20.

Gilligan, R. (1999) Enhancing the Resilience of Children and Young People in Public Care by Mentoring Their Talents and Interests. *Child and Family Social Work*. 4, 187–96.

Green, J. W. (1999) *Cultural Awareness in Human Services: A Multi-Ethnic Approach*. Englewood Cliffs, NJ: Prentice-Hall.

Krueger, M. (1994) Rhythm and Presence: Connecting With Children on the Edge. *Journal of Emotional and Behavioural Problems*. 3: 1, 49–51.

Lennhoff, F.G., and Lampen, J. (2000) *The Inherent Discipline of Crafts and Activities*. Retrieved Dec., 2002, from http://www.cyc-net.org/today/today000628.html.

Lopiano, D.A. (2002) *Advocating for Gender Equality in Sport: The Experience of the Women's Sport Foundation in the United States*. Retrieved Nov. 2003, from http://www.womenssportsfoundation.org/binary-data/WSF_ARTICLE/pdf_file/908.pdf

Maier, H.W. (1975) Learning to Learn and Living to Live in Residential Treatment. *Child Welfare*. 54: 6, 406–20.

Maier, H.W. (1981) Essential Components in Care and Treatment Environments for Children, in Ainsworth, L.C. (Ed.) *Group Care for Children: Concepts and Issues*. London: Tavistock.

McIlvanney, H. (1997) *McIlvanney on Football*. Edinburgh: Mainstream Publishing.

Rohnke, K. (1984) *Silver Bullets: A Guide to Initiative Problems, Adventure Games, Stunts and Trust Activities*. IO: Kendall Hunt Publishing.

Phelan, J. (2001). Another Look at Activities. *Journal of Child and Youth Care*. 14: 2, 1–7.

Pratt, S. (1990) Therapeutic Programming and Activities: Transitional Tools in the Treatment Process. in Anglin, J.P. et al. (Eds.) *Perspectives in Professional Child and Youth Care*. New York: Haworth Press.

Thompson, E. (2001) *Active Kids are Better off*. Retrieved Dec. 2002, from http://www.cyc-net.org/today/today010606.html.

Trieschman, A., Whittaker, J.K. and Brendtro, L.K. (1969) *The Other 23 Hours: Child-Care Work With Emotionally Disturbed Children in a Therapeutic Milieu*. New York: Aldine De Gruyter.

Trotter, C. (1999) *Working With Involuntary Clients: A Guide to Practice*. London: Sage.

VanderVen, K.D. (1985) Activity Programming: Its Developmental and Therapeutic Role in Group Care, in Fulcher, L.C. and Ainsworth, F. (Eds.) *Group Care Practice With Children*. London: Tavistock.

Ward, A. (2000) *Opportunity Led Work*. Norwich: University of East Anglia.

Zaff, J.F., Moore, K.A., Papillo, A.R. and Williams, S. (2003) Implications of Extracurricular Activity Participation During Adolescence on Positive Outcomes. *Journal of Adolescent Research*. 18: 6, 599–630.

Chapter Fourteen

New Developments in Care Planning for Children in Residential Care

Alison Williams

Introduction

There is obviously a proper pace at which matters should proceed for a child, a pace that provides enough time for the necessary assessments to be made, agreements obtained and reports submitted ... placements can be made too hurriedly as well as too slowly.

(Parker, 1999: 121)

This chapter examines the developments and initiatives in care planning over the last decade. The research, which has informed practice development will be evaluated. A model of care planning is proposed which brings together individual care planning for each looked after child and strategic planning and commissioning of services for looked after children. The model should assist all carers to contribute to and to implement the care plan.

Assessment and planning initiatives

The aim of care planning is to improve outcomes for looked after children and there have been a number of government initiatives to support this aim. At the individual level, the care plan is made up of a number of plans focused around particular developmental needs of children. The challenge for workers is to ensure that these education and health plans, for example, are integrated into the overall care plan.

The Integrated Children's System (www.dfes.gov.uk/integratedchildrenssystem) is designed to bring together the assessment framework for children in need with the looking after children materials in order to place a greater emphasis on needs based **assessment**, the importance of analysis of individual need and setting desired outcomes prior to deciding on the services required – **planning and intervention**. These, alongside monitoring and **review**, are the ingredients of qualitative care planning.

The Integrated Children's System pilots and the National Children's Bureau project to develop practice guidance and training in care planning aim to increase the focus and importance of the care plan. This work will provide tools for managers to analyse and collate management information about need from individual assessments and plans to inform their strategic plans and work on commissioning services. The aim is not just to provide information for the planning of services but also to ensure that each young person has a plan which assists them towards achieving stability, continuity and security in a life which has been very turbulent and traumatic. It is these experiences which have contributed to their becoming looked after and for many children their lives continue to be unstable and turbulent in care.

The government has set timescales for plans for permanence for all children (DoH, 2001). Achieving permanence requires proactive care planning prior to and after becoming looked after. Twin tracking must be used for children in care proceedings during the early stages of their entering care in order to evaluate whether returning home is possible whilst also setting in place plans to achieve permanence through a substitute family or other form of substitute care, if this fails. Additionally there are three programmes in England piloting concurrent planning for very young children (Monck et al., 2003). The objective of the adoption standards and these permanence initiatives is to reduce delay in these crucial months and years of a child's life. Social workers are also encouraged to have contingency plans in place for all children, which can be activated in the event of a plan or placement breaking down.

Standards for residential care came into force in 2002 (DoH, 2002) and children's homes and other residential settings are inspected against these standards. These include standards relevant to individual care and placement planning. They also emphasise the importance of the Statement of Purpose in enabling the service to set its own expectations concerning the needs it can and cannot meet.

At the same time as these initiatives were progressing, the courts became concerned *Re S and Re W* (sometimes referred to as Re W and B) about cases where care plans (Section 31 of the Children Act 1989) were not being followed and where the child did not have a route back into a court appeals process, without assistance. As the court has no power to monitor the care plan, questions were raised over the child's right to family life (Article 8, Human Rights Act 1998) and the right to a fair trial (Article 6) and whether these could be breached if they had no adult who could initiate a challenge. Although the House of Lords judgment in *Re S and W* clarifies that there was not a breach *per se* of human rights and that the Children Act 1989 was fully compatible with the Human Rights Act, the government decided to strengthen the importance of care plans and the role of Independent Reviewing Officers (IRO). Section 118 of the Adoption and Children Act 2002 amends Section 26 of the Children Act 1989 and requires IROs to act for the child and ensure that an appeal can be made if they consider a child's rights may have been breached.

At the strategic level, planning has in the past tended to be service led, based on the service providers' priorities, aims and objectives, eligibility criteria and, very often, a pressure to save money. Plans have failed to engage with the requirement for individual care planning for looked after children. Attention is now being given to creating more responsive children's planning mechanisms. This will now be carried forward within Children and Young People's Plans under the Children Act 2004. Planning at this strategic and macro level has been driven by the requirements of a government agenda for locally determined services, alongside more local and consumer led pressure to deliver better quality services and to achieve better value for money with improved outcomes.

The aim of all this work, whether at the strategic or individual level, is to improve the outcomes for children through delivering services which can meet their assessed developmental needs in the short and long term. The complexity of the task should not be underestimated but the importance of the ambition cannot be argued with and is based on a combination of legislation, planning systems, theory and research coming together to assist workers, managers and politicians to achieve the aim.

Theory and research

Attachment theory underpins these initiatives and practice for looked after children. This is clearly stated within the adoption agenda but a plan for residential care should also address how it will promote a child's attachment to a significant person or persons. The care plan is central to addressing how broken attachments are going to be mended or replacement figures used to promote new attachments and help the child to develop trust. Attachment theory has moved from its origins of biological attachment and has been adapted to reflect different attachment relationships. Howe (1996) has brought together a range of discursive work to apply attachment theory to modern day social work. He refers to attachment behaviour as:

> . . . *any form of behaviour which results in a person attaining or retaining proximity to some other differentiated and preferred individual, who is usually conceived as stronger and/or wiser.*
>
> (Howe, 1996: 4)

Bowlby's 1991 research, for example, demonstrated that children who do not have secure attachments are more likely to experience a range of difficulties including:

- An inability to form healthy relationships.
- Mental illness.
- An inability to communicate feelings but to display these through dysfunctional behaviour, aggression or withdrawal.

Rutter (1991) demonstrated that environment and interventions can influence and compensate for damaging experiences providing new pathways and opportunities for children to develop and achieve. The care of looked after children should provide these pathways and opportunities.

Research has increased our understanding of risk factors (see for example Haggerty et al., 1994; Garmezy, 1994; Rutter, 1994) concerning the accumulation of adversity and the presence and development of resilience and has provided some indications for effective practical interventions.

The individual subject's own ability to plan and therefore inject some control, rather than be a passive recipient, is a form of resilience (for example Rutter, 1994).

Jackson and Martin (1998) concluded that succeeding in education, combined with relationships with adults who helped them remain focussed on their desired educational outcomes, assisted children survive the care system.

Aldgate et al. (1992) found a relationship between stability within the placement and educational attainment.

Gilligan (2000) cites three key qualities which care should promote:

- A secure base.
- Self-esteem.
- Self efficacy through, for example, continuing contact with family members and others from a child's past, friendships with peers, helping others, a positive school experience, interests in hobbies and other activities, practice in problem solving and developing coping skills and strategies.

The resilience debate makes an important contribution to care planning. Services, which promote stability and continuity and the development and sustenance of relationships, will assist children to develop resilience. Studies, which examined the causes of placement moves and instability, help us to identify some of the barriers to achieving stability and continuity.

Jackson and Thomas' (1999) analysis of the research and literature concerning instability and placement changes identified the following indicators as contributors to instability:

- *placement at older age*
- *child's behaviour seen as problematic by carers*
- *placement in residential unit with frequent emergency admissions*
- *school problems, especially if leading to exclusion*
- *child separated from siblings*
- *foster parents' children very young or close in age to foster child*
- *lack of social work support*
- *exclusion of birth parents from placement*
- *child has a history of abuse or neglect*
- *early stage of placement*
- *poor co-ordination of services*

(Jackson and Thomas, 1999: 96)

Apart from some indicators, such as age and behaviour, the research is by no means conclusive. We do not as yet understand the relationship between the indicators and the reasons for individual success and failure where strong pro- or counter-indicators to stability exist.

Despite this lack of understanding of the interrelationship, there are clear messages concerning action which can be taken. It is important that workers take these messages into account whilst also evaluating them against the individual assessment of need for that particular child within their individual context. Strategic and individual plans should identify ways of

compensating for indicators which we know contribute to instability.

Harwin and Owen (2002) examined the process of implementing court care plans and their outcomes. Significantly, they found a relationship between the quality of the care plan and the likelihood of the placement being achieved. The more detail there was in the plan concerning:

- *type and details of the proposed placement*
- *arrangements for contact and reunification*
- *how the children's needs might be met*
- *services to be provided by the local authority*

(69)

the more likely it was to be achieved. The study found that external factors also affected the fulfilment of the plan. Resource shortages, in this study those of adoptive placements, and the profile of the child impacted on the achievement of plans for adoption. The plan for adoption was less likely to be achieved if the child was older, had a developmental delay, disability or belonged to a large sibling group. These findings are transferable to all children and indicate the importance of care planning and the attention to the detail of the plan, particularly when seeking a scarce resource.

Harwin and Owen also found that achievement of the plan had a significantly positive effect on the child's welfare outcome, irrespective of the type of placement. A continuous process of assessment and evaluation of the plan is required as plans are tried and tested to meet identified needs. Plans will change but these changes ought to be based on:

- An assessment of emerging need.
- An evaluation of the effectiveness of planned responses and services to meet these needs.
- A re-evaluation and review of whether the plan continues to meet the child's identified needs and is achievable.

The impact of availability of resources on the achievability of the plan will always need to be a consideration and may involve compromise or consideration of different ways in which needs can be met.

Ward and Skuse (2001) and Harwin and Owen (2002) found that initial plans at entry into care for return to parents changed to alternative permanent placements for a large proportion of their sample. Social workers tended to be over optimistic concerning the likelihood of achieving a plan to return a child to their parents. Greater use of assessment and analysis of parental ability to meet the child's needs, prior to the child becoming looked after, may prevent some of the delays caused by these changes of plans. High thresholds now exist which prevent children becoming looked after and new resources have been allocated to provide family support services to prevent family breakdown. This should mean that the social worker has more information and evidence available to accurately assess need and determine the plan at or soon after the point of becoming looked after. It may also mean that some children become looked after at a very late stage when it may be very difficult for services to address deficits of care and confirmed behaviour patterns.

It is possible to conclude that the work involved in care planning is more likely to achieve favourable outcomes for the child if the plan is timely, detailed and proactive, contains realistic timescales, identifies the risks and resource limitations and seeks to address these.

Children's views

Research into children's views of care planning and in particular the review process (see for example Grimshaw and Sinclair, 1997, and Thomas, 2000) is available to inform our understanding of how they want reviews conducted, how they want to participate, and what they want discussed. Children have difficulty in relating to 'a care plan' and what it means for them and when asked will often reply 'what care plan'. However, Thomas (2000) found that some children had a good understanding of what they wanted from the review process and meeting, who they wanted there and what decisions should be made. Some children recognised that there were some decisions which had to be made by adults:

> *I like them making decisions about when I go to my Mum and Dad's, because I find that difficult.*
>
> (144)

> *Getting my life in one piece, that's what's given me confidence.*
>
> (142)

Important decisions for them were about where they go and what they do and who they wanted to see, friends, school, time to come in, clothes and food. Others wanted to be involved in decisions about adoption, their social worker, contact and staying with friends:

> *it is our life – we have our own feelings, concerns and views, and the outcomes will affect us.*
>
> (151)

Parents' views

In contrast, there is very little research into parents' views of care planning and reviews. Grimshaw and Sinclair (1997) interviewed some parents as part of their study. They found that parents thought they had been consulted but had not received information beforehand, which might have enabled them to play a fuller part. If attendance at reviews is taken as an indicator of participation in care planning decisions, a worrying picture is presented of parents' attendance reducing relative to the age of the child, with 68 per cent of mothers and 36 per cent of fathers of children under five attending reducing to 30 per cent of mothers and 4 per cent of fathers of young people aged 16 and over. They were asked if social services explained reasons for decisions:

> *They never do. We just argue. I don't feel I have been given reasons for their thinking.*
>
> (162)

Components of care planning

This section will propose a care planning model for workers, carers and managers which addresses the complexity of care planning and which takes forward the messages from research and practice. The model has been developed within NCB, between 2001 and 2004, from the work we have conducted with a range of local authorities, training and development courses with workers and carers from all the agencies involved in care planning for looked after children. The model examines the different components of planning at the individual and strategic levels. If all these components are in place, the objective of having a proactive, child centred, needs based plan can be achieved. The model is not linear once needs and desired outcomes are set, and the process will need to be inclusive and evaluative whilst remaining within a framework, which is the overall care plan for the child.

Whilst the focus is residential child care as the setting, the model is transferable to other settings.

Principles

Inclusion and diversity

The model is applicable to children with very diverse needs. It allows for difference and is inclusive of disabled children as it focuses on the identification of developmental need, and the provision of services to meet these. The approach does not provide one racial or cultural perspective but allows for and encourages difference. The challenge is for workers and managers to engage with the racial, religious and cultural background and beliefs of the child and to assess their needs within this context.

It requires knowledgeable and enquiring workers, prepared to identify and acknowledge difference, and, in partnership with the child, their parents and all those involved in their care, discuss needs, set outcomes and consider services and plans which meet long and short term need.

Involving the child

The importance of involving and consulting the child throughout the process must be stressed. As discussed earlier, having some control over plans is one of the keys to developing resilience. Involving the child can help to achieve their ownership of the plan and their commitment to using the services and resources. They can identify their desired outcomes. They may not be ready to address some needs and this should be recorded and returned to at later reassessment and planning stages.

Advocacy or separate representation for children can assist their participation in decision-making. Children require choice about the ways in which they participate and whether they want to attend meetings or have someone speaking for them. Children communicate their views in different ways to different people and they may contradict themselves demonstrating how divided and torn they may feel by conflicting loyalties. Unravelling such views and wishes is a skilled task and providing them with someone independent can assist some children to sort out their views and make their wishes known. Carers also have an important role to play in representing the child as well as stating how they believe their needs can be best met. Advocacy or separate representation may be particularly important if the plan is not following the child's wishes and views or where there are conflicting views.

Ascertaining the views and wishes of children who do not use speech as their method of communication is particularly important. All children are able to communicate happiness and unhappiness. They may require people who understand their communication to represent their views. Parents and carers may not be able to do this as they may be representing their own needs and views which may be in conflict with those of the child. Similarly, for children whose first language is not English, it will be important that the interpreter is independent but understands the processes of planning and review.

Sometimes it's not the child that can't talk, it's adults that don't understand.
(quote from a child interviewed as part of the 'It's my turn to talk' project. NCB, 2004)

Explaining to children the boundaries of their involvement will help them to understand their contribution and influence. Whilst adults will listen and hear their views and take them into consideration, there will also be other factors for them to consider and weigh up, for example, whether it is safe for a child or young person to have their placement of choice. As children and young people grow and develop they gain information and understanding and their levels of influence may increase. Growing up is also about beginning to take more risks, seeing whether something will work, for example moving into a flat and putting support in place, whilst also preserving a safety net if it should fail:

There are some decisions that you can't make on your own. Like if you can't see your parents. You have to be sensible and learn to deal with that.
(quote from a child interviewed as part of the 'It's my turn to talk' project. NCB, 2004)

Young people will return and want to see their files later in their lives and they particularly want to be able to understand decisions that were made. Children can contribute to recording and not only sign key records but also add their comments. The national minimum standards for residential care (DoH 2002) encourage these positive practices.

Involving parents

Parents and children require information about the process of planning and decision making, as well as explanations of plans and reasons for decisions.

The same principles and practices for the child apply to the parents and those with parental responsibility. However, the child, as well as the social services department, should be able to express their views concerning the extent of the parents' involvement, if parental responsibility is shared.

Consultation with parents concerning the plan for their child is one of the basic principles of practice and of the Children Act 1989. Balancing the child's best interests and their wishes with the participation and involvement of their parents can often be a difficult exercise for all those who share parental responsibility.

Example

A child may want their parent to be present and involved in their reviews. It may not be safe to do this and a court may have decided that the child should have no contact with their parent. A reviewing officer may be able to make a bridge by seeing the child and the parent separately and holding the review in separate parts to enable all to participate.

Parents may have more or less involvement at different stages in a child's time in care.

Example

During care proceedings, when the level of conflict and emotions may be high, a parent may elect to communicate with the social worker only through the guardian or their solicitor. It will be important therefore that any care planning decision-making meetings involve the parent or their representative. After care proceedings, the parent may want to re-engage and work directly with the social worker, contributing to a plan to return the child or taking part in meetings, contributing information and materials concerning the child's history, to enable the child to move to a new family. It will be important that the social worker maintains contact throughout, irrespective of the parents' response, so that doors are kept open to enable such changes in levels of involvement and contribution.

Recording

Children and parents frequently complain that whilst they may have been consulted, they have not had decisions explained to them, particularly when these have not followed their expressed views and wishes:

> *You never get told what's going on anyway, never mind about what decisions are being made. So I think you know, they just do it anyway.*
> (quote from a child interviewed as part of the 'It's my turn to talk' project. NCB, 2004)

Reasons and plans are often contained in people's heads with records of these and their review taking too long to catch up. In the meantime this can mean that different workers and carers may be working to their understanding of the plan which may differ from that agreed at the review.

The principles of recording, irrespective of the documents and methods used, should include:

- An individual, clear, traceable record of assessment.
- Child and parents' views and wishes recorded as expressed.
- Collation and analysis of assessments and plans.
- A record of the discussion, decisions and the reasons for decisions.
- Transparency of decision making with all having access to these records whilst balancing this with individual confidentiality.
- Plans used as working documents.
- Records and decisions, notes of meetings written up within timescales and distributed to those who need them.
- Clarity concerning the processes of evaluation and review.
- Evidence of the managers' involvement, for example their agreement to the care plan.

Assessing need

Assessment is a dynamic and ongoing process.

The domains and dimensions of the Framework for the Assessment of Children in Need and their Families provide the potential for a holistic assessment.

A children's home or residential setting should both request a copy of the child's core assessment and should expect to contribute to its continuing development. As a placement develops the home will become the setting, which knows and understands the developmental needs of the

Figure 14.1 Assessment framework

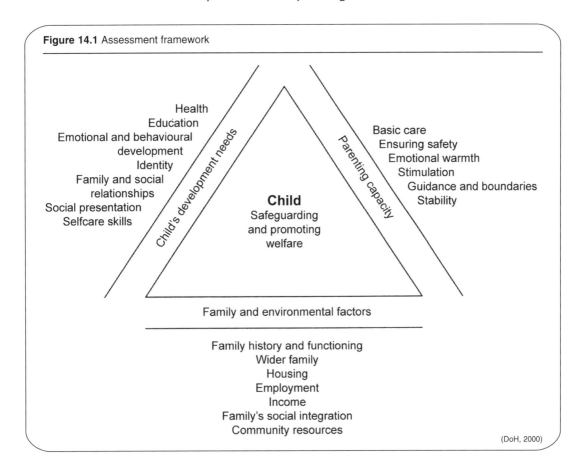

Health
Education
Emotional and behavioural
development
Identity
Family and social
relationships
Social presentation
Selfcare skills

Child's development needs

Parenting capacity

Basic care
Ensuring safety
Emotional warmth
Stimulation
Guidance and boundaries
Stability

Child
Safeguarding
and promoting
welfare

Family and environmental factors

Family history and functioning
Wider family
Housing
Employment
Income
Family's social integration
Community resources

(DoH, 2000)

child and can propose ways of meeting these needs inside and outside the home. Others, parents, social workers, may be in a better position to understand the parenting and family and environmental domains. The importance of combining and evaluating this information and knowledge within the assessment in order to evidence, explain and justify the care plan will be vital for all involved in delivering the plan, including the child and their parents.

A needs based approach is hard to achieve. Workers find themselves pushed too early into identifying services without having clearly articulated the need and outcomes the services should meet and achieve. There can be confusion over what is a need and what is a service, for example, needs might be described as:

Joseph needs to live somewhere where the boundaries and rules are very clear, where there are routines and the roles of staff and children are defined and are not confusing; where the expectations of his behaviour are defined and he is able to make relationships with children of his own age in a protected and safe environment.

Whilst:

Joseph needs a residential placement.

identifies a service.

Children can be very helpful in this process. They often find it easier to identify need than their workers who have been educated to think about services and social work jargon! Identifying need can be worrying for workers as they are concerned about raising expectations by identifying needs that can then not be met within the services or resources of their authority. However, the work can have the opposite effect, it may unlock skills and resources either within people or within the area, which have been untapped. Managers may be able to collate data concerning unmet need and commission services accordingly.

Whilst different agencies and people contribute to the assessment, one person, the social worker, should co-ordinate it and ensure that the child is not subjected to successive and repetitive assessments.

An example of a component of the education plan

Need: Sameera (age 9) needs to improve his reading
Assessed: as at level 2
Fit with care plan: will assist in meeting educational needs, attainment in all subject areas, developing self esteem, making friendships, inclusion at school, attachment to carer.
Outcomes: level 4 (KS 2) in reading by end of year 6, raised attainment levels in other subject areas, improved self esteem, friends, attachment to carer.
Services: extra tuition in reading twice a week, for half an hour each session; link with carer who will read to and with Sameera each evening; funded by SSD.
Evaluation and review: termly by carer, tutor and teacher reporting into the Personal

Education Plan process which will carry the authority to review services, relative to outcomes being achieved, reporting to the LAC review.

Some of this will be explicit and formal, some will involve checking out with Sameera where he thinks they have got to and feeding back, and looking back so that all can see the progress, for example:

Making sure that Sameera can see the progress he is making, which books he can now read that he could not read before, drawing Sameera's friendship network with him at the beginning and through the work, foster carer talking to Sameera about the relationship they have, what they talk about together, what they do together . . . Sameera boasting about what he can do!

Establishing desired outcomes

If needs are detailed, individual and specific then it is possible to set some achievable outcomes which relate to them. The child can say what their hopes are and what they want others to achieve for them or help them to achieve. The outcomes should be SMART:

- Specific
- Measurable
- Achievable
- Realistic
- Time-limited

Individual outcomes contribute to overall performance indicators and outcomes which a service or local authority must achieve to meet its set targets. Continuing the earlier example, outcomes for Joseph, might be:

> *He is clear about what happens in the home; he goes to bed and gets up at set times; he arrives at school on time; he knows what will happen if he misbehaves, breaks rules; he has made friends at school and in the community.*

Deciding on the care plan

The care plan should pull together and summarise the assessment – the detail of needs and outcomes – and ensure consistency between the parts and the whole.

It will indicate the overall aim of the plan for the child, for example, returning to their family or adoption. The plan may be for a further assessment in a residential setting or for the young person to live in a residential setting until they are ready to move to a more independent setting. Timescales should be given.

It must also consider the legal action necessary, if any, to support the plan.

The care plan details the specific services needed to meet the needs and desired outcomes.

It is vital that a named person is identified for each piece of work so that responsibilities are clear. Timings are important – children want to know how often they will see workers, they need to know what to expect of services, how long they will be receiving it and how and when it will be evaluated and reviewed.

Services for Joseph might include:

> *. . . placement in a children's home which only has planned admissions; high quality inspection reports, particularly to the standards which relate to behaviour and routines; an individual behaviour management plan which includes praise and reward and which all staff understand and follow; a timetable; a school place local to the home; able to invite friends to the home and can go to friends' homes.*

Placement plans

Whilst detail is important in the care plan, it is vital in placement plans. The latter should provide all the workers in the placement with detailed work plans for each individual child, to assist them in achieving the desired and specified outcomes. The plans must be reviewed regularly, within the review process so that progress is marked, acknowledged and rewarded for children and staff, and new outcomes set.

Managers of homes should also ensure that they have information systems for evaluating and assessing outcomes against needs to demonstrate delivery of services for the individual child as well as for the service as a whole.

Engaging the services

The work of engaging services must be led and co-ordinated by one person, usually the social worker. Children's homes may also need to commission extra services to meet the needs of the child and they are then responsible for managing the service and setting the timescales and desired outcomes. The services delivered may come from a number of different people or service providers.

Some authorities use panels to make decisions concerning the allocation of resources for children. These panels must be clear about their terms of reference. In particular, their objectives should be to:

- Share the responsibility for identifying and finding the right resources to meet the needs.
- Ensure that the views and wishes of the child, their family, those with parental responsibility are represented.
- Make the appropriate management decisions regarding the allocation of resources, regardless of which agency is providing them.

If identified needs remain unmet, particularly for resource reasons, panels should identify how the child or their family can appeal these decisions and ensure that their human rights are respected. Panels' relationship to the review process should be explicit, and reviews will need to be arranged if a care plan is significantly changed from that agreed as meeting the child's needs.

In order to assess whether services, particularly placement services, can meet the needs of a child it is helpful if each home's Statement of Purpose relates to the dimensions of children's developmental needs (DoH, 2000).

Reassessing, evaluating the plan

Assessment and evaluation of the plan and the work to achieve the plan all happen within a process of reviewing, a component of which may be a meeting or meetings. All the people working to the plan should be aware that their individual pieces of work relate to the child's whole care plan. Each person, including the child and their parents, has a responsibility to participate in assessing, to state what they want to achieve or be achieved, how they will contribute, evaluate, review and record. Each piece of work should have a clear focus.

How, where, in what meetings, care plans are decided should be clear to all participants in the planning process, for example, for children in care proceedings, the court decides upon the care plan but the social service department should be clear about the process for agreeing the plan it is putting to the court. Any process has to provide the child or young person and their family or those with parental responsibility with an opportunity to express their views and wishes as well as the people responsible for providing services.

Most of the work to evaluate the care plan which includes the health, education and pathway plans, should happen outside of the review meeting within the process of review. The care plan should be agreed at the review. The work of the review meeting should be kept to a minimum focusing on the care plan and the needs and views and wishes of the child. Children's participation in the meeting is enhanced if they have had a say in who attends, how they want the meeting conducted and if they are prepared:

> *If you are better prepared for the review then you'll come in confident, I mean we've heard about people just not being able to say what they can say. But if you're very well prepared for the review and you've got the confidence inside you, the chances are you'll have more of a successful review.*
> (from a child interviewed as part of the 'It's my turn to talk' project. NCB, 2004)

Collating management information concerning needs and services

All providers ranging from the small specialist provider to a large generic local authority, have a responsibility to analyse and collate information concerning met and unmet need. Reviewing the quality of services, evaluating services against outcomes, taking into account the views of consumers of the services, and inspection reports are all important processes for ensuring that services remain responsive to needs and improve the life chances of looked after children. This management information should be used to evaluate and review the Statements of Purpose for individual providers and contribute to development plans and the services commissioned by local authorities.

Children, young people, parents and carers are increasingly involved in these processes. Best practice includes giving them feedback concerning how their views have been taken into account following consultation events.

Role of the keyworker

The keyworker in a children's home or residential school is the person primarily responsible for leading the work with the child and carrying out individual one-to one work. They have the important role of holding on to the detail of the placement plan and keeping their eye on the overall care plan to ensure that each supports the other and that their objectives are compatible.

The skills of a keyworker are complex as they are managing a plan whilst working directly with the child to achieve it. They need to be able to step back and analyse and evaluate their own and others' work in the context of the information they are gaining from all who are working with the child. They are required to help the child to come to an informed view and sometimes represent this view whilst also stating what they believe to be in their best interests.

The keyworker has to be able to record this complexity, so that the child in the present, and in the future when they return to view their file, can understand decisions made and the reasons for them.

Conclusion

Good care planning is underpinned by a clear theoretical framework. Promoting the attachments of the child must be a central aim of all care plans. This chapter demonstrates both the importance and the complexity of high quality care planning. It relies on skilled workers with an understanding of the process, an ability to analyse the information gathered and to use theory and research to guide and evidence their assessments and plans.

The messages emerging from research emphasise the need for detail, clarity and

transparency in the systems of care planning. Children and parents should be involved through a careful consideration of their views and wishes together with a skilled needs based assessment, analysis and plan which sets individualised objectives and outcomes relevant to the situation and environment of the child. The resources required to implement the plan must be identified and available to meet agreed needs.

Residential care workers and managers should expect, ask for and contribute to clear care and placement plans to inform and to evidence the work they carry out with the child. This will enable them to provide new pathways and opportunities through a combination of the skills of staff, the personal relationships made and high quality provision.

Managers' responsibilities are to ensure that there are systems in place which support needs based assessment and planning and which collate met and unmet need to inform development plans and service commissioning. Staff development plans should support workers in their direct work with individual children.

Transparent decision-making systems, at individual and strategic levels, are essential for all involved in the planning process. Regular evaluation and review are key components of qualitative care planning and, whilst due process is important, it is equally important that time scales relate to the needs of the child and that valuable time is not lost through drift or focussing on the needs of others.

All the professional thoroughness and care in the world can be nullified if the child's emotional resources are over-taxed and the capacity to form healthy attachments is damaged.

(Lowe et al., 1999: 45)

References

Aldgate, J., Colton, M., Ghate, D. and Heath, A. (1992) Educational Attainment and Stability in Long-Term Foster Care. *Children & Society.* 6: 2, 91–103.

Bowlby, J. (1991) Postscript, in Murray-Parkes, C., Stevenson-Hinde, J. and Marris, P. (Eds.) *Attachment Across the Life Cycle.* London: Routledge.

DoH (2000) *Framework for the Assessment of Children in Need and their Families.* Norwich: The Stationery Office.

DoH (2001) *National Adoption Standards for England.* Norwich: The Stationery Office.

DoH (2002) *Children's Homes: National Minimum Standards and Children's Homes Regulations.* Norwich: The Stationery Office.

Garmezy, N. (1994) Reflections and Commentary on risk, resilience and development, in Haggerty, R.J., Sharrod, L.R., Garmezy, N. and Rutter, M. (Eds.) *Stress, Risk and Resilience in Children and Adolescents: Processes, Mechanisms and Interventions.* Cambridge University Press.

Gilligan, R. (2000) Promoting Resilience in Children in Foster Care, in Kelly, G. and Gilligan, R. (Eds.) *Issues in Foster Care: Policy, Practice and Research.* London: Jessica Kingsley.

Grimshaw, R. and Sinclair, R. (1997) *Planning to Care: Regulation, Procedure and Practice Under the Children Act 1989.* London: NCB.

Haggerty, R.J., Sharrod, L.R., Garmezy, N. and Rutter, M. (Eds.) (1994) *Stress, Risk and Resilience in Children and Adolescents: Processes, Mechanisms and Interventions.* Cambridge University Press.

Harwin, J. and Owen, M. (2002) A Study of Care Plans and Their Implementation and Relevance for *Re W and B and Re W (Care Plan)*, in Rt Hon Lord Justice Thorpe and Cowton, C. (Eds.) *Delight and Dole: The Children Act 10 years on.* Bristol: Jordan.

Howe, D. (1996) Attachment Theory in Child and Family Social Work, in Howe, D. (Ed.) *Attachment and Loss in Child and Family Social Work.* Ashgate: Aldershot.

Human Rights Act (1998) Norwich: The Stationery Office.

Jackson, S. and Martin, P.Y. (1998) Surviving the Care System: Education and Resilience. *Journal of Adolescence.* 21: 5, 569–83.

Jackson, S. and Thomas, N. (1999) *On the Move Again? What Works in Creating Stability for Looked After Children.* Ilford: Barnardo's.

Lowe, N. and Murch, M. (1999) *Supporting Adoption: Reframing the Approach.* London: BAAF.

Monck, E., Reynolds, J. and Wigfall, V. (2003) *The Role of Concurrent Planning: Making Permanent Placements for Young Children.* London: BAAF.

NCB (2004) *It's my Turn to Talk.* London: NCB.

Parker, R. (1999) *Adoption Now: Messages from Research.* Chichester: Wiley.

Rutter, M. (1991) A Fresh Look at Maternal Deprivation, in Bateson, P. (Ed.) *The Development and Integration of Behaviour.* Cambridge University Press.

Rutter, M. (1994) Stress Research: Accomplishments and Tasks Ahead, in Haggerty, R.J. et al. (Eds.) *Stress, Risk and Resilience in Children and Adolescents: Processes, Mechanisms and Interventions.* Cambridge University Press.

The Stationery Office (2002) *Adoption and Children Act 2002.* Norwich: The Stationery Office.

Thomas, N. (2000) *Children, Family and the State: Decision-making and Child Participation.* Basingstoke: MacMillan.

Ward, H. and Skuse, T. (2001) Performance Targets and Stability of Children Long Looked After Away from Home. *Children & Society.* 15, 333–46.

Part Five:
Improving the Educational Attainments of Looked After Children and Young People

Chapter Fifteen

Education and Residential Child Care in England: A Research Perspective

Isabelle Brodie

Introduction

Had this chapter been written a decade or more ago, the information available on this issue would have been sparse indeed. The question of the education of children looked after barely featured on the political radar, and was frequently absent from the majority of research concerning children living in public care. An exception to this was Jackson's (1987) seminal paper highlighting the generally low educational attainment of looked after children, and the role of the care system in creating and sustaining educational disadvantage amongst this group.

It is pleasing to write this chapter at a very different time, when the education of children looked after is an issue that is prominent in both policy and practice discussions. At a political level, concern about the issue has most recently been demonstrated by the publication of a report by the Social Exclusion Unit (SEU, 2003). There is also extensive evidence of a range of initiatives within local authorities throughout England which aim to improve educational outcomes for children looked after (SEU, 2003; Who Cares? Trust, 2001; DoH, 2003).

While these signs are extremely encouraging, it would be a mistake to view this as a problem that has essentially been 'solved'. There continues to be a significant gap between the educational performance of looked after and non-looked after children, and evidence continues to emerge of the poverty of educational experience that is the lot of many children and young people living in residential care. It is therefore important to review where change has occurred and where there is evidence of good practice.

This chapter begins by considering the background to the issue, and changes to the policy context that have taken place under New Labour. The discussion then turns to evidence of change, first in measurable outcomes for looked after children and then in relation to practice more generally.

The education of looked after children: background

During the 1970s and 1980s a trickle of research evidence pointed to the low educational achievement of children living in residential and foster care in comparison to their peers. Jackson (1987) presented a much more detailed case, describing not only the low educational attainment of children looked after but also the low expectations and lack of attention given to schooling by social workers, carers and other professionals.

There is little doubt that Jackson's conclusions struck a chord with practitioners and others, and educational issues began to feature more frequently in policy and research debates. Thus, for example, in 1995, a joint report from the Social Services Inspectorate and the Office for Standards in Education found that only a third of the 60 secondary-age looked after children whose cases they examined achieved satisfactory standards in terms of age and ability, and none were judged by their teachers as likely to achieve five subjects grade A–C at GCSE.

In explaining such outcomes two issues have been identified. Firstly, research has consistently found that children looked after come from very poor and disadvantaged backgrounds (see, for example, Bebbington and Miles, 1989). The majority of children living in residential care will have experienced family disruption, abuse or neglect of different kinds and emotional difficulties (DoH, 1998). These experiences and their possible effects need to be taken seriously, especially given a much wider body of evidence indicating the relationship between social and educational disadvantage more generally.

Secondly, the failure of the care system to promote education has been highlighted. Research into care leavers (Biehal et al., 1992) also demonstrated the almost total absence of care leavers achieving school qualifications. Qualitative findings highlighted the poor educational environment of many residential establishments and the fact that a disproportionate number of looked after children were excluded from or not attending school (Berridge and Brodie, 1998). Education was frequently given a low priority by field social workers and carers and, consequently, planning for education was often poor. Young people experienced a high number of placement moves, often accompanied by change of school, with negative effects on learning and on young people's opportunities to sit exams successfully (Fletcher-Campbell and Hall, 1990; Fletcher-Campbell, 1998).

At the same time education policy under the Conservative government during the 1980s and 1990s was viewed as unhelpful in promoting the educational welfare of looked after children. Indeed, Jackson's (1987) paper was singularly timely, appearing a year before the Conservative governments Education Reform Act in 1988. The provisions of this were subsequently seen to have had serious implications for the educational welfare of children looked after. The introduction of parental choice, based in part on published league tables, resulted in schools 'competing' for pupils, and a growing division between schools that were 'over-subscribed' and those who struggled to attract pupils. Children viewed as less desirable pupils, either on account of behavioural or other educational issues, appeared to be marginalised and even at increased risk of exclusion (Parffrey, 1994; Parsons et al., 1994). Children living in public care were frequently considered part of this category.

The improved evidence base regarding the education of looked after children provided an important foundation for policy change under New Labour. The next section describes what these changes have involved.

A change in policy direction

It is possible to identify three linked areas of policy change under Labour that have had the potential to improve educational outcomes for looked after children living in residential care. These are as follows:

Firstly, the education of looked after children has been given priority as a political issue. At national level this has been evident in the recognition of looked after children as a group that have experienced educational disadvantage. In fact, spurred by a cross-parliamentary report

on children in care (House of Commons Health Committee, 1998) this was evident from an early stage in New Labour's policy programme; for example, the first report from the Social Exclusion Unit (1998) focusing on truancy and school exclusion, identified children looked after as a group at particular risk. The development of the *Quality Protects* programme during 1997-98 and described in greater detail below, similarly highlighted the issue (DoH, 1998b).

This profile has been maintained: speaking at the launch of new guidance on the education of young people in public care, Schools Minister Jacqui Smith stated that:

Children in public care are at the heart of the Government's drive to raise educational standards for all children and tackle social exclusion, and their education is one of our greatest challenges ... it is clearly unacceptable that only about 1 in 4 children leaves care with qualifications.

(DfES, 2001)

More recently, the change in policy direction has been evident in a further Social Exclusion Unit report in 2003 and, at the time of writing, the introduction of the Children Act 2004 section 52 amendment to the Children Act 1989, placing a duty on local authorities to promote the educational attainment of children looked after. While contradictions between this and other areas of policy should not be ignored, the attention given to the issue – and the resources that have resulted from this – have represented a welcome investment in the looked after group.

At local level, greater emphasis has been given to the role of elected members in monitoring local authority progress concerning the education of looked after children. This shift can also be traced to central government, specifically a letter to councillors from the Secretary of State for Health in 1998, drawing their attention to this issue, outlining their responsibilities and listing a series of questions that they should use to guide their monitoring of local authorities' work in this area (see reproduction of this letter in DfEE/DoH, 2000). An important consequence of this has also been that, not only is more activity directed at the education of looked after children, but this is more strategically directed. Whereas in the past one or two measures might have been in place, decision making concerning the education of looked after children now tends to take place at a higher level of management and has a generally higher priority in policy making.

Secondly, links have been made between the educational experiences of looked after children and other aspects of the educational system. The overall drive to improve standards and address problems of disaffection can be seen as relevant to the looked after population. Policy relating to young people with special needs has also been important. The 1997 Green Paper on Special Educational Needs was a significant turning point in this respect, in emphasising the importance of 'inclusion' as an idea to underpin work with children who presented special educational needs. While many young people would experience difficulties during the course of their school careers, these need not be permanent and that support could be offered without resort to segregation and exclusion. It also highlighted the need for early intervention and improved co-ordination between education, health and social services in meeting children's special educational needs. Such messages were reflected in other legislation and guidance, such as that relating to pupils with behavioural problems who were at risk of non-attendance and exclusion. The *Social Exclusion: Pupil Support guidance* (DfES, 2001) again stressed the need for early intervention and preventative action, including thorough planning that set strategies for dealing with problems and contained clear targets and timescales for action.

Thirdly, specific initiatives have been introduced that are designed to improve the education of looked after children and young people. Three of these are described below: the child care initiative *Quality Protects*, guidance on the education of looked after children and legislation for care leavers.

Quality Protects

The Quality Protects initiative involved an investment by government of £375 million with the intention of 'transforming the management of delivery of children's social services' (DoH, 1999: 10) and in turn to improve their effectiveness. Ring-fenced funding for the initiative ends in 2004, but the thinking behind the programme has been important in local attempts to improve the education of looked after children.

The initiative was organised under 11 objectives, each of which was linked to a series of sub-objectives and performance indicators. To some extent all of these objectives could be seen as relevant to improving the educational

experience and attainments of looked after children, in the light of the evidence already discussed – for example, objectives covered areas including stability, improvement of the educational attainment of children in need, and the participation of children in the planning, delivery and review of services. Local councils were required to submit annual management action plans explaining how they intended to achieve targets, and reviewing progress made.

The specific objective relating to the education of looked after children was:

> . . . *to ensure that children looked after gain maximum life chance benefits from educational opportunities, health care and social care.*

with the sub-objective:

> . . . *to bring the overall performance of children looked after, for a year or more, in National Curriculum tests closer into line with local children.*

The more familiar target associated with this was to 'Improve the educational attainment of children looked after, by increasing to at least 50 per cent by 2001 the proportion of children leaving care at 16 with a GCSE or GNVQ qualification; and to 75 per cent by 2003'. As with most targets, this was controversial, and the programme has been more generally criticised for its emphasis on targets as against process. More specifically, it was argued that the target reinforced low expectations regarding the educational abilities of children looked after. Others felt that the focus on academic achievement was too narrow and failed to take account of talents that might be expressed in other ways.

Guidance on the Education of Young People in Public Care (DfEE and DoH, 2000)

This was the first detailed guidance to be issued regarding the education of looked after children, and has been given a high profile. Its implementation was also supported at regional level by the 'Education Protects' programme – networks which were intended to help disseminate good practice and help progress implementation of the guidance. The guidance seeks to address many of the difficulties identified above, emphasising the need to improve stability of both care and school placements and the importance of inter-professional collaboration. Underpinning this is the view that education is essential to a young person's life chances, and that this is one of the most important ways in which corporate parents can support a child. Other key elements of the guidance are:

- Each school must have a designated teacher with special responsibility for children looked after.
- Education should be a primary consideration when changes to care placements are being planned.
- There is a statutory requirement that each child should have a Personal Education Plan (PEP) through which planning and review of their educational progress takes place.
- There is a time limit of 20 school days within which children in care who change school must be found an education placement.
- There should be an expectation that children will attend school and efforts made to support their achievement, for example by assisting with homework and study support. High expectations should be clearly communicated and achievement celebrated and rewarded.

The Leaving Care Act 2000

Research has consistently pointed to the fact that few care leavers progress to further or higher education and that employment outcomes are typically poor. Only 12–19 per cent of looked after children go on immediately to further education compared with 68 per cent of the general population (DfEE/DoH, 2000) and only one in 100 looked after children reach university compared to one in three of all pupils (Jackson and Sachdev, 2001).

The Leaving Care Act 2000 aims to improve both planning and provision in this area. All young people covered by the Act must have a Pathway Plan that replaces other forms of care planning and is in place until the young person is at least 21. A personal advisor should assist the young person in drawing up the plan, which should cover education, training, career plans and the support that is required in this. The Act also introduces a statutory requirement that social services departments encourage young people to remain in further and higher education, and provide financial assistance for this up until the end of the course or programme being followed by the young person.

What has changed?: educational outcomes

These policy changes have not been rewarded by immediate changes in educational outcomes for looked after children – though improvements in recording and data collection at least mean that it is possible to measure this with greater confidence than in the past.

Statistics (DoH, 2003) for 2001/2002, indicate that looked after children continue to underperform in comparison with their peers. In school year 11, 53 per cent of looked after children obtained at least one GCSE or GNVQ compared to 95 per cent of all school children. Only 8 per cent of looked after children obtained at least five GCSEs at grades A*–C, compared with 50 per cent of all children. There are also significant gaps in test results at other stages of schooling.

Examination of rates of special educational needs and exclusion and attendance rates yields similar inequalities. Twenty-seven per cent of looked after children had statements of special educational needs compared to three per cent in the general school population, while one per cent of looked after children had been permanently excluded, compared to a national rate of 0.1 per cent. Twelve per cent of looked after children missed more that 25 days of school in 2001/2002 (comparable figures on attendance are not collected for all children by the DfES).

In the light of this information, a new government target for the education of looked after children has been set, namely to improve life changes for children, to 'narrow the gap in educational achievement between looked after children and their peers, and improve their educational support and the stability of their lives, so that by 2008, 80 per cent of children under 16 who have been looked after for 2.5 or more years will have been living in the same placement for at least two years, or are placed for adoption'. The view that there is a strong link between placement stability and educational progress is therefore explicitly made, and is further reflected in the indicators through which local authorities will measure performance, namely:

- The percentage of children aged 11, looked after for at least 12 months, who obtain level 4 in Key Stage 2 English and Maths.
- The percentage of young people, looked after for at least 12 months, who reach school

leaving age without having sat at GCSE equivalent exam.

- The percentage of young people, looked after for at least 12 months, and in Year 11, who achieve 5 or more GCSEs graded A*–C or equivalent.
- Participation of care leavers aged 19 in education, employment and training.

There is therefore greater acknowledgement of the fact that the care system is not the only influence on a child's education, and should not be assessed on the experience of children and young people looked after for only short periods of time. As noted previously, the Children Act 2004 places a new duty on local authorities to promote the education of looked after children. New guidance on the education of looked after children will be issued in mid-2005.

Changes in practice

The difficulties encountered in achieving a significant shift in the educational outcomes for looked after children might beg the question of why change is so difficult. In answering this it is important to return to the explanations that have been offered for looked after children's under-achievement more generally. The first of these relates to the complex set of circumstances which lead young people into residential care in the first place. Relationship difficulties at home and abuse and neglect feature strongly in the backgrounds of a high proportion of those living in residential accommodation. Many will bring pre-existing behavioural and educational problems to a placement. Research continues to highlight the fact that the residential group continue to present a greater combination of problems than their peers in foster care (DoH, 1998; Berridge et al., 2002).

As discussed earlier, the care system has often been at fault in failing to prioritise education and creating environments in which children can progress at school. However, in view of the prior experiences of young people, it is also essential that the care and education systems are able to provide support that helps *compensate* for earlier disadvantage (Heath, Colton and Aldgate, 1994). This means that efforts need to be made that are over and above what is offered to children more generally. This is clearly a major challenge, given that the care system has often struggled to provide what might be considered 'normal' parenting.

Certain features of the care system continue to make this difficult. For example, despite efforts under the *Quality Protects* initiative, placement change continues to be a significant feature of the lives of many looked after children. Department of Health (2002) statistics indicate that the number of children having three or more placement moves fell from 19 per cent in 1999/2000 to 15 per cent in 2001/2002. The Social Exclusion Unit (2003) suggests that 52 per cent of looked after children experience one or more changes of school as a result of placement moves. Young people living in residential accommodation appear to be especially vulnerable to placement change. Berridge et al. (2002) found that despite being separated from their families at a later age than those in foster care, young people in residential accommodation experienced a greater number of moves. Placement change also presents challenges for residential staff, as they seek to manage the dynamics of a changing resident group.

It would be a mistake, however, to view the lack of dramatic change in measurable outcomes as an indication that no activity has been taking place at local level. The final review of management action plans (DoH, 2003) noted that, while councils have not reached the attainment targets set out by *Quality Protects*, more councils are achieving improved educational results, and fewer have very poor educational results. Councils identify a range of measures which appear significant in making improvements, including support and training for carers, consistent planning and review in relation to education, practical support services such as homework clubs and access to IT, and prioritisation of looked after children in school admissions policies. Implementation and monitoring of the measures of the new guidance is also considered central.

There is also evidence in terms of practice that some change has taken place, and the following sections examine this in greater detail.

Residential staff and education

An overall concern has been the priority given to education by carers within residential settings, especially in the light of the relatively low levels of qualifications within the residential sector generally. More specifically, research has found a lack of clarity amongst residential staff concerning their roles and responsibilities in regard to educational issues (Brodie, 2001), often linked to feelings of powerlessness in the face of difficulties in finding young people a school place or getting those young people out-of-school back into education.

Certainly the contribution of residential staff to the educational welfare of young people should not be underestimated. One study (Harker et al., 2004) found that young people feel that encouragement from carers – residential and foster – is the most important factor in enabling them to progress educationally. Research also continues to show that, generally, relationships between young people and residential carers are positive and valued, thereby placing residential social workers in a strong position to provide educational support for residents (Hicks et al., 2003).

However, support for carers will be less effective without input from other professionals, especially where young people are experiencing difficulties with their education. While there is a lack of detailed evidence on this issue, anecdotal information and some research data indicates that children's homes are developing better links with other professionals who can provide information or work directly with young people in regard to their education. In an exploratory study of services for adolescents living away from home, Berridge et al. (2002) found that children's homes increasingly have access to teachers and other education staff who are employed with specific responsibilities for looked after children. These links were valued by residential managers and staff, and were considered particularly beneficial in terms of finding educational placements or developing alternative programmes of work for children out-of-school. This latter point is important, especially in the light of a recent survey of residential staff which found many still frustrated by the patchy nature of provision for children not attending school (Mainey, 2003).

It is important to link the experiences of residential staff in relation to education with the provision of care much more broadly. Research has generally shown quality of care to be uneven, and there are many differences between residential units in their response to schooling and education. Progress in relation to educational issues is likely to take place in a context where the overall quality of care is good. High quality of care is associated with clarity of objectives and methods (Berridge and Brodie, 1998; Sinclair and

Gibbs, 1998; Hicks et al., 2003). Where managers have well-developed strategies for dealing with behavioural and educational issues, staff are likely to feel more confident in dealing with these matters. In turn, clarity of procedures in dealing with problems such as school exclusion mean that these difficulties are more likely to be avoided in the first place, and cultures of non-attendance not permitted to develop. At the same time, attention needs to be given to the qualitative perceptions of residential staff in terms of what they understand to be good quality care. As Watson (2003) points out, residential social workers have frequently been detached from wider debates about this. In the context of this paper, it is essential that there is scope for discussion and training regarding educational issues, and the role of education – in its broadest sense – in promoting the welfare of young people.

Support for learning

These messages also have a bearing on the extent to which the residential environment supports young people educationally. Jackson (1989) highlighted the absence of basic facilities, such as a desk and quiet space for homework, in many residential units while Berridge and Brodie (1998) found that many homes, especially those catering for adolescents were 'frankly dull places in which to live' with few books, newspapers or games and no computers.

Emerging evidence suggests that some progress has been made in this area. Money from the *Quality Protects* initiative has been especially important in this regard, providing many homes with books, computers and other resources (Berridge et al., 2002). In some local authorities additional funding has been available to support such developments, for example providing IT support for children's homes and developing links with local libraries (Harker et. al., 2004).

The issue of a supportive educational environment is especially important in view of the numbers of young people living in residential care who do not attend school. There is some evidence that a greater number of options are available for this group, in terms of special projects that provide alternative educational activities. Some authorities have also employed additional 'link teachers' for looked after children who will provide additional support should a young person be out of school, and also help to enable re-integration when a school place becomes available. It is important, however, that local authorities are clear on the amount and quality of education a young person is receiving, and that alternative arrangements for schooling are regularly reviewed through planning processes.

Recognising achievement

Measures of academic success are, of course, only one way of understanding achievement, and the importance of developing abilities in out-of-school activities should not be underestimated. Gilligan (2000) emphasises the need to enable young people to develop a wide range of interests in order to develop their overall resilience. Jackson and Martin (1998), in their study of care leavers who had achieved highly at school, found that involvement in extra-curricular activities and hobbies was an important element in young people's academic success.

Children's homes have been criticised for their relative isolation from community activities (Berridge and Brodie, 1998). Research into adolescents excluded from school and living in residential accommodation found that they tended to lack occupation and were therefore more vulnerable to getting into trouble (Brodie, 2001). Recording of information about children and young people has often focused on problems rather than the individual's strengths and achievements.

These issues are difficult to measure, but there are some research findings that cast some light on this area. The Social Exclusion Unit (2003) found that three-quarters of children and young people questioned in their survey had access to after-school activities and clubs, and about two-thirds of those – about half of all respondents – used them. However, those in foster care were more likely to have access to these activities than those living in residential care or with their families. Other research (Berridge et al., 2002) found that there was an increased awareness and recording of achievements in other spheres in files and in discussions with residential carers. A number of local authorities have taken the issue of recognising achievement further, by introducing award ceremonies for looked after children. Evaluation of these indicates that such events are greatly appreciated by young people, and indeed make a difference to the way in which they feel about themselves (Harker et al., 2004).

This finding is an important one, suggesting that the development of children's strengths is central to direct work in a residential context.

Inter-professional working

Previous research has highlighted a range of difficulties connected with inter-professional working, especially that between education and social services. These problems have included:

● A lack of understanding of the respective roles of social workers, carers and teachers in respect to the education of looked after children.
● A lack of specialist input, and a lack of understanding of what this could offer. Thus, for example, social workers might believe that a child needed an educational psychologist without any clear idea of what this would achieve.
● On the part of some professionals, stigmatising of looked after children – for example, the belief that children living in children's homes had committed a crime of some sort.
● The absence of a strategic approach to the education of looked after children at managerial level.
● Poor collection and sharing of key information about the education of children looked after – for example, the educational placements of children who had been permanently excluded from school.

Encouragingly, research evidence suggests that some progress has been made in this area of work, though there are differences in the amount of work that has taken place in different local authorities. One recent report (OFSTED, 2004) comments that inter-professional working in relation to looked after children who are not attending school tends to be more effective than that for children out of school more generally. Overall it seems that new guidance has had some effect and considerable efforts have been made in terms of developing policies at local level. These have been aided by structural changes such as the merging of social services and education departments in some areas. These developments are likely to be advanced further in the light of the recent Green Paper on children's services. More contentious is the matter of information sharing. The development of databases and other systems that permit the exchange of information continues to be problematic, not least in the light of concerns about the ethics and indeed legality of such sharing (Harker et al., 2004; Fletcher-Campbell, Archer and Tomlinson, 2003).

The challenge continues to lie in ensuring that inter-professional working takes place at all levels of policy and practice. This is especially difficult in regard to field social workers, in that staff shortages and local authority reorganisation frequently mean that good practice in working with other professionals does not have time to develop. On the other hand, research into the role of schools in supporting the education of children in public care suggests that schools have taken seriously their new responsibilities in relation to this group, and go to 'considerable lengths' to ease transitions for those changing schools and in monitoring support needs. Designated teachers play a key role in working with other professionals and carers, advocating for young people and maintaining an overview of young people's progress (Fletcher-Campbell, Archer and Tomlinson, 2003). As noted earlier, children's homes staff also appear to have access to a broader range of professionals.

Conclusion

This chapter has argued that, although far from uniform or complete, progress has been made in respect to the education of looked after children living in residential accommodation. Research has played an important role in this. During the 1990s the focus was primarily on providing evidence of the nature of the problem; more recently growing attention has been given to monitoring change. Some work has taken place on evaluating the effectiveness of interventions, though there is scope for much more work in this area. It is also important to remember that significant gaps remain in our understanding of the educational issues affecting children and young people living in residential settings. Information about the educational experiences of young people looked after in out-of-authority placements, for example, continues to be sparse, as does understanding of ways in which questions of gender and ethnicity interact with the care experience. It also continues to be important that links are made between what we know about the education of looked after children and other research into schools and the education of children more generally.

However, it is also important that efforts are made to build on the positive messages that exist about good practice in regard to the education of

looked after children living in residential accommodation. Above all, perhaps, it is essential that greater consistency is achieved across the residential sector in terms of practice in this area. Without this, young people living in residential care will not be guaranteed the standard of care and support they deserve.

References

Bebbington, A. and Miles, J. (1989) The Background of Children who Enter Local Authority Care. *British Journal of Social Work.* 19, 349–68.

Berridge, D. and Brodie, I. (1998) *Children's Homes Revisited.* London: Jessica Kingsley.

Berridge, D., Beecham, J., Brodie, I., Cole, T., Daniels, H., Knapp, M. and MacNeill, V. (2002) *Costs and Consequences of Services for Troubled Adolescents: Report to the Department of Health.* Luton: University of Luton.

Biehal, N., Clayden, J., Stein, M. and Wade, J. (1992) *Prepared for Living? A Survey of Young People Leaving the Care of Three Local Authorities.* London: NCB.

Brodie, I. (2001) *Children's Homes and School Exclusion: Redefining the Problem.* London: Jessica Kingsley.

DfEE/DoH (2000) *Guidance on the Education of Young People in Public Care.* London: HMSO.

DfES (2001) *Press Notice 2001/0194.* London: DfES.

DfES (2001) *Social Exclusion: Pupil Support.* London: DfES.

DoH (1998) *Caring for Children Living Away from Home.* Chichester: Wiley.

DoH (1998b) *The Quality Protects Programme: Transforming Children's Services.* London: DoH.

DoH (1999) *The Government's Objectives for Children's Social Services.* London: DoH.

DoH (2002) *Social Services Performance Assessment Framework Indicators 2001/2002.* London: DoH.

DoH (2003) *Transforming Children's Services: An Evaluation of Local Responses to the Quality Protects Programme, Year 4.* London: DoH.

Fletcher-Campbell, F. and Hall, C. (1990) *Changing Schools? Changing People? The Education of Children in Care.* Slough: National Foundation for Educational Research.

Fletcher-Campbell, F. (1998) Progress or Procrastination? The Education of Children Who Are Looked After. *Children and Society.* 12, 3–11.

Fletcher-Campbell, F., Archer, T. and Tomlinson, K. (2003) *The Role of the School In Supporting the*

Education of Children in Public Care. RB498. London: DfES.

Gilligan, R. (1998) The Importance of Schools and Teachers in Child Welfare. *Child and Family Social Work.* 3, 13–25.

Harker, R., Dobel-Ober, D., Berridge, D. and Sinclair, R. (2004) *Taking Care of Education.* London: NCB.

Heath, A., Colton, M. and Aldgate, J. (1994) Failure to Escape: A Longitudinal Study of Foster Children's Educational Attainment. *British Journal of Social Work.* 24, 241–60.

Hicks, L., Gibbs, I., Byford, S. and Weatherly, H. (2003) *Leadership and Resources in Children's Homes.* London: DoH.

House of Commons Health Committee (1998) *Children Looked After By Local Authorities. Volume 1: Report and Proceedings of the Committee.* London: The Stationery Office.

Jackson, S. (1987) *The Education of Children in Care.* University of Bristol, School of Applied Social Studies.

Jackson, S. (1998) *High Achievers: A Study of Young People Who Have Been in Residential or Foster Care. Final Report to the Leverhulme Trust.* Swansea: University of Wales.

Jackson, S. (1989) Residential Care and Education. *Children and Society.* 2: 4, 335–40.

Jackson, S., and Martin, P.Y. (1998) Surviving the Care System: Education and Resilience. *Journal of Adolescence.* 21, 569–83.

Jackson, S. and Sachdev, D. (2001) *Better Education, Better Futures.* London: Barnardo's.

Mainey, A. (2003) *Better than you think: staff morale, qualifications and retention in residential child care.* London: National Children's Bureau.

OFSTED (2004) *Out of School: A survey of the Educational Support and Provision for Pupils Not in School.* London: OFSTED.

Parffrey, V. (1994) Exclusion: failed Children or Systems Failure? *School Organisation.* 14: 2, 107–20.

Parsons, C. with Benns, L., Hailes, J. and Howlett, K. (1994) *Excluding Primary School Children.* London: Family Policy Studies Centre.

Sinclair, I. and Gibbs, I. (1998) *Children's Homes: A Study in Diversity.* Chichester: Wiley.

Social Exclusion Unit (2003) *A Better Education for Children in Care.* London: Social Exclusion Unit.

Social Exclusion Unit (1998) *Truancy and School Exclusion: Report by the Social Exclusion Unit.* Cm 3957. London: The Stationery Office.

Watson, D. (2003) Defining Quality Care for Looked After Children: Frontline Workers Perspectives on Standards and All That? *Children and Family Social Work.* 8: 1, 67–77.

Who Cares? Trust (2001) *Right to Read.* London: Who Cares? Trust.

Chapter Sixteen

Still Room for Improvement? The Educational Experiences of Looked After Children in Scotland

Kirstie Maclean and Graham Connelly

Introduction and background

Concern about the educational experiences and outcomes of looked after children has gathered momentum over the last 10–15 years. Whilst there had been awareness in Scotland of the relevant research and inspection findings elsewhere in the UK, there was a tendency to think we might be different – perhaps our looked after children were better served by an educational system widely considered to be in good shape. In 1998, the then Scottish Office commissioned a review of research, policy and practice in the education of looked after children (Borland et al., 1998). While the review found that research findings in Scotland were sparse and supplemented them with findings from England and Wales, the authors concluded that there was no room for complacency. There was considerable evidence that being looked after away from home in Scotland constituted an educational hazard, thus adding to the disadvantage entailed in removal from home.

As a result of the review, ministers decided that there should be an inspection in Scotland of the educational experiences of children looked after away from home, conducted jointly by the Social Work Services Inspectorate (SWSI) and HM Inspectorate of Education (HMIE). Two of the authors of the resulting report, *Learning with Care* (HMI and SWSI, 2001), found there was: 'room both for improvement and for cautious optimism' (Maclean and Gunion, 2003)

In a number of areas the findings of the inspection came as no surprise:

- Care and placement planning were often not in evidence and, even where they were, education was rarely addressed in sufficient detail. Social workers and carers were often vague and over optimistic about children's attainments. There had previously been very similar findings in England and Wales (Jackson, 1989; Fletcher-Campbell and Hall, 1990; Aldgate et al., 1993; OFSTED/SSI, 1995; Skuse and Evans, 2001).

- There were high levels of exclusion. Twenty one out of 50 children in the inspection sample had been excluded at least once and some had been excluded many times or for lengthy periods. During the course of the inspection the statistic that looked after children in Scotland – one per cent of the school population – accounted for 13 per cent of exclusions had been published (Scottish Executive, 2000). Other Scottish research found a similar or even gloomier picture (Maginnis, 1993; Dixon and Stein, 2002).

- Slightly more than half of the 25 primary age children in the sample were under-achieving in the 5–14 curriculum in comparison with their peers. About one fifth were attaining one level below and about one third were attaining two or more levels below. Whilst most research into attainments has concerned young people undertaking qualifications, at least two previous studies have found significant underperformance by younger looked after children (Essen et al., 1976; Aldgate et al., 1993).

- Children and young people were, sometimes with good reason, concerned about how confidential information would be used by teachers. This had also been a finding in the OFSTED/SSI (1995) inspection and in English and Scottish research (Berridge et al., 1996; Gallagher, 1996).

- Hardly any social workers, carers or teachers had received training, either in their qualifying courses or since, concerning the education of looked after children.

- There was a lack of recognition of the positive role parents could play in the education of their looked after children and most felt excluded from this aspect of their child's care. This has also been a finding in England and Wales (OFSTED/SSI, 1995; Martin and Jackson, 2002).

- Local authorities were unlikely to have specific policies on the education of looked after children or to collect relevant data about their attainments. Whilst some progress has been made in England and Wales: 'the majority of recorded information cannot be used to assess the progress of individual children' (OFSTED, 2001: 7).

In other areas, however, findings in the inspection were more promising than previous research findings:

- Attendance, availability of school places and continuity of education, for instance by using taxis over substantial distances in rural areas to retain children at their original schools, were better than could have been anticipated from previous English and Scottish research (Maginnis, 1993; Kendrick, 1995; OFSTED/SSI 1995; Lockhart et al., 1996; Borland et al., 1998; Dixon and Stein, 2002)

- Three-quarters (19 out of 25) of the sample young people in secondary school gained at least the national target for looked after young people of two Standard Grades. However, only eight out of 25 obtained the national average of seven Standard Grades and only three achieved the national average of three awards at 'credit' level. These results were considerably better than could have been anticipated from research findings (Stein and Carey, 1986; Biehal et al., 1992; Garnett, 1992) However, the sample was small and subsequent research and statistics (see below) have not found such a positive picture.

- There was no indication in the inspection that bullying concerning their looked after status was an issue for any of the children and young people. This was in contrast to other research studies both from Scotland and England (Fletcher, 1993; Berridge et al., 1996; Dixon and Stein, 2002).

- The sample children all had good access to extra-curricular activities, some provided by carers and some by schools. There were good examples, particularly in rural areas, of children being introduced to a wide range of musical, sporting and cultural activities. One primary age boy played in football and shinty teams, attended four different youth clubs, was learning the chanter (bagpipes), had given a Gaelic recitation at the Mod (a cultural festival held annually in Scotland) and still found time to read for pleasure.

- Strong educational support was provided by all the foster and relative carers and they generally engaged very positively with the children's schools, although some of them, particularly the relative carers, needed more information and practical help from the social work departments in order to do this. However, the educational needs of the children in the sample made it unlikely that carers' undoubted commitment, on its own, would be sufficient to help the children overcome their educational difficulties. The educational support provided in residential units was more variable than in foster homes. Some provided educationally rich environments with considerable emphasis placed on valuing education and study support but others were providing educationally poor environments. Whilst this was a mixed picture, it was somewhat better than had been anticipated from previous inspection and research (OFSTED/SSI, 1995; Berridge et al., 1996).

- Working relationships between senior managers in education and social work appeared close – this was often contrasted with a more negative picture from a few years previously when, as one manager described it: 'we never actually met but would fight about money or placements'. A more negative picture would have been anticipated from research (Kendrick et al., 1996; Fletcher-Campbell, 1997).

What do we know about attainments?

Statistical data concerning the educational attainments of looked after children in Scotland was published for the first time in 2002 (Scottish Executive, 2002a) Not all local authorities were able to make a return and only 'headline' figures were published. Of 16 and 17 year old care leavers in 2001–2002, six out of ten did not achieve any qualifications. Only 27 per cent achieved the Scottish Executive target of both English and maths at Standard Grade.

The 2003 statistics (Scottish Executive, 2003a) were considerably more detailed but showed little if any improvement. However, whilst only 41 per cent of looked after young people achieved any qualifications as opposed to 92 per cent of young people in the general population who achieved 5+ Standard Grade awards at level 3 or above, 50 per cent of young people looked after away from home achieved qualifications as opposed to only 30 per cent of those on home supervision requirements. The Scottish Credit and Qualifications Framework (see www.scqf.org.uk) is a system of attainment from Access 1 (level 1) to doctorate (level 12) Standard Grade

Table 16.1 Comparison of S4 general population attainments and the attainments of 16 and 17 year old looked after young people for 2002–2003, in local authorities with 50 or more 16 and 17 year old looked after school leavers

Local authority	General population 5+ awards at level 3 or higher (%)	Position out of 32 local authorities	Looked after young people some qualifications (%)	Position out of 29 local authorities (data were not available for 3 authorities)	Looked after children in residential care (%)
Aberdeen	91	19	76	4	14
Dundee	82	32	28	24	14
Edinburgh	88	27	44	14	15
Glasgow	85	30	39	19	13
Inverclyde	95	4	21	27	17
North Lanarkshire	92	13	20	28	14
Renfrewshire	93	8	43	16	18
West Lothian	92	13	27	25	10

courses (roughly equivalent to GCSE) taken by 14–16 year olds lead to awards at three levels: foundation (level 3), general (level 4) and credit (level 5). Likewise, 35 per cent of young people looked after away from home achieved the target of English and maths Standard Grades, whereas only 19 per cent of those looked after at home did. Although further research is needed, this difference may indicate that care away from home does help young people recover, at least to some extent, from educational disadvantage.

A further interesting finding is that although there is some disparity between authorities in Scotland in the proportions of young people in the general population who achieved qualifications, ranging from 82–97 per cent who achieved 5+ awards at level 3 or above in 2002–03 (Scottish Executive, 2003a), there is enormous disparity between authorities' looked after children's attainments – 18–100 per cent achieved some qualifications (Scottish Executive, 2003b). There does not appear to be any correlation between authorities whose general population of young people do well and those whose looked after young people do well. Some of this disparity can probably be explained by the fact that many authorities have very small numbers of 16 and 17 year old care leavers and, therefore, results are likely to fluctuate year on year. However, if results from local authorities that have at least 50 16–17 year old care leavers are taken, the disparity still remains stark.

Table 16.1 demonstrates that results achieved by looked after young people appear not to be dependent on general educational outcomes but are more likely to depend on other factors. One

hypothesis is that this may relate to particular and successful efforts that have been made in some local authorities to improve educational outcomes for looked after children. Another hypothesis might be that authorities with a higher proportion of young people in residential care would have worse attainments, but that relationship is not apparent in the above table.

What about attainments of young people in residential child care?

Within the general results for looked after children in Scotland there is not yet very much specific information about how young people in residential care fare. A recent small study (O'Hagan, 2003) found that 44 per cent of a sample of 88 young people looked after away from home aged 15–18 had achieved some Standard Grades (an average of four against the national average of seven). However, only 29 per cent of young people in residential units had achieved some Standard Grades as against 67 per cent of young people in foster care. Results from England (DoH, 2001) point to young people in residential care having much poorer attainments than young people in foster care. Only 32 per cent of care leavers in the year ending 31 March 2000 had any GCSE or GNVQ qualifications. However, 42 per cent of care leavers from foster care had such qualifications whereas only 18 per cent from children's homes and 7 per cent from residential schools did. Although *Learning with Care* (HMI and SWSI, 2001: 36) did not provide percentages, it found that:

Table 16.2 Standard Grade results at Oakbank School (compiled from data provided by the school's Principal)

1995	2002
Pupils were entered for Standard Grade examinations in English, mathematics, science and craft and design.	Pupils were entered for Standard Grade examinations in English, mathematics, science, art and design, craft and design, history, modern studies, French and German.
Of the pupils entered for four subjects, 75 per cent gained passes at Grade 6 and above. Of the pupils entered for three subjects, 100 per cent gained passes at Grade 6 and above.	100 per cent of pupils who had been on the roll from August 2001 and who were still on the roll at examination time, gained five or more passes at Grade 6 or above. Two pupils gained eight passes; four pupils gained seven passes; three pupils gained six passes; one pupil gained five passes. All pupils who joined the school late or who had not maintained their place gained passes at Grade 6 or above in two, three or four subjects.

Children in residential care were, on the whole, those with more educational difficulties and lower educational achievements. It was beyond the scope of the inspection to evaluate whether they were placed in residential care because of their educational difficulties, or whether their difficulties were caused or exacerbated by their placement in residential care.

The *Learning with Care* report only considered children attending schools in the community from residential units or foster or relative placements. It did not consider children placed in residential schools. Statistics provided by Glasgow City Council (2003a) show that 44 out of 56 (77 per cent) secondary 4 pupils (i.e. age 15/16) living in residential schools were presented for Standard Grades compared with only 14 out of 38 (37 per cent) living in children's units. The proportion of those entered gaining an award was comparable in the two settings. Residential schools have traditionally provided a narrower curriculum than mainstream secondary schools, though this is changing. Some residential schools have been able to provide a broader curriculum and improve attainments. Table 16.2 shows some examples of the attainments of pupils at Oakbank School in Aberdeen, an independent secondary-stage residential school with provision for around 40 young people experiencing significant social, emotional and behavioural difficulties. In an inspection of the school in September 2003, inspectors highlighted: 'The high regard the young people had of the quality of education they received and their opportunities for achieving qualifications' (Care Commission and HM Inspectorate of Education, 2003: 6)

This picture contrasts with the statistics from England (see above) and may indicate that the smaller residential school sector in England is primarily used for children with learning disabilities rather than children with social, emotional and behavioural difficulties.

Although the evidence is still incomplete, it would appear that young people placed in residential care in Scotland attain considerably less well than young people in foster care. This may partly be a reflection of their difficulties but may also be a reflection that considerable numbers of residential settings are not yet educationally rich environments. Young people in residential schools appear to attain better than young people in residential units. This may reflect both the difficulties that some units have in getting young people to attend school and looked after young people's perception that some mainstream schools see them as more trouble than they are worth and quickly exclude them 'for daft things' (Dixon and Stein, 2002). This point is illustrated by the following extract from a case study of a 12 year old looked after boy with ADHD and Asperger's Syndrome:

Sam (name changed) was excluded from school three times. On two of these occasions the exclusion took place prior to 9 am. These two exclusions were both as a result of him being on top of the school roof and refusing to come down, disobeying the head teacher and causing disruption in the playground. Upon investigation it transpired that Sam got dropped off at school by taxi at 8.20 am. He then spent the time between 8.20 am and 8.55 am unsupervised in the playground. Sam was often a victim of 'fun-taking' in the playground and inevitably reacted to being bullied/wound up by other pupils.

What helps?

It is easy to be critical of the attainments of looked after children, particularly those living in

Table 16.3 Extract from pilot testing of the self-evaluation instrument in one residential unit

Key feature	Description	Level (1–4)	Comment
Books, newspapers, computers and educational, artistic and other cultural materials are available	Young people need to have access to writing and drawing materials, reference books and computers to help in completing homework and for intellectual stimulation. Carers should actively encourage young people to purchase books of their own.	2 1	(**carer**) 'Presently books, computers, space available for study is not adequate and craft materials not always in use due to other priorities. New educational room described before will address this as will an allocation of money to each young person . . .' (**young person**) 'We need more books and magazines.'

residential units. However, there are also reasons to be optimistic for the future as a result of work in progress aimed at raising the attainments of accommodated children and young people, particularly approaches designed to create educationally rich environments in residential care settings. A number of illustrative examples of such work are now discussed.

Assessing the educational richness of the home environment

The Scottish Executive funded the development of information and training materials aimed at carers and teachers (Ritchie, Morrison and Paterson, 2003; Hudson et al., 2003; Connelly, 2003). The materials included self-evaluation indicators which could be used by a range of care settings, by schools and by local authority managers to monitor the quality of support provided to help children and young people to have satisfying school experiences, attain qualifications, and develop cultural and sporting interests (HM Inspectors of Education, 2003). The instrument is based on the framework of *How Good is Our School?* (HM Inspectors of Schools, 2000, 2001) which has gained widespread respect in Scottish education. It provides indicators to help practitioners recognise key strengths, identify areas where good quality needs to be maintained or where improvement is needed, identify priorities for a development plan, and report on standards and quality. In essence, the audit process invites staff groups to ask themselves three questions: How are we doing? How do we know? What are we going to do?

At the time of writing it was too soon to evaluate the impact of the instrument but pilot work undertaken in residential units provided encouraging results. In one unit, senior staff completed the audit document independently. In another the audit was debated at an open staff meeting, while in a third unit both staff and young people completed the audit independently. Table 16.3 shows for illustration a comparison between the ratings and comments given by a carer and those of a 16 year-old in relation to one aspect of the pilot instrument. In this case both agree that the availability of educational materials such as books represents a weakness in practice, though the young person rates it more severely.

One of the authors has provided the services of a 'critical friend' for a residential unit involved in the pilot, meeting occasionally with the unit manager and deputy to discuss progress on action points identified by the self-evaluation exercise. Action included conducting staff briefing using the *Learning with Care* information booklet (Connelly et al., 2003), more focussed staff development centred on providing home support for young people (aged 14–16) in relation to Standard Grade English, and setting up a room dedicated to homework.

Jackson (1989) observed that when education is made the central purpose, residential care can be a positive factor in enhancing a child's progress. In her case study of one home it was found that two key factors contributed to improved attitudes to learning, school attendance and attainment: the commitment and background of the head of home; and the appointment of a liaison teacher. Both factors are now more common features in care settings and one might expect that they would begin to impact on the educational experience of looked after children and young people. A number of interventions is likely to be required, however, and Connelly et al. (2003: 17) provide the following suggestions of things carers can do to help improve the educational richness of the home environment.

- Collaborate with teachers to ensure the child attends school regularly.
- Become familiar with the courses, qualifications and attainment targets relevant to individual children.
- Help the child or young person with personal organisation (e.g. planning homework and study, using a homework diary, having the correct books and equipment).
- Keep in contact with the school (and individual teachers, if appropriate) and act early to avoid escalation of difficulties.
- Offer support and encouragement.
- Encourage intellectual activity (e.g. discussion of news, watching TV documentaries, provision of books and newspapers, reading to young children).
- Share enthusiasm for learning or particular expertise in a school subject, creative pursuit or sport with children in your care.

The general atmosphere of the unit and the expectations of carers appear to be crucial factors in both influencing and supporting the educational aspirations of looked after young people. Although it is a major challenge to overcome years of disadvantage, a stable home life can make a huge difference. Who Cares? Scotland and Save the Children (Ritchie, 2003) surveyed the perceptions of young people on their educational experiences while in care. While they found that most of the children aged under 12 surveyed were positive about the help they received from residential care staff, older young people were more variable in their experiences of support. The discrepancy is largely unexplained but may be due to older children presenting greater social and educational challenges for care staff. Nevertheless, the contrasting experiences illustrated below in the words of the young people themselves, begs the question that if some

looked after children can describe supportive actions should these conditions not be available to all (ibid.: 34)?

They don't really know when I've got homework or not . . . They don't ask me, I just do it of my own accord. I do it a bit late night, I suppose, last minute, like 2 o'clock I'm working on something for the next morning.

(male, 15)

For my latest project I got one of the staff to help, and because of all my hard work and his hard work, I got an A+ for it and I was over the moon.

(female, 15)

Providing educational support

The Care Commission (www.carecommission. com) was set up to regulate and inspect care services. In particular, the Commission takes account of National Care Standards in evaluating provision. Standard 13 of the care standards for residential homes for children (Scottish Executive, 2002b: 32) includes the promise that care staff will:

. . . encourage and support you in school and homework activities. They work with the school or college so they know how to help to meet your learning needs. Books, newspapers, computers and educational, artistic and other cultural materials are available in the care home.

The staff in one children's unit, asked to describe 'good experiences' and 'difficulties' associated with their attempts to provide an educationally rich home environment, provided the account shown in Table 16.4.

A number of Scottish local authorities have instituted the role of link teacher, working directly with accommodated children in their placements, supporting teachers and liaising between schools and carers. In one authority with 190 looked after children (around 80 accommodated) a looked after children's team of teachers and support workers has been

Table 16.4 Support for school and homework

Good experiences	Difficulties
There is an expectation that children will do homework when they come in from school. Staff check homework diaries and assist where possible, and they ensure that homework is completed to an acceptable standard (e.g. neat writing).	There is one communal computer. This is adequate because computers are available at schools and in the public library. However, there is no internet access in the home because the council has not been satisfied that it can comply with safe care requirements.
A link teacher visits the home every Monday to help in homework supervision.	
All children are members of the local public library and staff accompany children on informal visits to look for resources.	

established. Unusually, they work not just with accommodated children but with children on home supervision and with children living in accommodation for the homeless. The work of the team is monitored by an inter-departmental forum that meets monthly. This provides a reviewing mechanism which emphasises the authority's corporate role in raising attainments of children in their care:

> *Each referral is referred to a multi-agency planning meeting and an Intensive Support Programme (ISP) is developed in full co-operation with the pupil and parents/carers. Each ISP is re-integrative in nature and is part of the continuum of support which is available in South Ayrshire. Many younger children are referred with the aim of early intervention and many children and families require the intensive support which an ISP offers on a long term basis.*

All looked after children in the authority have Personal Education Plans (PEPs) and the looked after children's team provides support for school staff preparing PEPs, and also has a mechanism for reviewing progress annually. Parents are involved in the development of PEPs and the plans identify the people who should receive communication from the school, the arrangements for doing this, and who should take responsibility in care issues.

Another local authority employs a full-time teacher whose job is to work directly with children accommodated in the authority's three residential units. The teacher has advised on the purchase of books and toys, the supply of computer equipment and arranging safe internet access. She describes her role (personal communication) as follows:

- Planning and implementing of individual school placements.
- Communication: inter-agency/young people/parents.
- School/class support: learning/behaviour/ mentoring/nurturing.
- Promoting high expectations within the units.
- Home-school liaison.
- Management of exclusions: provision of educational materials and one-to-one tuition; provision of daily timetables.
- Homework: monitoring/assistance/liaison.
- Standard Grades: folios/revision materials/supported study/ensuring attendance at exams.
- Ensuring attendance at school events.
- Attendance at statutory meetings.
- Contributing to residential assessments.

This is clearly a very demanding role. No individual teacher can easily cover both primary and secondary stages across the entire breadth of the curriculum, as well as offering consultancy to teachers and carers. However, an important aspect of this role is the task of proselytising: literally countering the grim messages of research and experience, and encouraging fellow professionals to show faith in the capacity of looked after children to achieve – essentially providing a culture which values education (Lindsay and Foley, 1999). Teachers and carers need to believe that they can make a difference. Gilligan (2000) argues for the value of promoting resilience, the capacity of young people to do well despite adverse experience, a condition he suggests comes from carers, teachers and social workers investing interest, concern and personal commitment:

> *The rituals, the smiles, the interest in the little things, the daily routines, the talents they nurture, the interests they stimulate, the hobbies they encourage, the friendships they support, the sibling ties they preserve make a difference. All of these things may foster in a child the vital senses of belonging, of mattering, of counting.*
>
> (ibid.: 45)

Educational attainment grant

In October 2001, the Scottish Executive's then education minister, Jack McConnell, announced a single grant allocation: 'to provide books, equipment and homework materials for every looked after child in Scotland'. The funding allocation was based on a sum of £2,500 for every child in residential care and £500 for each child in foster care or living with their family or relative carers, and the total allocation across Scotland amounted to around £10 million. Approximately half of the money was spent on purchasing computer equipment and software and arranging internet access. The funding was also used to purchase books, reference materials, art and craft materials, musical instruments, digital cameras and furniture to facilitate private study. Table 16.5 provides illustrative extracts taken from the summaries of the use made of the specific grant money by two local authorities in the government's official report (Scottish Executive, 2003c).

Despite a general welcome for the additional funding, there were criticisms from many quarters concerning the nature of the grant: it was short-term; expenditure had to be approved and

Table 16.5 Example of the use of the educational attainment grant

Local authority	Allocation	Report summaries
Moray	£113,000	ICT equipment. Licence for IEP (Individualised Educational Programme) Writer 2 has been purchased for each of their schools and each school will attend an in-service training day. 4 children currently studying for higher education will be loaned a PC laptop for the duration of their higher education studies. The three children's homes in Moray were allocated £25,000 to develop their range of ICT and general educational resources. £12,500 was allocated to out-of-Moray residential establishments.
West Dunbartonshire	£265,000	Residential Units – £67,500. All units received new computer equipment for sole use by young people. This covered: new computers, printers, scanners and equipment like tables etc. Money was spent on the creation of quiet areas in units for the use of the equipment for study, homework etc. All units have been hooked up to a permanent internet connection with payment for the first year's usage. Have also purchased access to a web resource for accommodated children from a local company Spark of Genius (Training) Ltd. This entails young people getting access to a web site with an electronic library of teaching materials and lessons. The extra funding also covered the following: each unit having a stock of reading material (educational and leisure); educational software; subscription to magazines; educational equipment (packs of material for each young person admitted); tutoring for individual young people (including homework sessions in units); rewards for young people achieving exam results.

spent in a very short time frame (around 10 weeks); and the capital investment left local authorities with responsibilities to fund future maintenance and replacement. A report by the advocacy organisation Who Cares? Scotland (O'Hagan, 2003) indicated that of 170 young people surveyed, 98 (58 per cent) were unaware that money had recently been invested in their educational attainment, and that few (22 per cent) had been given a say in the spending. Among other criticisms expressed, some young people were disappointed that the expenditure did not appear to benefit them directly.

My £500 was spent on a laptop which the school kept. I only got to use it once before I moved school.

(female, 12)

Money was given to [name] high School in April which was the same time plans were made for me to leave this school.

(female, 14)

Some criticisms are surely justified: short-term fixes cannot solve overnight more intractable problems; the haste with which the money had to be spent was not a good example of strategic planning; and there is a bitter irony in the apparent lack of consultation with young people, though the need to act swiftly will have contributed to this omission. Nevertheless, the whole exercise arguably had a number of positive outcomes. Firstly, there was considerable capital spend on a neglected aspect of care provision. Secondly, the exercise itself acted as a form of audit of the resource needs to underpin the educational attainment of looked after children. Finally, it identified a number of creative uses of funding by some authorities which could be taken up by others. For example, one authority purchased corporate membership of leisure centres to encourage access to sport and physical activity, another provided each looked after child with a £10 book token every month for a year, and several paid for extra tuition or music lessons for individual children.

Local authority monitoring and reporting

Collaboration between key services is critical to the success of any developments aimed at improving the educational attainment of looked after children. To provide an illustration of the approach taken by one local authority, we report briefly on work by Glasgow City Council (2003b) which has 'corporate parent' responsibility for around a quarter of all looked after children in Scotland. The authority has developed its strategic response in three key ways: by appointing a senior officer to liaise between education and social work services; by developing a joint protocol of guidance to inform the working practice of both departments; and by developing an electronic means of monitoring attendance, exclusion and attainment.

The electronic reporting system works by creating a link between the social work and education management information systems. For example, the system ensures that when a child becomes looked after, or experiences a change in status or a change of placement, once the relevant information is entered by social workers certain fields are automatically updated in the education database and the child's school is alerted to consider what action might be required. Similarly, that child or young person's academic records become available to the Senior Officer (Educational Outcomes). The information created can be used for monitoring the progress of individual children and for providing reports for operational planning or research purposes. One practical application of the system is the collaboration between the authority and the University of Strathclyde which runs a Summer Academy (see: http://www.strath.ac.uk/summeracademy/). The Academy is aimed at 15 year-old pupils entering the fourth year of secondary education who for various reasons could benefit from additional motivation to aspire to further and higher education. The existence of the database allows easy identification of target children, ensuring that carers are aware of the opportunity and can encourage young people in their care to apply to take part.

Conclusion

The title of this chapter is 'Still room for improvement?' Attainments of looked after children in Scotland would certainly indicate that this is the case. There has been considerable support from the Scottish Executive and children's organisations to improve the situation. A number of local authorities have clearly taken on board the recommendations of the *Learning with Care* report and a range of projects and developments are in place. It is important that the effectiveness of these different approaches is evaluated so that it will be possible to take forward approaches that demonstrably make a difference for looked after children and young people.

Looked after children and young people are attaining much better in some local authorities than others. There is no reason why the results in the poorest cannot be brought up to the level of the best and why the best cannot improve further. This undoubtedly presents a challenge but results achieved so far show that improvement is both entirely possible and vital if the life chances of the children and young people concerned are to be transformed. We need to be able to report 'Fully reaching their potential' rather than 'Still room for improvement'.

Acknowledgements

The authors gratefully acknowledge the assistance and advice of Jane Arrowsmith, Lorraine Jardine, Graham McCann, Mona McCulloch, Sandra McLaughlin, Pauline O'Hagan and Esther Roughsedge.

The chapter published in this volume was written while Kirstie Maclean was Director of SIRCC. The views expressed are her own and do not represent the views of Her Majesty's Inspectorate of Education.

References

Aldgate, J. (1990) Foster Children at School: Success or Failure? The 1990 Hilda Lewis Memorial Lecture. *Adoption and Fostering*, 14: 4, 38–49.

Aldgate, J., Heath, A., Colton, M. and Simm, M. (1993) Social Work and Education in Foster Care. *Adoption and Fostering*, 17: 3, 25–34.

Berridge, D., Brodie, I., Ayre, P., Barrett, D., Henderson, B. and Wenman, H. (1996) *Is Anybody Listening? The Education of Young People in Residential Care*. University of Luton.

Biehal, N., Claydon, J., Stein, M. and Wade, J. (1992) *Prepared for Living?* London: NCB.

Borland, M., Pearson, C., Hill, M., Bloomfield, I. (1998) *Education and Care Away From Home: A Review of Policy, Practice and Research*. Edinburgh: Scottish Council for Research in Education.

Care Commission and HM Inspectorate of Education (2003) *Integrated Inspection by The Care Commission and HM Inspectorate of Education of Oakbank School, Aberdeen*. Edinburgh: Scottish Executive. www.hmie.gov.uk/documents/inspection/Oakbank%205282349.pdf

Connelly, G. (2003) Developing Quality Indicators for Learning With Care. *Scottish Journal of Residential Child Care*. 2: 2, 69–78.

Connelly, G., Mckay, E. and O'Hagan, P. (2003) *Learning With Care: Information for Carers, Social*

Workers and Teachers Concerning The Education of Looked After Children and Young People. Edinburgh: HMIE/SWSI. www.hmie.gov.uk/documents/publication/5679text.pdf

DoH (2001) *Guidance on The Education of Young People in Public Care.* London: DoH/Dfee.

Dixon, J. and Stein, M. (2002) *Still A Bairn: Throughcare and Aftercare Services in Scotland.* Edinburgh: Scottish Executive. www.york.ac.uk/inst/swrdu/Publications/stillabairn.pdf

Essen, J., Lambert, L. and Head (1976) School Attainment of Children Who Have Been in Care. *Child Care, Health and Development.* 2: 339–51.

Fletcher, B. (1993) *Not Just A Name: The Views of Young People in Foster and Residential Care.* London: National Consumer Council/Who Cares? Trust.

Fletcher-Campbell, F. and Hall, C. (1990) *Changing Schools? Changing People? The Education of Children in Care.* Slough: National Foundation for Educational Research.

Fletcher-Campbell, F. (1997) *The Education of Children Who Are Looked After.* Slough: National Foundation for Educational Research.

Furnivall, J. and Hudson, B. (2003) The Learning With Care Training Materials. *Scottish Journal of Residential Child Care.* 2: 2, 63–8.

Gallagher, R. (1996) *Confidentiality in Schools.* Unpublished Report. Glasgow: Scottish Child Law Centre.

Garnett, L. (1992) *Leaving Care and After: A Follow-Up Study to the Placement Outcomes Project.* London: NCB.

Gilligan, R. (2000) Adversity, Resilience and Young People: The Protective Value of Positive School and Spare Time Experiences. *Children and Society.* 14, 37–47.

Glasgow City Council (2003a) *The Education of Glasgow's Looked After Children.* Glasgow City Council Social Work Services.

Glasgow City Council (2003b) *Educational and Social Work Services Joint Protocol: Education of Looked After Children.* Glasgow City Council.

HM Inspectors of Schools (2000) *The Quality Initiative in Scottish Schools.* Edinburgh: Scottish Executive. www.campus-oei.org/calidad/paper.PDF

HM Inspectors of Education (2001) *How Good is Our School? 2002 Edition: Self-Evaluation Using Quality Indicators*, Norwich: HMSO. www.hmie.gov.uk/documents/publication/HGIOS.pdf

HMI and SWSI (2001) *Learning With Care: The Education of Children Looked After Away From Home by Local Authorities.* Edinburgh: Scottish Executive. www.Scotland.Gov.Uk/Library3/Education/Lacr-00.Asp

HM Inspectorate of Education (2003) *Inclusion and Equality, Part 1: Evaluating Education and Care Placements for Looked After Children and Young People.* Edinburgh: HM Inspectorate of Education. www.hmie.gov.uk/documents/publication/hgioslac.pdf

Hudson, B. Furnivall, J. Paterson, S. Livingston, K. Maclean, K. (2003) *Learning With Care: Training Materials for Carers, Social Workers and Teachers Concerning The Education of Looked After Children and Young People.* Glasgow: University of Strathclyde.

Jackson, S. (1989) Residential Care and Education. *Children and Society.* 2: 4, 335–50.

Kendrick, A. (1995) *Residential Care in The Integration of Child Care Services.* Research Findings 5. Edinburgh: Scottish Office Central Research Unit.

Kendrick, A., Simpson, M. and Mapstone, E. (1996) *Getting it Together: Changing Services for Children and Young People in Difficulty.* York: Joseph Rowntree Foundation. homepages.strath.ac.uk/¬zns01101/jrf.htm

Lindsay, M. and Foley, T. (1999) Getting Them Back to School: Touchstones of Good Practice in the Residential Care of Young People. *Children and Society.* 13, 192–202.

Lockhart, F., Swanson, M. and Freeman, I. (1996) *Strathclyde Regional Council Social Work Department School Training Employment Survey.* Glasgow: Strathclyde Regional Council.

Maclean, K. and Gunion, M. (2003) Learning With Care: The Education of Children Looked After Away From Home by Local Authorities in Scotland. *Adoption and Fostering.* 27: 2, 20–31.

Maginnis, E. (1993) *An Inter-Agency Response to Children With Special Needs: The Lothian Experience – A Scottish Perspective.* Paper presented at Exclusions From Schools: Bridging The Gap Between Policy and Practice Conference, 13 Jul, NCB.

Martin, P. and Jackson, S. (2002) Educational Success for Children in Public Care: Advice From a Group of High Achievers. *Child and Family Social Work.* 7: 2, 121–30.

OFSTED/SSI (1995) *The Education of Children Who Are Looked-After by Local Authorities.* London: OFSTED/SSI.

OFSTED (2001) *Raising Achievement of Children in Public Care*. Report From the Office of HM Chief Inspector of Schools. London: OFSTED/SSI.

O'Hagan, P. (2003) *A Different Class? Educational Attainment: The Views and Experiences of Looked After Young People*. Glasgow: Who Cares? Scotland.

Ritchie, A. (2003) Care to Learn? *The Educational Experiences of Children and Young People Who Are Looked After*. Edinburgh: Who Cares? Scotland and Save The Children.

Ritchie, A., Morrison, E., Paterson, S. (2003) Care to Learn? The Educational Experiences of Children and Young People Who Are Looked After. *Scottish Journal of Residential Child Care*. 2: 2, 51–62.

Scottish Executive (2000) *Exclusions From Schools, 1998/99*. Edinburgh: Scottish Executive. www.scotland.gov.uk/stats/bulletins/0007-00.asp.

Scottish Executive (2002a) *Children's Social Work Statistics 2001–02*. Edinburgh: Scottish Executive.

Scottish Executive (2002b) *National Care Standards: Care Homes for Children and Young People*. Edinburgh: Scottish Executive. www.carecommission.com/CareComm.Web/Uploads/Documents/ncs care homes for young.pdf

Scottish Executive (2003a) *SQA Examination Results in Scottish Schools 2002–03*. Edinburgh: Scottish Executive.

Scottish Executive (2003b) *Children's Social Work Statistics 2002–03*. Edinburgh: Scottish Executive.

Scottish Executive (2003c) *Report on Educational Attainment of Looked After Children*. Edinburgh: Scottish Executive. www.scotland.gov.uk/library5/education/ealac.pdf

Skuse, T. and Evans, R. (2001) Directing Social Work Attention to Education: The Role of the Looking After Children Materials. in Jackson, S. (Ed.) *Nobody Ever Told Us School Mattered: Raising the Educational Attainments of Children in Care*. London: BAAF.

Stein, M. and Carey, K. (1986) *Leaving Care*. Oxford: Basil Blackwell.

Part Six:
Locking Up Children and Young People Who Offend

Chapter Seventeen

The Dismal State of the Secure Estate

John Pitts

Introduction

The past decade has witnessed a huge increase in the incarceration of children and young people in trouble with the law in England and Wales. Between 1992 and 2002, the number of children and young people aged 10–17 sentenced to custody in the 'juvenile secure estate' (Young Offender Institutions [YOIs], Local Authority Secure Units [LASUs] and Secure Training Centres [STCs]) rose by almost 90 per cent (Home Office, 2003; Youth Justice Board, 2004). During this period, the number of children aged between 10 and 14 years increased by, a remarkable, 800 per cent (Bateman, 2003). Although around 80 per cent of these young inmates were boys, from 1992, the number of girls aged 10 to 17 entering the system rose 600 per cent, albeit from a relatively low base (Nacro, 2004). And, although they constitute only 2.7 per cent of the 10–17 year old population in England and Wales, 'black' or 'black British' children and young people accounted for 6 per cent of all youth court disposals, 11 per cent of all custodial disposals and 20 per cent of those given orders for long-term detention (Youth Justice Board, 2003); a substantial increase since the implementation of the Crime and Disorder Act in 1998 (Audit Commission, 2004). Drawing upon the available data, it appears that by 2003 the level of child and youth incarceration in England and Wales vis-à-vis the under 18 population as a whole was four times that of France, ten times that of Spain and one hundred times that of Finland (Nacro, 2003). Not only are more children and young people entering the secure estate, they are also staying longer. Between 1992 and 2002 the average custodial sentence for 15–17 year old boys increased from 5.6 months to 10.3 months and for girls; from 5.5 months to 7.1 months (Pitts, 2003).

This growing influx of children and young people into the 'secure estate', since the early 1990s, has exacerbated the problems of management and control already evident in its institutions. In consequence, in 2003, 3,337 children thought to be too vulnerable for custody were, nonetheless, placed in Prison Department YOIs. From their introduction in the mid-1990s, the STCs have been dogged by violent disturbances and allegations of heavy-handedness by staff in their attempts to contain and restrain the 12–15 year old inmates (Pitts, 2003). And, in 2004, two children died in STCs, one, Gareth Myatt (15), as a result of restraint by staff at Rainsbrook; the other Adam Rickwood (14), a known suicide risk, who hanged himself in Hassocksfield. Tim Bateman (2004) has observed that self-harm in the secure estate is running at record levels:

Between January 1998 and January 2002, there were 1,111 reported incidents of young people harming themselves while in a YOI. Given the nature of official recording, it is reasonable to assume that a considerable number of lesser injuries went unreported. More telling still, is the stark fact that 12 boys took their own lives while in custody during those four years.

At the turn of the century, most Young Offender Institutions (YOIs) in England were seriously overcrowded, significantly under-resourced, and growing numbers were showing signs of being mismanaged (Goldson and Peters, 2000). Even in the better institutions, only around 30 per cent of young prisoners now receive any education. At Feltham YOI in 2001, only 10 per cent of inmates were attending education classes despite the fact that in the system generally, 54 per cent of inmates score below level one (GCSE standard) in reading ability. These problems are compounded by widespread drug abuse, racism, violence and intimidation.

Reviewing recent reports by Her Majesty's Chief Inspector of Prisons in December 2002, Mr Justice Munby, concluded that their findings:

. . . shame us all. They ought to be – I hope they are – matters of the very greatest concern to . . . society at large. For these are things being done to children by the State – by all of us – in circumstances where the State appears to be failing badly and in some instances failing very badly, in its duties to vulnerable and damaged children.

(R v Home Department (2002) cited in Bateman, 2004)

In a similar vein, in its 2002 report, the United Nations Committee on the Rights of the Child expressed concern at:

> ... the high and increasing numbers of children in custody generally, at earlier ages for lesser offences, and for longer sentences imposed by the recently increased court powers ... [I]t is the concern of the Committee that deprivation of liberty is not being used only as a measure of last resort and for the shortest possible appropriate period of time, in violation of Article 37(b) of the United Nations Convention on the Rights of the Child.

The committee also noted that the situation had worsened since its previous report in 1995.

But is this 'carceral bonanza' (Pitts, 2003) an effect of the harshness of recent legislation and heavier sentencing, as many reformers believe, a product of changes in the volume and nature of youth crime and disorder, as the government contends, or incompetence and mismanagement, as the parliamentary opposition and many in local government would have it? Or could it be all three?

Is the youth justice system becoming harsher?

Beatrix Campbell (1993) has observed that the murder, in 1993, of two year old James Bulger by two truanting 10 year olds, served as a catalyst for the emergence of a new-style, 'realistic', 'compassionate' yet 'hard headed', Labour Party. 'New Labour' repudiated the traditional party political divisions which cast the Conservatives as 'the natural party of law and order' and Labour as the party of penal reform. They promised to mobilise the family and the community against what they described as a growing and unchecked problem of crime and disorder amongst the young, and to 'strengthen' the youth justice system. In so doing, New Labour endeavoured to integrate popular Conservative 'law and order' themes with a new emphasis upon 'evidence-led policy' and 'evidence-based practice'. In its *Crime and Disorder Act* (1998) (CDA), New Labour established elaborate new administrative structures, designed to 'deliver' these reforms with optimal 'economy, efficiency and effectiveness' (Pitts, 2003).

The CDA marked a reaction against both 1960s 'welfarism' and 1980s 'progressive minimalism' (Currie, 1985). As the title of the White Paper that preceded it, *No More Excuses*, suggests, the idea of youth crime as a product of poverty, social inequality or psychological disadvantage, which informed the 'welfarist' policies of the 1960s, is supplanted by an emphasis upon individual and family responsibility. Whereas the minimalist strategies of the 1980s and 1990s aimed to divert youngsters in trouble away from the justice system in order to deal with them informally within mainstream services, the 1998 Act abandoned both diversion and normalisation in favour of a strategy which aimed to bring both first-time offenders and troublesome youngsters below the age of criminal responsibility into the ambit of the criminal justice system. Indeed, a guiding precept of the *No More Excuses* White Paper is that early exposure to, and swift processing through, the youth justice system is likely to have long-term deterrent and rehabilitative effects. Whereas welfarism and progressive minimalism both strove to minimise the stigma associated with involvement in the youth justice system, the CDA employs stigma as a deterrent strategy, allowing the anonymity traditionally afforded to juvenile offenders to be waived, if such 'naming and shaming' is deemed to be in the public interest.

The effects of these changes are evident in the redistribution of penalties that followed the implementation of the CDA. Between 1995 and 2002, cautions, reprimands and final warnings administered to 10–17 year olds fell by 40 per cent, while the numbers of 10–17 year olds sentenced in court rose by 25 per cent (Home Office, 2002). The CDA increased the number of offences for which juveniles could be imprisoned, increased sentence lengths, extended the 'grave crimes' provisions (i.e. offences which in the case of an adult would attract a maximum sentence of 15 years) to children of 10, extended the powers of Youth Courts to remand children and young people directly into secure and penal establishments, introduced 'fast-tracking' for persistent young offenders and lowered the age at which young people in trouble could be incarcerated. It also abandoned specific 'community alternatives to custody'. This has, as Burnett and Appleton (2004) discovered, drawn substantial numbers of younger and less serious offenders, into the secure estate; causing both surprise and concern amongst parents, YOT workers and the staff of secure and custodial institutions.

Youth Court magistrates interviewed by Burnett and Appleton (2004) claimed that their sentencing had grown no more severe over the period and that custodial sentences were only imposed when absolutely necessary. However, both statistical sources and anecdotal evidence suggest that the bench greeted their new powers to remand children directly into custody and the Detention and Training Order, introduced in 1998, with enthusiasm, and proceeded to consign many children and young people, who would previously have been dealt with in the community, to custodial institutions. More generally, it appears that when the bench is handed increased power to imprison, particularly in an environment in which politicians are 'talking-up' the problem of crime, as was the case in the late 1990s, it has used them (Pitts 1998, 2003). Leaving the actions of politicians and the bench to one side, however, these dramatic changes in the numbers of juveniles entering the secure estate inevitably beg the question as to whether youth crime was, as many commentators have asserted, getting worse.

Is youth crime getting worse?

It is, on the face of it, remarkable that the unprecedented 'toughening' of the English youth justice system in the past decade, described above, has paralleled a 25 per cent fall in the number of recorded crimes committed by children and young people (Bateman, 2003). This fact, alone, would appear to support the view that the youth justice reforms of 1998 were essentially symbolic, concerned first and foremost, to secure the ephemeral loyalties of erstwhile Conservative voters rather than curb the excesses of the nation's youth; suggesting, as several criminologists have noted (Muncie and Hughes, 2002; Pitts, 2003) that the relationship between crime and control is, at best, a tenuous one.

However, while the fall in the recorded youth crime rate since the early 1990s is real enough, it is a gradual fall from the all-time high it reached in 1992. Moreover, there is evidence that, over the last two decades, the nature, not just the volume, of youth crime has been changing. Thus, the earlier rise and the present fall in the volume of youth crime have been paralleled by a steady increase in the proportion of youth crime which is violent, sexual and drug-driven. In 2002/3 in the justice system as a whole, arrests for sexual offences rose 15 per cent, arrests for drug-related offences 12 per cent and arrests for violence against the person 9 per cent. Although children and young people aged 10–17 are less likely than

young adults to be involved in these more serious offences they are, nevertheless, involved. In the past decade, the use of firearms in pursuance of crime has grown significantly and 2001/2002 saw a 34 per cent increase, with a further 2 per cent rise recorded in 2002/2003 (Home Office, 2004). Tilley and Bullock (2003), in their study of gang-related shootings in the black community in south Manchester, a 'firearms hotspot', found that in one gang '. . . members (were) evenly spread from their early teens to 20s: two to four at every age between 15 and 23'. Since the mid-1990s, the deregulation of the 'night-time economy' has generated unprecedented levels of violence and disorder, much of it involving young people and young adults. The last two decades have also witnessed a remarkable increase in the availability and use of class A drugs; heroin, cocaine and crack cocaine, with a concomitant increase in the numbers appearing in court for drug-related or drug-driven offences (Parker et al., 1998; Hammersley et al., 2002). Just under a quarter of all the juvenile arrestees surveyed by Trevor Bennett and his colleagues (2002) had used opiates in the preceding seven days and the 9 per cent of those using more than one such 'class A' drug were responsible for 52 per cent of all offences recorded. They were also five times more likely to have committed robbery. The British Crime Survey 2002–2003 revealed that 6 per cent of 16–19 year olds had used a class A drug in the preceding year, while recent Chief Inspector of Prisons reports confirm that almost two-thirds of young people held in Young Offender Institutions are known to have serious drink and drug problems which are associated with their offending (Home Office, 2002). The origins of these changes in the nature of youth crime must be sought in the seismic social economic and cultural changes that occurred in the UK in the 1980s.

The legacy of the 1980s

Between 1982 and 1992 recorded crime in England and Wales rose by, an unprecedented, 111 per cent and during this period the nature and distribution of crime also changed. The 1992 British Crime Survey revealed that while, in the preceding decade, the chances of a resident in the lowest crime neighbourhood ever being assaulted had fallen to a point where it was barely measurable, residents in the highest crime neighbourhoods now risked being assaulted twice a year. These findings pointed to a significant redistribution of victimisation towards the poorest and most vulnerable over the period.

These changes in the volume and distribution of crime were paralleled by equally dramatic changes in the distribution of wealth and the growth of both absolute and relative deprivation. Between 1981 and 1991 the number of workers earning half the national average wage or less, the Council of Europe poverty line, rose from 900,000 to 2.4 million. In the same period those earning over twice the national average rose from 1.8 to 3.1 million. These seismic economic shifts were paralleled in the UK by fundamental policy changes, involving the introduction of market mechanisms into the management of public sector housing, via 'Right to Buy' schemes, which diminished the amount of available housing, and 'Tenant Incentive' schemes which shifted more affluent tenants into the private sector (Page, 1993; Hope, 1994). As the 1980s progressed, relatively prosperous, middle-aged, higher-income families left social housing, to be replaced by poorer, younger, often lone parent, families (Page, 1993). Whereas in the 1980s and 1990s, 40 per cent of heads of households in social housing were aged 65 or over, 75 per cent of newly formed households entering social housing were headed by someone aged between 16 and 29. A high proportion of these new residents were unemployed, not least because they included a heavy concentration of lone parents.

In its report, *Bringing Britain Together*, the Social Exclusion Unit (1998) identified 1,370 housing estates in Britain which it characterised as 'poor neighbourhoods' which have 'poverty, unemployment, and poor health in common, and crime usually comes high on any list of residents' concerns'.

The neighbourhoods that experienced the greatest changes saw increasing concentrations of children, teenagers, young single adults and young single parent families. Old social ties, constructed of kinship, friendship or familiarity withered away to be replaced by transience, isolation and mutual suspicion. Neighbours no longer watched out for one another's property or their shared amenities. Nor did they approach strangers, rowdy adolescents or naughty children, for fear of reprisals. As a result, anti-social behaviour went unchecked. In their study of one such estate, Tim Hope and Janet Foster (1992) discovered a five-fold increase in burglaries over a three-year period. Between 1981

and 1991 in Britain, those people most vulnerable to criminal victimisation, and those most likely to victimise them, were progressively thrown together on the poorest housing estates in Britain. By 1997, 25 per cent of the children and young people under 16 in the UK were living in these neighbourhoods (Burroughs, 1998). As Tim Hope (2003: 15) has argued:

> It is no exaggeration to say that we are now two nations as far as crime victimisation is concerned. Half the country suffers more than four fifths of the total amount of household property crime, while the other half makes do with the remaining 15 per cent.

A disproportionate amount of the crime in these destabilised urban neighbourhoods was youthful, violent and implosive, in that it is usually committed by, and against, local residents in general and local young people in particular. This intra-neighbourhood crime pattern became a distinguishing characteristic of high-crime areas in Britain at the end of the 20th century (Forrester et al., 1990). Its other distinguishing feature was that the young people involved in such crime appeared not to grow out of it (Graham and Bowling, 1995). Being locked in a state of perpetual adolescence, these young people did not 'grow up'. And because 'growing up', the assumption of adult roles, rights and responsibilities, usually accompanies 'growing out of crime' (Rutherford, 1986; Sampson and Laub, 1993) they did not. So, as Graham and Bowling (1995) suggest, they continued to perpetrate 'youth crime' into their twenties and beyond. As John Hagan (1993) has observed, pre-eminent among the factors which make for higher levels of crime in destabilised neighbourhoods is that young people who, under other circumstances, would have grown out of crime, leaving it behind with other adolescent enthusiasms, become more deeply and more seriously embedded in a criminal way of life. The problems of crime in these neighbourhoods were compounded from the mid-1980s as opiate use and addiction migrated from the West End of London to the poorest neighbourhoods in the UK (Pearson, 1987). Once there, it transformed faltering local economies. In mining areas, in the late 1980s and early 1990s, the transition from coal to coke occurred at mind-numbing speed.

The demographic and cultural changes occurring in these neighbourhoods have had a profound impact upon the schools that serve them. In an Inner London school, where the present author and his colleagues undertook a study of student violence, the transience of the housing estates which fed the school was reflected, in the late 1990s, in a turnover in the school roll between years 7 and 11 of around 50 per cent. One consequence of these changes was to keep the informal 'pecking order' of the school in a state of permanent flux, resulting in an increase in the numbers of serious fights, and inter-racial group conflict in particular. This violence, which may have started in the school or in the neighbourhood, would quickly attract older adolescents and young adults from the surrounding area who, having nothing better to do, would get 'stuck in'. This violence contributed significantly to the risks faced by school students who were not directly involved in it. Indeed, in a one-year period at the end of the 1990s, 41 per cent of year 11 students were assaulted, with 30 per cent of these assaults occurring in the vicinity of the school or on the way home from school, in the hour or so following the end of the school day (Pitts, 2003).

Eventually, like similar schools around the country, the London school was assigned its own police officer. While this was a source of consternation to many criminologists, staff and students of the London school, as well as parents, were very relieved because they had been asking for a police presence, to protect staff and students from attack, for several years.

The picture is a complex one. While the youth justice system did get tougher from the early 1990s and overall recorded youth crime dropped significantly, the volume of serious youth crime appears to have risen. Although, between 1992 and 2002, the numbers of children and young people entering the courts remained fairly constant, the proportion of defendants sentenced to custody rose from 44 per cent to 63 per cent (Home Office, 2003). While it is true that the government extended the 'grave crimes' provision from 15 to 12 year olds, thus drawing a handful of younger children into the Crown Court for sentencing, between 1992 and 2002 the numbers of children and young people remitted to Crown Court for sentencing, because the seriousness of their offences appeared to merit a more severe penalty than the Youth Court was able to impose, rose by 30 per cent (Home Office, 2003). While some of this increase may be attributable to a changed penal atmosphere, it is unlikely that all of it is.

As we have noted above, the youth justice system of England and Wales imprisons more children and young people than any other EU state and tops the league for adult incarceration as well. With 108.2 prisoners for every 100,000 of the population, the justice system of England and Wales appears to be the most punitive in Europe. However, as Kommer (2004) has observed, when we compare prison numbers with convictions and arrests for serious offences across Europe, England and Wales emerges as a significantly less punitive country than raw imprisonment rates would suggest (Pease, 1994). Yet, as we note below, while some forms of youth crime are a cause for serious concern there appears to be a worrying mismatch between the seriousness of a child's offending and the likelihood of them being imprisoned. Beyond this, of course, is the question of what, in the case of more serious young offenders, incarceration is supposed to achieve, a question to which we return at the end of this paper.

A culture of control?

It is something of an academic anomaly that, in the past few decades, the criminological debate about the changing contours of control systems in Britain and the USA has proceeded with scant reference to the changing contours of crime (Matthews, 1999). One of the results of this has been that governmental responses to crime have tended to be explained in terms of the changing zeitgeist in which anxieties precipitated by social, economic or cultural change, and amplified by a sensation-seeking media, are projected onto certain categories of 'others', against whom governments then feel constrained to act. Only criminologists, it seems, are able to grasp the reality that nothing much has changed; that the threat posed to the public by crime is vastly exaggerated and that governmental responses are almost invariably disproportionate and essentially symbolic.

In his highly influential *The Culture of Control* (2001) David Garland argues that, in 'Anglo-America' in the recent period, we have witnessed the decline of the rehabilitative ideal, a renewed emphasis upon punitive sanctions, dramatic changes in the emotional tone of criminal justice policy and the emergence of a 'penal populism' in which the 'victim' becomes the central focus of criminal justice policy. It is certainly the case that we appear to be living in an era of 'government through crime' (Muncie and Hughes, 2002) in which every government department and government initiative is required to demonstrate how it is contributing to crime reduction and community safety. Commentators speak about the 'criminalisation of social policy' (Crawford, 1998) but a concern with crime infuses policy in the areas of health, housing, education, economic regeneration, and beyond. Moreover, from the 1997 general election campaign onwards, we can cite many examples of the government trading upon what Ulrich Beck (1992) has called the 'negative solidarity of fear' generated by anxieties about crime, to build a new 'constituency of the centre' (Pitts, 2003).

However, these accounts of the utility of 'youth crime' to ambitious politicians and political parties tend to ignore the fact that political responses are seldom clear-cut. While these accounts offer some insight into the forces driving New Labour policy they remain partial. Although the New Labour government may have misunderstood the true nature of the problem of youth crime at the turn of the century, and although it expressed a largely unwarranted confidence in the measures it introduced to contain it, governmental concerns were rooted in the essentially accurate perception that youth crime and disorder was changing and, in certain instances, becoming more serious. That their responses were frequently pragmatic, often contradictory and sometimes counter-productive, does not detract from the fact that New Labour's youth justice policy, whatever else it aimed to achieve, also represented a response to a real and, as far as we can tell, growing problem.

In reality, New Labour appears to have been at least ambivalent and often very torn on the issue of youth crime. While the liberal critique of contemporary UK youth justice policy suggests that burgeoning youth custody rates 'work' for a government which achieved office by wresting the mantle of 'law and order' from the Conservative Party (Pitts, 2003), the reality is far more complex. Thus, while in 2002 the Prime Minister, the Home Secretary the Chair of the Youth Justice Board and the Lord Chief Justice all called for tougher custodial penalties for 'mobile phone thieves', in the face of steadily rising street crime, in the same year they also bemoaned the rising level of youth incarceration (Pitts, 2003). Moreover, New Labour has introduced measures to reduce the numbers of fine-defaulters consigned to gaol and the length of many prison sentences with early release schemes. In the youth justice system they have developed Intensive Supervision and Surveillance Programmes (ISSPs) to reduce the numbers of serious and persistent young offenders sent into security and custody. Although this 'liberalisation' has been motivated in no small part by the unprecedented influx of prisoners into the system, a government wedded to the draconian, US-style, penal policies described by Garland, would have acted very differently.

Rising numbers notwithstanding, the government's stated policy remains to '. . . limit the number of young people who are in custodial provision' (Home Office, 2002) and the Youth Justice Board has repeatedly stated that for most young people community sentences are '. . . more effective in reducing offending and are better value for money' (Youth Justice Board, 2003). Indeed, two of the key performance targets the Board has set for the multi-agency Youth Offending Teams (YOTs), established in 1998, are designed to limit the demand for custody on the part of the Bench. While this hardly represents a wholehearted onslaught on youth incarceration, the fact that the two key organs of government in this field, the Home Office and the Youth Justice Board, have stated formally that they regard present levels of incarceration as problematic suggests a very un-American ambivalence on this issue.

The fact that UK politicians talk, and sometimes try to act, 'tough' on youth crime may be obscuring the reality that, in 1998, New Labour ministers actually believed that, over time, the raft of child and youth focussed social initiatives they were introducing and the new 'evidence-based' youth justice system they had brought into being would reduce the numbers entering the system and 'turn around' the remaining few who did. It may also be true that they wished to improve the system and render it more humane. Following its election in 1997, New Labour established a youth justice taskforce to report upon the juvenile secure estate. This taskforce concluded that:

> *The different types of facilities for young people that constitute the secure estate are in need of major reform. Current arrangements are both inconsistent and unsatisfactory. Young offender institutions are too large. Bullying and abuse of one young offender by another occurs too often while the education offered is often poor.*

Responsibility for transforming the 'secure estate' into a coherent system with 'a structured and caring environment', that 'addresses the individual needs and welfare of the young people and the risk of harm they pose to themselves', and which 'reduces offending behaviour' was handed to the newly constituted Youth Justice Board of England and Wales (YJB). If, in the intervening period, the population of the secure estate had fallen, or even remained the same, the YJB might have stood a chance of achieving its objectives but the, probably unintended, consequences of the government's robust criminal justice legislation put paid to these hopes.

While it is evident, as Garland (2001) suggests, that in the past two decades, the UK has looked to the USA rather than Europe in fashioning its criminal justice policies and legislation, there are crucial differences between the two countries. In the USA, for example, the distinction between adult and juvenile jurisdictions has been progressively blurred; explicitly cruel measures have been introduced into adult and youth jurisdictions and constitutional protections demolished. In the UK, by contrast, ever more rights have been granted to juvenile and adult subjects of justice systems. In 1990, unlike the USA, Margaret Thatcher's government signed the UN Convention on the Rights of the Child, although, as we have noted, the recent UN Committee report finds the UK wanting in its treatment of young offenders (United Nations, 2002). The Human Rights Act (1998), which incorporated many of the provisions of the European Convention on Human Rights into English Law, reinforced this stated commitment to children's rights. The first Prisons Ombudsman was appointed in the UK in the mid-1990s and an eminent penal reformer has recently been appointed to the role of Chief Inspector of Prisons by the government. In the Secure Training Centres, developed by the New Labour government, elaborate arrangements for independent inspection and institutional transparency have been instituted, although they have subsequently been found wanting. Yet more recently, in 2003, a judicial review, albeit one contested by the Home Office Prisons Department, ruled that the provisions of the Children Act (1989) should apply to Prison Department Young Offender Institutions. Unlike the United States, in the UK courts have been active in defending and extending the rights of children and young people held in security and custody.

Autocracy, ambivalence or amateurism

The CDA, because it represented a far more robust response to youth offending, provided a stage upon which New Labour could demonstrate its political grit. However, it also aimed to remedy long-standing judicial, administrative and logistical shortcomings in the existing system. Indeed, the reforms were hailed as a 'new dawn', not just by government but also by practitioners, magistrates and many criminologists. The architects of the CDA certainly appear to have believed that early intervention, coupled with the proven efficacy of the 'evidence-based' programmes which underpinned the new community-based penalties introduced by the CDA, would ensure that only a handful of the most intractable offenders would need to be contained within secure or penal institutions. Indeed the whole logic of the 1998 Act is predicated upon the success of these measures. (The shortcomings of these measures and the flaws in the evidence which supports them are discussed at length in Pawson and Tilley, 1997; Matthews and Pitts, 2000; Pitts, 2003; Bateman and Pitts, 2004.)

Not least of the problems afflicting the CDA is that it was put together in a hurry. Rushed drafting of the legislation has meant, for example, that substantial numbers of young people charged with, but unwilling to admit, very trivial offences were finding themselves in youth courts where they were made the subject to the new three-month referral orders with the prospect of a custodial sentence if they breached its many conditions (Burnett and Appleton, 2004).

Moreover, scant attention was paid to the most basic logistics of the system that was being brought into being. The government was determined to 'sell' its new Detention and Training Order (DTO) to the Youth Court bench, on the basis that it would be the means whereby the educational problems experienced by many of the young people passing through the system would be resolved. However, within this government committed to 'economy, efficiency and effectiveness', not to mention 'education, education, education', nobody appears to have calculated whether the educational component of DTOs could be 'delivered' within existing resources, let alone what would happen if the government's attempts to popularise the DTO with the Youth Court bench were successful which, of course, they were. Equally embarrassing for a government elected on a promise of 'evidence-led policy and 'evidence-based practice' was the fact that nobody in government, before or since the advent of the DTO, has ever cited any evidence to suggest that similar regimes introduced in other juvenile jurisdictions had met with any success. In fact, this was all wishful thinking, a successful 'pitch' by one group of amateurs, in government, to another group of amateurs on the juvenile bench. This particular outbreak of amateurism had very serious consequences for many children and young people appearing in the Youth Court, as a respondent cited by Burnett and Appleton (2004) observed:

> It is hard to believe sometimes. You think, are they really, really considering giving someone a DTO for stealing four CDs out of HMV? Perhaps they are! And that's a worrying thing. There does seem to be an inconsistency in the sentencing of younger and older offenders and a tendency to give DTOs prematurely. There's almost an eagerness to dish out DTOs.

A staff member in a Young Offender Institution whom they interviewed noted that:

> The biggest changes are the increase in first-time, out-of-nowhere young people, in that previously kids would have gone through a whole series of court proceedings. That doesn't happen anymore. They come very quickly into custody – and it is a shock. We get a lot of kids very distressed, shocked, families shocked, saying 'I can't believe this has happened!' very un-streetwise young people – a high increase in vulnerable young people.

Latterly, the Anti-social Behaviour Order (ASBO), a civil injunction that carries a penal sanction, has become a motor for incarceration because, after five years of under-use, following a concerted campaign mediated via regional *ASBO Academies*, the government has required police authorities to meet their ASBO quotas on pain of financial cutbacks. This means that children and adolescents with no prior criminal offences, but who cause a nuisance to their neighbours, are now entering penal institutions in growing numbers.

Youth justice systems, like all bureaucratic systems, have a logic of their own. Yet it appears to have occurred to nobody in government in 1997 that early induction into the system might, through a combination of stigmatisation, 'deviancy amplification' and administrative inertia, accelerate young people's progress

through it. (Pitts, 1988). However, the CDA was rooted in the counter-evidential belief (cf Kemp et al., 2002 for example) that early exposure to the youth justice system, if linked with evidence-based programmes of intervention, would have long-term deterrent and rehabilitative effects.

These problems appear to have been compounded by the uncritical enthusiasm of the New Labour government for market solutions, which has had the effect of sidelining professionalism in the secure estate and establishing contract compliance as the key criteria of effectiveness. Highly prescriptive contracts which, quite literally, reward 'contractors' for 'keeping the lid on' troublesome incidents and troublesome young people, rather than 'working through' their problems, have severely limited the scope for change, development and innovation in the secure estate.

Despite an early recognition that standards within the secure estate were declining as a result of the unanticipated increase in throughput, that violence and abuse were commonplace and that management was often ineffective, New Labour's commitment to 'market' solutions has meant that it has relinquished direct managerial control of a growing number of institutions, relying instead on a variety of inspection and audit regimes which utilise financial penalties to ensure contract compliance. Thus, in the face of neglect and brutality at Ashfield YOI, deemed at the time to be one of the worst run prison department establishments in Britain, the YJB was only able to:

> (Reduce) the number of places purchased at Ashfield YOI (by) 60 ... The Board will for the foreseeable future purchase 240 places at Ashfield in an effort to improve the situation by effectively raising the staff/young person ratio. The decision follows two in-depth benchmark reports which indicated that Ashfield was signally failing to comply with the Board's Service Level Agreement with the Prison Service. Meanwhile, the Board has lifted a Compliance Failure Notice issued in respect of Onley YOI near Rugby as it is considered that sufficient improvements have been made by the governor and staff which is improving the quality of the regime.
> (Youth Justice Board News, 14 Sep. 2002: 1)

The only leverage available to the Prison Service, which purchased the service from Ashfield's private sector proprietors, prior to selling this service on to the YJB (sic) was to require their bankers to appoint a new contractor. These constraints have meant that, from time to time, the various institutions that constitute the secure estate are afflicted by carbon copy crises of control or abuse, to which they apply carbon copy solutions, which don't work (Pitts, 2003).

The worsening crisis in the secure estate appears to be due variously to the poor drafting of, sometimes contradictory, youth justice law, contradictory administrative imperatives and sentences and interventions, many of which were chosen on the whim of ministers or their political advisers with an eye to how they would 'play' in the Tory heartlands rather than their 'systemic effects'. However, because New Labour ministers were more receptive to the good news offered by their inexperienced political advisers than the misgivings of civil servants, justice system professionals and some academic criminologists, they failed to spot that the new system's plumbing was awry. These problems were compounded by an aggressive governmental posture on youth crime, which produced a penal atmosphere in which the sentencing of children and young people became harsher. As we have seen, this hastily constructed, and toughened, system had the effect of drawing larger numbers of relatively unproblematic young people deeper into the system and accelerating their progress through it. Paradoxically, however, it was also able to divert some far more serious and persistent offenders into community-based ISSPs. (Pitts, 2003; Kemp et al., 2003; Burnett and Appleton, 2004). Alongside this, we have witnessed a series of idiosyncratic interventions by the Home Secretary or the Prime Minister in response to real and imagined crises (Allen, 2004). Thus, in 2001, children and young people serving sentences for murder and grievous bodily harm were released early to accommodate the swathe of young mobile phone thieves swept into security and custody by Home Secretary David Blunkett's *Street Crime Initiative*. Thus it appears that the criminogenic 'chaos of reward', which Jock Young (1999) identifies as a defining characteristic of late modernity, finds its corollary in a chaos of punishment in the youth justice system. These problems are compounded by an unwillingness on the part of government to assume direct responsibility for and control over the secure estate, apparent complacency amongst some of those commissioning and inspecting correctional services, a blatant disregard by government for international standards, the displacement of professional and humanitarian considerations by political and administrative imperatives, institutional inertia, an over-reliance

upon an under-trained and transient workforce and idiosyncratic local management.

Surveying these developments it does not appear that we are witnessing the straightforward imposition, by an autocratic government, of draconian penalties upon the children of the underclass, as some commentators appear to be suggesting (Goldson, 1999). While New Labour is frequently authoritarian, the emerging picture is more one of ambivalence and ambiguity and of a government that appears to be overwhelmed by the complexities of criminal justice policy, its implementation and its administration.

In order to exert greater control over these processes New Labour initially embraced what Mair (2000) has called a strategy of 'good governance' which eschewed direct 'government' in favour of arms-length 'governance' via a 'steering and rowing' relationship with service providers, in the public or private sectors. In fact, because of New Labour's profound mistrust of civil servants, local government and public professionals, whom they have often viewed as actively resistant, if not subversive to, their public sector reforms (Pitts, 2003), it has been drawn ever-deeper into the micro-management of public services through the elaboration of a complex apparatus of contracts, targets, performance indicators, audits and inspections. Its other, counter-insurgency, strategy has been to place political 'friends' in key positions previously occupied by civil servants and justice system professionals. In doing so, New Labour has brought into being a new political class, part political apparatchik and part public servant whose commitment to the New Labour 'project' has sometimes been in inverse relation to their grasp of the administrative and operational issues for which they have responsibility. These friends appear to share a commitment to speed and simplicity in the transformation of public services and are not particularly interested in what happened in the past, especially if it appears to raise doubts about the policies they are charged with 'driving through'. So, rather than stepping back from the executive and administrative functions of government, as the ideology of good governance would appear to indicate, New Labour has effectively annexed and politicised them, and nowhere more so than in the youth justice system. In so doing, it has tended to erode such transparency and accountability as existed in this sector. However, by 2004, with burgeoning youth incarceration, record re-conviction rates and similarly dismal findings from the evaluations of community penalties (Bateman and Pitts, 2004), New Labour appears to be casting around for solutions.

In a previous era both Labour and Conservative governments have relied upon the political dexterity of their civil servants to manage, rationalise and, indeed, reform, the youth justice system. As part of this process, the executive has maintained a dialogue with the judiciary, criminal justice professionals, penal pressure groups and academic researchers. Thus, Mrs Thatcher's 'law and order' rhetoric effectively served as a cover for the pragmatic rationalisation, and de facto reform, of the youth justice system in the 1980s (Pitts, 1988; 2003). In this period, successive Conservative Home Secretaries were able to ignore their leader's, blood-curdling, 'window dressing' and pay attention instead to the professionals. In this period of what is sometimes called 'elitist', as distinct from populist, policy formation, the impetus for change flowed upwards, via the civil service, to an intermittently receptive government whereas, at present, the impetus for change flows only downwards, often circumventing the civil service and the judiciary, not to mention the Youth Justice Board, and prescription has taken the place of dialogue (Pitts, 1988). And it hasn't worked. Put simply, as a result of inexperience and an apparent unwillingness to learn the lessons of the past, the present government has painted itself into a corner on the issue of youth justice and it now badly needs skilled professional assistance to extricate itself with its dignity and political credibility intact.

The future of the secure estate

If New Labour is to disentangle itself from its present predicament it will, like the Wilson and Thatcher administrations, need to de-politicise youth crime and justice. The legal, administrative and logistical problems it confronts notwithstanding, at present the major obstacles to the realisation of an optimal secure estate are ideological and political. In the recent period, UK governments, like those in the United States and some other European countries (Muncie, forthcoming) have effectively placed youth crime and their capacity to deal with it at the centre of the political stage while, in the case of New Labour, elevating domination of the daily news

agenda to a paramount political virtue. If the government is to rationalise its youth justice strategy, while honouring its commitment to 'evidence-led policy' and 'evidenced-based practice', this will require a change in political culture. Such a strategy could involve a repudiation of US-style penal populism and the restoration of an 'elitist' model of policy-making of the kind that prevailed in the UK between the end of the second world war and the early 1990s which is, as Mick Ryan (1999) has observed, '. . . often attributed with defending and promoting liberal, humane and welfarist policies against the demands of a more punitive public culture.'

An alternative model, which would circumvent the lack of transparency and accountability endemic to the elitist model, would be to 'professionalise' the youth justice policy-making process. A useful model for such professionalisation might be derived from the Bank of England's monetary policy committee. This committee, established by Chancellor of the Exchequer Gordon Brown in 1997, is composed of five leading economists, 'the five wise men', who are appointed precisely because they have different views about how economies should be managed. The committee is charged with establishing a bank rate that works in the long-term economic interest of the country rather than the short-term political interests of the government. And, of course, it is precisely because the economy is such a highly politicised sphere of government activity that New Labour, in an effort to achieve greater political legitimacy and duck undue political flack, decided to introduce this neutral element into the policy-making process.

Ideally, like the Bank of England's monetary policy committee, a re-configured Youth Justice Board would be able to step out of the shadow of the Home Office and New Labour's political machine, and embrace a far broader range of views about how youth justice systems operate and how they might best be managed and developed. Cultivating such a dialogue would do much to re-establish the credibility of both the Board and the government in this problematic policy area.

Precedents for such professionalisation can be found in several other European states (Muncie, forthcoming). In Finland, for example, a state with very low imprisonment rates, penal management and reform has traditionally been the province of a relatively small group of professional and academic criminal policy experts. This group has maintained close links with successive Ministers of Justice some of whom have themselves been researchers and criminologists. This has meant that criminal justice policy has remained relatively depoliticised and attempts to insinuate 'heavyweight', US-style, 'law and order' measures like 'three strikes' and 'truth in sentencing' have been thwarted at an early stage (Kuure, 2002).

If such a shift, from populist to professional youth justice policy-making, under the auspices of a reconfigured YJB, were to be achieved, one of their first jobs would be to specify what deterrent, incapacitative or rehabilitative, as distinct from political, effects the incarceration of children and young people might realistically be expected to achieve. In the face of powerful evidence of:

- The ineffectiveness of custodial sentences for juveniles in terms of rehabilitative impact, re-conviction, the diminution of the seriousness and persistence of their subsequent offending the protection of potential victims and general deterrence.
- The apparent long-term damage, distress and debilitation that incarceration in the existing custodial apparatus inflicts upon juveniles in terms of drug use, mental health, violent victimisation and educational and vocational attainment, all factors closely associated with desistance from, or persistence in, crime.
- The deleterious impact upon young offenders' family relationships a factor known to be closely associated with recidivism.

The reconfigured Youth Justice Board would therefore need to specify:

- The purposes to be served and the goals to be achieved by the placement of juveniles in the various institutions that comprise the juvenile secure estate.
- The characteristics of the children and young people who would constitute appropriate subjects for such placement and evidence of the deterrent, incapacitative or rehabilitative effects upon similar children and young people in analogous contexts.
- The optimal institutional regimes for achieving these effects with these children and young people.
- How such changes might articulate with National and International Children's Rights

Conventions and Standards and the Children Act (1989).

Underlying such a strategy is a more fundamental question however; one which concerns what the incarceration of children and young people, a 19th century mode of penal intervention, can be expected to achieve in the 21st century. Finding an answer to this question would appear to be a core task, perhaps the core task, of policy makers.

References

Allen, R. (2004) The Role of Central Government and the Youth Justice Board, in Bateman, T. and Pitts, J. *The Russell House Companion to Youth Justice*. Lyme Regis: Russell House Publishing.

Audit Commission (2004) *Youth Justice 2004: A Review of the Youth Justice Reforms*. London: Audit Commission.

Bateman, T. (2003) *Locked-up Children: A Failure of (Youth) Justice?* London: NACRO.

Bateman, T. (2004) Custody and Policy, in Bateman, T. and Pitts, J. *The Russell House Companion to Youth Justice*. Lyme Regis: Russell House Publishing.

Bateman, T. and Pitts, J. (2004) (Eds.) *The Russell House Companion to Youth Justice*. Lyme Regis: Russell House Publishing.

Beck, U. (1992) *The Risk Society: Towards a New Modernity*. London: Sage.

Bennett, T. et al. (2000) *Drugs and Crime: The Results of the Second Stage of the NEW ADAM Programme*. London: Home Office.

Burnett, R. and Appleton, C. (2004) *Joined-up Youth Justice*. Lyme Regis: Russell House Publishing.

Burroughs, D. (1998) *Contemporary Patterns of Residential Mobility*, in Campbell B. (1993) *Goliath: Britain's Dangerous Places*. London: Methuen.

Campbell, B. (1993) *Goliath: Britain's Dangerous Places*. London: Methuen..

Crawford, A. (1998) *Crime Prevention and Community Safety*. London: Longman.

Currie, E. (1985) *Confronting Crime: An American Challenge*. New York: Pantheon.

Forrester, D., Frenz, S., O'Connell, M. and Pease, K. (1990) *The Kirkholt Burglary Prevention Project: Phase II*. London: Home Office.

Garland, D. (2001) *The Culture of Control: Crime and Social Order in Contemporary Society*. Oxford University Press.

Goldson, B. (1999) Youth (In)justice: Contemporary Developments in Policy and Practice, in Goldson, B. (Ed.) *Youth Justice: Contemporary Policy and Practice.* London: Ashgate.

Goldson, B. and Peters, E. (2000) *Tough Justice: Responding to Children in Trouble.* The Children's Society.

Graham, J. and Bowling, B. (1995) *Young People and Crime.* London: Home Office.

Hagan, J. (1993) The Social Embeddedness of Crime and Unemployment. *Criminology.* 31: 455–91.

Hammersley, R., Marsland, L. and Reid, M. (2003) *Substance Use by Young Offenders: The Impact of Normalisation of Drug Use in the Early 21st Century.* London: Home Office RDS.

Home Office (2002) *Justice for All.* White Paper. London: Home Office.

Home Office (2003) *The Criminal Statistics.* London: Home Office.

Home Office (2004) *Firearms Related Crime.* London, Home Office.

Hope, T. and Foster, J. (1992) Conflicting Forces: Changing Dynamics of Crime and Community on a Problem Estate, *B.J. Criminology.*

Hope, T. (2003) The Crime Drop in Britain. *Community Safety Journal.* 2: 4, 32.

Kemp, V., Sorsby, A., Liddle, M. and Merrington, S. (2002) *Assessing Responses to Youth Offending in Northamptonshire.* London, NACRO.

Kommer, M. (2004) Punitiveness in Europe Revisited. *Criminology in Europe.* 3: 1, Feb.

Kuure, T. (2002) *Reducing Custodial Sentencing for Young Offenders: The European Experience.* London: NACRO.

Mair, P. (2000) Partyless Democracy. *New Left Review.* March/June.

Matthews, R. (1999) *Doing Time: An Introduction to the Sociology of Imprisonment.* Basingstoke: Palgrave.

Matthews, R. and Pitts, J. (1998) Rehabilitation, Recidivism and Realism: Evaluating Violence Reduction Programs in Prison. *The Prison Journal.* 78: 4, 390–405.

Muncie, J. and Hughes, G. (2002) *Modes of Youth Governance,* in Muncie, J., Huges, G. and McLaughlin, E. *Youth Justice: Critical Readings.* London: Sage.

Muncie, J. (forthcoming) *Repenalisation and Rights: Explorations in Comparative Youth Criminology.* Milton Keynes: Open University.

Nacro (2003) *A Failure of Justice: Reducing Child Imprisonment.* London: NACRO.

Nacro (2004) *Some Facts About Young People Who Offend – 2002.* London: NACRO.

Page, D. (1993) *Building for Communities: A Study of New Housing Association Estates.* York: Joseph Rowntree Foundation Hope.

Parker, H., Aldridge, J. and Measham, F. (1998) *Illegal Leisure, The Normalisation of Adolescent Recreational Drug Use.* London: Routledge.

Pawson, R. and Tilley, N. (1997) *Realistic Evaluation.* London: Sage.

Pearson, G. (1987) *The New Heroin Users.* London: Batsford.

Pease, K. (1994) Cross National Imprisonment Rates, in King, R. and Maguire, M. (Eds.) *Prisons in Context.* Oxford: Clarendon Press.

Pitts, J. (1988) *The Politics of Juvenile Crime.* London: Sage Publications.

Pitts, J. (2003) *The New Politics of Youth Crime: Discipline or Solidarity.* Lyme Regis: Russell House Publishing.

Rutherford, A. (1986) *Growing Out of Crime.* Harmondsworth: Penguin.

Rutherford, A. (2002) Youth Justice and Social Inclusion. *Youth Justice.* 2: 2, Oct.

Ryan, M. (1999) Penal Policy Making Towards the Millennium: Elites and Populists: New Labour and the New Criminology. *International Journal of the Sociology of Law.* 27: 1, 1–22.

Sampson, R. and Laub, J. (1993) *Crime in the Making: Pathways and Turning Points.* Harvard University Press.

Social Exclusion Unit (1998) *Bringing Britain Together: A National Strategy for Neighbourhood Renewal.* Social Exclusion Unit.

Tilley, N. and Bullock, K. (2003) *Shootings, Gangs and Violent Incidents in Manchester: Developing a Crime Reduction Strategy.* London: Home Office.

UN Committee on the Rights of the Child (2002) *Concluding Observations of the Committee on the Rights of the Child: United Kingdom of Great Britain and Northern Ireland.* Geneva: United Nations.

Young, J. (1999) *The Exclusive Society.* London: Sage Publications.

Youth Justice Board (2003) Improvements to the Juvenile Secure Estate. *Youth Justice Board News.* 19.

Youth Justice Board (2004) *Youth Justice Board Cuts Places in young Offender institutions.* Press release, 21 Jan.

Index